Much appreciation

THE

FORTY-
FOURTH

THE FORTY-FOURTH

A Perspective on the Odyssey of President Barack Obama (2008–2016) with Reflections on Lincoln Parallels

ALICE RHODES HINSLEY, EdD

Mountain Arbor
    Press
Alpharetta, GA

The author has made every effort to give credit to the source of any images, quotes, or other material contained within and obtain permissions when feasible.

Copyright © 2019 by Alice Rhodes Hinsley

All rights reserved. No part of this book may be reproduced or transmitted in any form or by any means, electronic or mechanical, including photocopying, recording, or any information storage and retrieval system, without permission in writing from the author.

ISBN: 978-1-63183-498-1 - Paperback
eISBN: 978-1-63183-499-8 - ePub
eISBN: 978-1-63183-500-1 - Mobi

Library of Congress Control Number: 2019932857

10 9 8 7 6 5 4 3 2   070819

Printed in the United States of America

⊗This paper meets the requirements of ANSI/NISO Z39.48-1992 (Permanence of Paper)

To my son, Kemperal, my brothers, Marvin, Hiram Jr., and all of my family/friends living or in memoriam.

To be part of the national conversation about Lincoln's unfinished work when there is a black president who is going to take the oath of office on Lincoln's Bible is—well . . .

—Theresa Caldwell

The election of Barack Obama is a major step forward in the accomplishment of the ultimate objective of this country, to exist as a unified America, regardless of racial or ethnic differences.

—William F. Winter

Obama's inauguration was America's moment to commemorate the election of the first African American president. Yet it was also the opportunity to indulge in an enduring American passion: honoring the 16th president, who salvaged a divided Union, liberated millions of slaves, and seven generations later, made Obama's rise possible.

—Washington Post

TABLE OF CONTENTS

Preface xi
Acknowledgments xix

Introduction: Launching from Illinois as Political Seat 1

Chapter One: Family Origin and Early Years 23
    Heritage and Birth 23
    The Progenitors 28
    Lincoln's Mother 32
    Obama's Mother 45
    The Stepparents 52
    One-Parent Household(s) 57
    The Father Image 62

Chapter Two: Education Defective and Education Par Excellence 75
    Early Childhood Education 77
    Self-Taught vs. Formal Training 84
    Thirst-for-Knowledge Parallels 88

Chapter Three: Crossing Career Paths 95
    Profession: Legal Practice 108
    Political: Rising Politicians 111

Interlude: In Retrospect—On the Iconic 1960s Political and Social Figures of Change: JFK/MLK/RFK 121

Chapter Four: Faith and Religion 129

Chapter Five: On Politics and Government 141

Chapter Six: In Pursuit of the White House 157
    Prefatory 157

Presidential Campaign Challenges	171
The Party Nominations of 2008 and 1860	203
Convention 1860 vs. 2008	211

A Conclusion and a Transition   235

Bibliography   245

PREFACE

When I first heard about this young Illinois senator of black mixed heritage who had made his way into the State House, then on up to Capitol Hill—I was impressed. Later, his memoirs hit the bestseller list with fervor and I purchased each of them, immediately.

However, when later hearing about his considering running for the presidency of the United States of America, I became enthusiastically curious. Indeed, other African Americans had given running for president a try while I observed their ambition with interest—even voted for one of them in the presidential primary of 1988—because I believe that it should be the case, rightfully speaking, for any qualified patriotic American citizen to have the opportunity to seek the presidency regardless of color, gender, faith, or family.

Therefore, historically speaking, to see such an incredible promise of diversity emerge back in 1972,[1] 1984, 1988,[2] and again in 2004[3] presented a sense of pride among citizens throughout this country, even though a century or more had passed since the founding of this great republic and no evidential trace of diversity existed in the line of those forty-three men elected to presidency.

Indeed, from the day Barack Obama announced his candidacy in 2007, my allegiance and hope never wavered or faltered. Why? Because it was time—time to turn the forty-three pages of presidential history forward, and not remain stagnant.

Subsequently, this book speaks about the American dream and presents a perspective on Barack Obama not as a pure biography or from a chronological viewpoint, but instead uses an element of relevancy to approach the meaningful parallelism and interrelationships found in this unique presidential narrative encircling two outstanding heroic American statesmen: Barack Obama and Abraham Lincoln. Each man stepped forth to resolve or fix the political state of affairs that were hinging on troubling, divisive circumstances causing times of unpredictable conflict. Moreover, because of their high levels of ability and wisdom, such qualities resulted in their exemplary performance and leadership. Their leadership had stunning impact upon the nation compounded with strong and effective outcomes directly intended for the will and interests of the common people. Each president soared above party politics. Obama, like Lincoln, was courageous enough to stand for what was morally right; even amongst oppositional partisan debate, each was consistent as communicators while governing with thoughtful deliberation as opposed to thoughtless raging, explosive, and impulsive actions that overlook the most vulnerable and hardworking classes of people.

Summarily, each of these presidents served his country with presidential dignity and balance, which primarily rested on having an inspiring combination of confidence complemented with an aura of graceful humility regardless of either one's personal strength, power, and gifted servant leadership. Each may be defined as exceedingly transformational presidents of change who built on a purpose-driven presidential agenda to appeal to the populace.

Tracing the odyssey of Barack Obama in his epic journey from obscurity to notability, pivoting him into the highest office of the nation by becoming the president of the United States for two consequential terms (2008–2016) and making him the first African American to achieve a *turn* to serve his country in this unprecedented capacity, marks the most controversial presidential transition ever in America. Although he was an unlikely candidate on the basis of heritage, politics, and class, so were some other unlikely candidates in modern times who rose to the presidency. Focus on the case of Harry Truman (thirty-third), John Kennedy (thirty-fifth), Lyndon Baines Johnson (thirty-sixth), Jimmy Carter (thirty-ninth), and Bill Clinton (forty-second). Kennedy was Catholic; Truman dropped out of college; while Johnson, Carter, and Clinton came from the rural South. Then, there is number sixteen: Abraham Lincoln. Kentucky born, no education, little experience, no pedigree, yet arguably, America's greatest president.

From number one (George Washington) to number forty-three (George Bush), each of the forty-three presidents had one characteristic in common, and that commonality was that he was a white male who served his term as president of the United States of America. Although, among the majority of the candidates who made it to the presidency, some endured more difficulties than their counterparts. For example, Abraham Lincoln was one admonished on the basis of his anti-slavery stand, causing him to encounter ridicule, hatred, and subsequent assassination. So, Abraham Lincoln and Barack Obama rose to their official terms by becoming the most consequential presidents despite hostile critics and mounting oppositions against them, which contribute to the eminence of their legacies.

Both presidents followed a moral compass leading them to humanitarian destinations and mantles high above mindless or shallow materialism coupled with hindering walls of exclusion. From Springfield to DC, Obama took his turn as president with honor and dignity. He was, in addition, a man of the common folk who salvaged an economic crisis, rose above color barriers, healed a nation with Obamacare (Affordable Healthcare Act), gave dreams of promise for innocent children born in the United States to parents who came across the border undocumented, and opened the doors to freedom for all groups of people regardless of their personal orientation or preferences, meaning he shepherded into legislation the legalization of gay marriages. In addition, Obama curtailed war when he pulled troops out of Afghanistan from an unpopular battle inherited from his predecessor.

Of course, the development of this book's title came through a myriad of changes in an effort to capture an accurate meaning of the presidency executed by Barack Obama, which encompasses a promising beginning compounded by an effective closing at the end of his eight years in office. The real truth is that Barack Obama's successful nomination led to his becoming the forty-fourth president of the United States, which is phenomenal because of several unlikely reasons primarily associated with him. Also compelling is the existence of parallels connecting Obama to one of the greatest presidents of this country, Abraham Lincoln. It is this perspective from which I write. Indeed, the election consequences inspired journalists/writers to pen narratives and critiques about the new president. Everyone seemed to catch the fever to probe and weave long narratives about the historic first event of an African American to occupy the Oval Office. As stated earlier, numerically, America has seen a number of presidents from 1789 through 2008: forty-four presidents came forth and took the Oath of Office to lead the nation to the best of their abilities.

A president is customarily identified, in a popular sense, numerically in successive order of servant leadership. Nevertheless, most of us know that George Washington is known as the first president or identified as number one in the American presidential order. Additionally, some may know that Thomas Jefferson became the third president in number—even if many may not always know that the second president was John Adams. This simply means that some presidents are more well-known than others by name or by number. Of course, Abraham Lincoln is most well-known, and everyone seems to know that he served as president during the Civil War. However, we're not sure that they always realize that he served as the sixteenth president. Currently, in numerical order, everyone knows that Barack Obama followed the forty-third president: George W. Bush.

Typically, numbers are definitive, representative, symbolic, substantive, generational, chronological, and transitional while serving as meaningful, universal tools applied in human lives. Indeed, numbers accurately determine—and document—who we are, where we are, where we've been, and often indicate where we're going. We live numerically in terms of life-span, from birth to death or number of years.

Numbers applied for whatever purpose, actually, become more than a mere figure; in this particular case, a number is a rank, a place, or a turn for change. Perhaps that is why in 1846, numbers were on Lincoln's side when his political friends favored him for congressional office over a popular candidate, reminding the party leaders that "turnabout is fair play—it's Abraham's turn now."⁴ Quite similarly, an Obama surrogate wisely commented about the future president, "He knows it's his time," suggesting the affecting seasons of time that impact significantly upon a person's life. By and by each man stood ready to move in seasonable time regardless of hard times or troublesome situations.

In writing this presidential narrative, my purpose has been to examine significant aspects of the historic realms of America while capturing the spirit of change and its effect on the populace. By engaging the essence of this text into historical nonfiction tradition, I join in a corporate spirit with other writers in this particular genre who have immense interest in Barack Obama and Abraham Lincoln. Among an elite plethora of writers—primarily white males—who have penned thoughtful, inspirational, critical, and informative volumes of presidential narratives about Abraham Lincoln and later to include Barack Obama, I consider this an amazing privilege for me to gain a niche in such literary theory by carving out a place for me to interpret and record legendary history for the people.

Furthermore, I am distinctive in this field on the basis of being an African American woman who purposefully writes about and admires Abraham Lincoln for his significant contribution to America. However, both presidents are a part of my story as an African American because each affected my family in compelling ways. For example, in 1839 and 1854, both of my great-grandmothers were born into enslavement there in the depths of the confederacy—Georgia—and my maternal great-grandmother became free at the age of eleven, while the freedom of my paternal great-grandmother only arrived when she became a young woman of twenty-six years old. Such long-awaited emancipation came as a result of President Lincoln's steady, influential hands on the legislation of the Thirteenth Amendment (1865), sustaining his earlier (1863) proclamation ending chattel slavery. On the other hand, in 2014 when my little great-nephew was born, unlike his great-great-great-grandmothers, this child opened his eyes into a world of freedom under the forty-fourth president—Barack Obama—and awoke into a nation with North and South unitedly settled because of Abraham Lincoln, while not overlooking that some one hundred years later the impact of the 1960s civil rights movement led by Dr. Martin Luther King Jr. nonviolently connected the links of freedom, so that my little nephew and other children like him could follow in the footsteps of other giant figures such as a Barack Obama, Dr. Martin King, or even a Lincoln. Yes, the genius of Lincoln and King began the winding pathway that vicariously led to one—Barack Obama—victoriously becoming the first African American to serve two successful terms in office as president of the United States. Again, as an African American woman writing in this prolific field heavily distinguished by white males on United States presidential lore, I find myself uniquely breaking the norm, so to speak. Yes, I conclude that both presidents are a part of my story as an African American woman, because each affected my personal family in consequential ways and touched the African American family as a whole.

Barack Obama fosters pride among the nation and peoples of color based on equality and inclusion by restricting limits and supremacy on the basis of race, gender, culture, or wealth. Of course, reflections on President Lincoln, the sixteenth president, symbolize the interrelatedness of these iconic American presidents: President Barack Obama and President Abraham Lincoln. In addition, both ascended to the presidency from Illinois as their adoptive home state, launching their careers while there. Not to mention that both rose above struggling odds to the presidency, which is reason enough to salute their impressive achievement. Indeed, for Barack Obama, the challenge of becoming the first African American to achieve the office of president of the United States is dramatically colossal because his election fulfills countless deferred dreams and centuries of unanswered prayers in the African American struggle. Gloriously—yet didactic—his powerful resolve to persuade and instruct America to believe that *"Yes, we can"* transform America now and forever will become stacked in the depths of his legacy in

America and globally. As a result of his charismatic election as a number one among forty-three numbers elected before, Barack Hussein Obama is the forty-fourth president of the United States. Clearly, America is the beacon of hope among all nations.

NOTES

Preface

1. Shirley Anita Chisholm (1924–2005): 1968, first African American woman elected to United States Congress (New York); 1972, she became the first African American candidate for a major party's nomination for president of United States and the first woman to run for the Democratic Party's presidential nomination.
2. Rev. Jesse Louis Jackson Sr. (1941–): Baptist minister (Chicago) served as a shadow United States senator for District of Columbia from 1991 to 1997. In 1984 and 1988, he became the second African American candidate for Democratic presidential nomination. Civil rights activist and founder of PUSH (People United to Save Humanity).
3. Rev. Al (Alfred) Charles Sharpton Jr. (1954–): An American civil rights activist and Baptist minister (New York), television/radio talk show host. In 2004, he was a candidate for the Democratic nomination for United States presidential election.
4. David Herbert Donald, *Lincoln* (New York: Simon and Schuster, 1995), 113.

ACKNOWLEDGMENTS

I am grateful for the opportunity to acknowledge the impactful encouragement, technical assistance, and strong belief in me influencing my literary goal: the publication of this book. To all my family, students, friends, librarians, colleagues, Obama loyalists, Lincoln enthusiasts, and the Mountain Arbor Press publishing staff, I appreciate your assurance in my ability to write about history in the genre of a presidential narrative.

In particular, I wish to thank my brother Marvin, who praised my efforts and recognized my desire to engage in this project while graciously compensating in the initial move. Additionally, it was so helpful to me when Ms. Kim Sheffield, one of my church members, cooperatively provided technical service of typing my manuscript, although my longhand was difficult penmanship for her to translate, believe me. Roberta, my sister-in-law, as well as my nephews Louis and Jason, patiently listened to me present ideas to them or had to sit down and listen to me do impromptu readings even though they had other things to do, which was gratifying to me. Of course, my son, Kemperal, singularly and consistently supported me and my literary theory, more or less, as a devoted and loving son. Several members of the Lincoln Forum Symposium were encouraging and thought that I should pursue this project. Dr. Anderson of Morris Brown College, occasionally, allowed me to share excerpts of my idea with colleagues during faculty meetings, which provided an academic audience for me.

Finally, as their eldest child, I feel indebted to remember my late parents: my beloved mother, Minnie C. Rhodes, and my father, Rev. H. A. Rhodes; nor can I forget my grandmother Alice Kemp Lawrence, as her namesake, who played an important role in my life. Indeed, the strides she made in my formative years are

ALICE RHODES HINSLEY, EdD

eternally etched in my spirit, and as her only granddaughter, I love her dearly and will never forget her, including the love she shared with her family.

INTRODUCTION

LAUNCHING FROM ILLINOIS AS POLITICAL SEAT

There's a wisdom there and a humility that I find in his approach to government, even before he was president.
—President-elect Obama
on President Lincoln (Nov. 2008)

In a sense, the 2008 race for president has historical parallels to the 1860 race, because at each time the country faced polarizing domestic issues tragically dividing a progressive new nation, a nation suffering from the lack of purposeful leadership to unify and resolve the sectional class divides and ideological differences invading the organizing center causing conflict in national and global affairs. Unfortunately, the country's suffering resurfaced at the end of the elected two-term president in 2016 as well as the unexpected presidential tragedy in 1865. Without keener vision and commanding activism from a strong new leader who would effectively change the direction of the country, America faced a collapse influenced by the pressure of failing to hold up the democratic principles on which it was founded. Was America threatening to fall like the Byzantine Empire? The decline of the Roman Empire was a gradual process beginning in the third century BC until the fifth century BC, when the western part of the empire was lost and the eastern part weakened, resulting in a progressive estrangement between the two halves. Was that happening in the mid-nineteenth century to the new nation a little over two hundred years old? A transformation was needed toward a unified whole, with the asserted antecedent "A House Divided Cannot Stand," if the South and North would be saved from the Union breaking up. Does that threat repeat itself today in the early twenty-first century, some one hundred fifty or more years later? The political divisions between the liberals and the conservatives, economic divides between the haves and the have-nots, dramatically resemble the antebellum period of discontent. Here was a new nation built on representative democracy and participatory citizenship descending into the pit of a chaotic, embattled national state that needed fixing. Is that what exists today in the close of the second decade of the twenty-first century? Issues of unstable economics, impending wars, anti-immigration laws by separating small children from families, clouds of racism, and dangerous terrorism all have marred the values for which we as a people stand. Maintaining America's status as the best and brightest hope in the world, while conspiratorial schemes creep in to remove its first-class position in the Free World and opposing factors deteriorate this nation's infrastructures, thrusting it into fierce infighting and devastating materialistic views versus the humanitarian approach of unity is baffling, to say the least. The debates of partisanship are constantly being argued until we are forced to doubt and fear the call of who shall stand. The compelling questions are, will we stand or will we fall as a nation to a lesser level by losing the nobility of our foundation? Is it not time for us to revisit the dream, restore the call of honor for a new birth of freedom, rebuild and reinforce our principled constructs, reevaluate doctrines in order to revive the fallen? Or do we simply sit passively by amidst partisan deals for the sake of unscrupulous doctrines in order to ignore the reality? Or do we overlook unethical political deals made in the interest of, perhaps, the privileged few? Are we advocates of reaching across the aisle joining hands in bipartisan practices benefitting the good of the people, or are we content to remain stuck in the mud and mire of status quo or lesser motives? Indeed, such critical matters pose a tumultuous crisis. Theories vary as explanations differ on causes of decadence and even triumph within a government. However, it is for sure that a head of state such as a leader—more specifically speaking, in this case, presidential leadership—becomes the key element in a functioning executive office of duties of responsibility resulting in accountabilities enriched by vision and the talent of creative leadership/wisdom with designs to achieve productive and measurable goals to implement significant change in the best interest of its people and country. In other words, consequential leadership led by sound judgment and disciplined, pragmatic decision-making must prevail. Now, the voices of the people thrust a crucial question. Does such an inspired pulse of leadership even exist? And if so, will that leader be acceptable to the people for electability as a president to save the country from the mounting trepidations crushing its survival? Or rather, will this person become the central agent of imperial powers instead? Historian Thomas McPherson reminds us that the issues facing our nation are, after all, profoundly affected by political power.[1] Since political power affects the state of the nation, those elected to office are accountable for the social history in whatever elected office held. The dynamics of politics are intriguing and demanding on the basis of one being able to win and hold the control of governmental office. Customarily, often contriving and competing forces for multiple reasons impede a candidate's quest to hold such an empowered office. During an election, candidates prepare to run by soliciting support from constituents and their party affiliate based on the candidates' qualifications of experience, popularity in name recognition, the art of timing, and meeting the believable robust characteristics of a likely candidate. Obviously, it is customary for likely candidates to step forth to run for an office primarily on assumptions that their experience and family pedigree traditionally tied to a political or commercial business dynasty entitle them to hold whatever office they seek. If that is the case, then, how can one leap from obscurity to luminary status? Is it traditional? Is it attainable? Furthermore, is it common? Is it likely? It should be a civil right to run for office according to the democracy and origin of the United States Constitution. Elections are free and fair in a democracy, and it matters not who you are except that you are a citizen. However, if a candidate's likelihood is not externally apparent, then a conflicting struggle ensues regardless of the internal qualities that are not so visible and likely of the candidate. Moreover, the subtle repetitive course of history delves into the motives of Abraham Lincoln and Barack Obama—unknowns—who captured the position of the highest office in the land. Abraham Lincoln launched his political career on frontier America in the midwestern state of Illinois. Winning in the Illinois legislature in 1834 where he served four consecutive terms, he became a leading party affiliate and a follower of Henry Clay of Kentucky. Former National Republicans Henry Clay and John Quincy Adams formed the Whig Party in 1834.

Clay started the party built on the ideals of an American system. This system emphasized government support for education, internal improvements, banking, and economic development. Lincoln viewed this system as a means of upward mobility for the working class, providing them with economic opportunity to improve their condition and move up the ladder toward success. He argued that the true test of American democracy would only be achieved when all of its people had the equal opportunity to participate in upward mobility regardless of class or color of their skin. Lincoln believed that the ideals of an American system meant improving the conditions of all humans, but that such ideals could not be reached within a system that enslaved others, thus, preventing their access to the same opportunity as other people. Progressively enlightened ideas marked the ideology of the Whig Party, attracting Lincoln to its polity because to him such practice "gives hope to all, and energy, and progress, and improvement of condition to all."[2]

Abraham Lincoln's struggle for nomination by his party (Whig) in 1843 to represent the Seventh District (Sangamon and Morgan Counties) in the United States Congress demonstrated the passion he held in becoming involved in the political process. After stepping back so many times before, Lincoln generously waited several years for his turn to run for United States Congress. His initial decision to run for a representative seat in United States Congress came about after John Todd Stuart announced that he was not going to seek reelection after his term (1839–1843) expired as a United States congressman from Illinois. As a result, the well-educated and experienced John Hardin, and the pompous Edward Baker, along with the dedicated Whig Party loyalist, the humble, loyal Abraham Lincoln, all ran for United States Congress from Illinois. As the party loyalist, Lincoln was dedicated, and one on whom the Whigs relied to get the work done because he did not mind toiling hard and long for his party. And he was effectively purpose driven. Although others were running, Lincoln hoped that he would be rewarded with the support of his party members and that he would be the one to gain the nomination over Hardin or Baker. Like Obama, who served two terms as an Illinois state senator before moving up to the Senate on Capitol Hill, Lincoln served his four terms in the Illinois state legislature (1841) and was now ready to go beyond the State House in Springfield to Congress in Washington, DC. The newly created Seventh Congressional District (Sangamon County/Springfield and Morgan County/Jacksonville) held a majority of prospective votes. Lincoln then decided to put his hat in the ring and run for the hotly contested seat representing the Seventh District (Illinois). However, it became a nasty struggle for Lincoln even among his own political party members, namely Hardin and Baker, who stacked up insults against him threatening any potential support holds that the unsung hero had. When Barack Obama ran for Congress (2000) against incumbent Bobby Rush, a former Black Panther who held status among many blacks and was favorably strong along with his popularity among his peers, Obama was likewise opposed as a candidate from Chicago by the media and those in his own race. Primarily questioning his blackness and connection to the folks of the "hood" by characterizing Obama on the basis of his education from elite institutions and how he spent so much time in the elitism of academia, specifically Harvard and Columbia Universities including the University of Chicago as well, became problematic for the young politician against the more well-known Bobby Rush, a former militant activist—a Black Panther.[3] Lincoln, too, had been disappointed as well when he first ran for a congressional office in 1843. The Congress seat was denied him when Edward Baker, behind his back, undermined Lincoln with accusations or a whispering campaign citing Lincoln's marriage into the wealthy, exclusive Edwards-Stuart elite family. Baker's surrogates characterized Lincoln "as the candidate of pride, wealth, and aristocratic family distinction."[4] Of course, the stunned Lincoln was baffled and could not understand why such accusations about him could be made by anyone, because he thought that surely everyone knew that he was a self-made man with humble origins. Confiding his trepidations to James Matheny, a lawyer, Lincoln in his honest laments confides, "Jim, I am now and always will be the same Abe Lincoln that I always was," but the charge stuck anyhow.[5] By contrast, Lincoln was the workhorse of the party, and Edward Baker, the flamboyant orator. Perhaps Barack Obama became troubled, too, in the Congress race (2000) against the former Black Panther Bobby Rush, who systematically and unhesitatingly came forth with negative comments about Obama. Such accusations like "His enemies also say he's too white and too bright." More media alerts sparked adversities against him. "There are whispers that Obama is being funded by a 'Hyde Park mafiam' a cabal of University of Chicago types, and that there's an 'Obama Project' masterminded by whites who want to push him up the political ladder."[6] John Hardin won the election for congressman over Baker and Lincoln in 1843. Edward Baker followed Hardin as congressman (Illinois). History records that when the time came for Lincoln's nomination to succeed Edward Baker in 1845, Lincoln then sought the former Congressman John Hardin specifically to request his support, only to be disappointed once more when Hardin surprisingly informed the aspiring candidate that he planned to run again. Indeed, Hardin's intention was a blow to Lincoln and could have been a setback for someone less determined and willing to tackle adversity when such conflicts hit them. On the contrary, Lincoln sought to saddle his shoulders with the strength of his hard labors on the prairie in spite of himself, for he was a man acquainted with rejection, grief, and disappointment; thus, he would not turn away, he would not walk away. Abraham Lincoln would not fall, nor be beaten or defeated. His will was to press on, and in the words of the old traditional spiritual, "Run on to see what the end might be . . . Somethin' in the end there is waitin' for me." With Hardin's decision to reenter the race, Lincoln realized that, unfortunately, the former congressman had broken the pledge according to the principle of rotation-in-office policy formed earlier by the party delegates. With the rotational policy, according to its rule and followed in many states,[7] Lincoln would have almost been guaranteed the nomination to succeed Edward Baker. Consequently, to counteract Hardin's decision, Lincoln promptly organized effective strategies to gain him the endorsement from significant leading men in the newly created Seventh District of Illinois before anyone was aware that Hardin wanted to return to Congress. Clearly, Lincoln was noted for his efficacy and intensively consistent labor on behalf of the Whig Party. No, he was not going to give up on his own political aspirations this time. In opposition to Hardin, Lincoln engaged in focused, steadfast competition and did not miss any opportunities of support, winning counties in the northern part of the district. Afterward, appealing to the state senator, Dr. Robert Boal, Lincoln tactfully wrote: "My allegiance for a fair shake (and I want nothing more) in your county is chiefly on you, because of your position and standing, and because I am acquainted with so few others."[8] Lincoln was careful to warn others that he did not want to speak against Hardin and described the former congressman as "talented, energetic, usually generous and magnanimous." His campaign was not to smear his opponent, but Lincoln's *claim* to the nomination was based on the principle that "turnabout is fair play."[9] Meanwhile, Lincoln continued plugging and pushing toward his political aspiration by strategically planning and campaigning energetically. Fortunately, at this time, his party had adopted the convention approach that the majority (Democrat and Republican) had utilized for their forum of nomination. To his advantage, Lincoln continued to promote himself in the political arena, exercising skillful strategies and proactive maneuvering over John Hardin. One can see that Lincoln did not allow "dust to grow under his feet," racing ahead of Hardin, who was just beginning to launch his campaign for reelection. Hardin, of course, was in for a rude awakening and quite astonished to learn from the Whig Party leaders that the party nominee was going to be Abraham Lincoln this time. Thus, the general opinion circulated among the Whigs that Hardin was "a good fellow and Lincoln was too.... But, Lincoln has worked hard and faithfully for the Party, if he desires to go to Congress let him go this time, turnabout is fair play."[10] Thus, surprisingly informing Hardin, "Our people think that it's Abraham's turn now."[11] The people had spoken. And so it was. Abraham Lincoln entered into his first term as Congressman Abraham Lincoln, and he was the *only* Whig from Illinois in the House representing Sangamon and Morgan Counties of the Thirtieth Congress convening in December 1857—fourteen or fifteen years later after his first try. Just as Lincoln was the *only* Whig from Illinois in the House, Obama was the *only* African American in the Senate from Illinois since Reconstruction. A century or so later in 2007, when Barack Obama launched his run for president, some Midwest investment managers and West Coast private-equity advisers supported him financially. The result shocked traditional political experts. Barack Obama, who came from nowhere and raised more money, matching or surpassing his rival, the presumed Democrat front-runner Hillary Rodham Clinton. Before the first vote had been cast, Barack Obama was already a serious contender. Indeed, Obama was proactive and strategized to expand his base to the common people of America, who actively contributed to his campaign, starting as small as a five-dollar bill and swelling the coffers to millions upon millions of dollars from digitally resourced funds from all across the United States through the mass medium of the internet, obviously stunning the icons and upsetting the conventional political structure. When Hillary Clinton announced her run for president, her apparent confidence indicated that she expected to become the presumed front-runner of the Democratic Party without any threat of losing rank to *anyone*, and certainly not to an unknown and unlikely candidate—such as one Barack Obama. Indeed, the chorus of inquiry by many Americans rang clear and loud with resonating sounds: "Barack? *Ba-rack who?* Who *is* Barack Obama? I have never heard of 'im before. Who is *heeeee?* Anyway. I don't know nothin' 'bout him. Mmmm . . . Ba-RAck O-BA-ma" came the puzzled questions and whispers heard amidst the crevices and across byways/highways from too many Americans. The aspect of Lincoln conquering the lead in a race of well-known, polished candidates in the contest for congressman brings us to frontier Illinois, where it was comparable for Lincoln as he emerged and ventured forth amongst the simplicity of the common people, traveling the remote villages in southern Illinois and riding the circuit as a country lawyer. The scenery was different then; modes of transportation were typical horse-drawn wagons/buggies, traversing miles by horseback, or walking/crossing rivers by boat because the railroad system rested in the infantile stage when Abraham Lincoln began as a young leader with his political aspirations and interests. Lincoln made stump speeches on behalf of his party or in support of party candidates for president, as well as speaking for himself whenever he was involved in his own election to the State House of Representatives.[12] He was among the people in the rugged lands of the backwoods and dirt farms located in the county seats on his judicial circuit. In contrast, the twenty-first century's high technology generated a highway of fast transportation and the advancement of air travel, contrary to slower and less advanced means of moving from one location to the next. Far from the frontier life inhabited in Illinois by Abe Lincoln, Barack Obama, a rising Democrat, experienced the benefits of more modern electronic technology—televised speeches, internet, cell phones—highly publicizing Obama's message far and wide, moving him to hope and believe all the way back to the Old State Capitol building in Springfield—launching his political aspirations in 2007. The Springfield Abraham Lincoln knew some centuries ago in the nineteenth century included Victorian customs and traditions, with developing towns/communities, which had not acquiesced to the modern populated city that it is today. In 1840, the population of Springfield was a mere 2,579.[13] Obama initiated his presidential political role in Springfield consisting of approximately 200,000 or more; by July 1, 2009, an estimate placed the population at 208,182.[14] Couched in obscurity, emerging from an ancient log cabin in Kentucky, Abraham Lincoln sprang from humble beginnings, although empowered by an ambition ferociously disciplined to take on challenges seemingly impossible. The touchstone of their destinies was shaped by hope cast in the steel of unbending willpower. Obama and Lincoln launched political careers right there in the Prairie State on the State Square at Springfield, Illinois. Each had migrated from other parts of the country before adopting the state of Illinois; each had lived and worked in Springfield and Chicago. Springfield is the capital of Illinois, but this was not so initially. The capital was once Vandalia, a small town of fewer than one thousand residents located in the southern parts of this frontier state. In fact, it was Abraham Lincoln's leadership, along with state politicians, that negotiated the capital's move from Vandalia to the center of Illinois in Springfield (February 1837) to provide more accessibility of the capital for its citizens. Does history repeat itself? Are there parallels, similarities, contrasts, differences, prophecies, dreams, mythical charms, illusive visions, abstract idealism, and/or concrete facts wrapped separately in the package of potentiality intended to come together bearing the quality of wholeness as a gift to the world? In truth, aspects of qualities and flaws connect humanity to humanity as we draw from one another to effect change, and they possess needs that make us believe that no generation is a remote island. "No man is an island." The past yesteryears somehow meet the present day blending into future tomorrows, displaying the wits and nuances that frame greatness, for who would have thought that an African American male with the Swahili name of Barack Obama could draw such parallels and assume bold, distinct contrasts to a European American male with the Hebrew/English name of Abraham Lincoln? Who would have thought their historical/political paths would cross into the boundaries of president? Is that likely? Is it attainable? Regardless of their race, annals of time, or whatever in common, both can be deemed as unlikely candidates who stepped forth to take their turn among opponents more likely than unlikely to be included in the race. And the people were skeptical at first, but found it necessary and right to affirm each because it was simply fair to do so. Of course, we do understand that the other 2008 candidates were very good and admirable Americans and patriots as well. Nonetheless, in 2008, again, the people spoke: It *is* Obama's turn now. "Turnabout is fair play." From the presidential perspective, the likelihood of Barack Obama or Abraham Lincoln being viewed as candidates could not be favorable, hinging on the basis of stereotypical, political, electorate, and contemporaneous issues. However, the essence of the phrase "It's Abraham's turn now" becomes "It's Obama's turn now" and is as relevant today as it was back in Lincoln's day, meaning that the ethical truth of fair play, opportunity, and inclusion may be universally applied in 2008, 1860, 1845, 2012, or any other time in a democratic contestant field. Former Senator Bob Kerrey once remarked about Obama in similar terms as Lincoln's people did about him; Senator Kerrey said of Obama, "He realizes that this is his time."[15] Above all, the underlying narrative is about inclusion as opposed to exclusion. It stirs up the awareness of truth of duty to the democratic polity of the United States as a republic. In symbolic terms, each of these featured candidates (Lincoln and Obama) called on the American electorate to cast their ballots and entrust them as their presidential leaders. Symbolically insisting, "Just give me a chance. Don't push me back. I've worked hard and effectively. It's only fair that I have a turn now to step up to the Oval Office." But not only that, beneath the excitement and wonder of announcing his decision to run for the president of the United States of America, Senator Barack Obama moved to spring his campaign from the steps of the historical Old State Capitol building in Springfield, Illinois, on February 10, 2007. At the same spot, Abraham Lincoln delivered his famous "House Divided" speech in 1858 as the country reeled and rocked on the verge of falling apart faced by riveting issues of division and injustices. In contemporary times, we are forced to reflect on history once more: Was Barack Obama the next dynamic promise from

Illinois to unite a divided America since President Abraham Lincoln? Using the site where Lincoln once served during the mid-nineteenth century, Obama turned the pages of history in America as he ventured forth, in the early twenty-first century, from Springfield like his predecessor long ago. As unlikely candidates, their odyssey began at the lap of America's humble plain-folk scenario, traveling on the trails of challenges in the country, walking through opposition, and yet equipped with a launching pad of determined willpower sustaining them—Obama and Lincoln—experiencing similar and different orbiting circumstances defining their more dramatic commonality than most of the cadre of the other presidents of the United States can ever claim. The Democratic Party was especially predominant as a major party in the South for discriminatory reasons, then changing its course to more progressively liberal politics with the emergence of President Franklin D. Roosevelt (thirty-second president) in the 1930s and early 1940s when President Roosevelt masterminded the salvation of the country with the New Deal economic package that effectively erased and eased the suffering pains of the Great Depression. Within President Roosevelt's White House years, a host of black Americans who once gave their allegiance to the Republican Party because of Abraham Lincoln switched their allegiance to the Democratic Party, even though many blacks still were not permitted to vote as late as the early decades within the twentieth century. With the thrust of the civil rights movement in the mid-twentieth century came white flight from the Democratic Party in the Deep South as Southern states rallied around the Republican Party, which had begun to take on more conservative politics. In 1965, the Voting Rights Act passed in Congress and was signed by President Lyndon Baines Johnson (thirty-fifth president), ensuring the legal right for all Americans to vote without the barriers of poll taxes and literacy tests used to bar blacks from voting in the South. Upon President Johnson signing that significant document, he openly warned and recognized that he had signed the South over to the Republicans. One hundred years before the Voting Rights Bill, back in 1865, Abraham Lincoln (sixteenth president) initiated strong forces to aggressively amend the Constitution of the United States of America by shepherding in the Thirteenth Amendment through United States Congress to give sustainability and permanence to the Emancipation Proclamation's ringing and consoling words "Forever Free," which would permanently stand! Upon signing the Emancipation Proclamation in 1863, Lincoln told those who witnessed this humanitarian act: "I never, in my life, felt more certain that I was doing the right thing than I do in signing this paper. If my name ever goes into history, it will be for this act, and my whole soul is in it."[16] In efforts to sustain blacks in their rightful human dignity and the liberty of their natural rights, Lincoln instituted the Reconstruction Policy.

Unfortunately, after Lincoln's assassination, the Reconstruction Period (1865–1878) was short-lived, failing to champion in the fullness of a "new birth of freedom and a more perfect union" that America's sixteenth president so valiantly instructed and invoked the national leaders to activate. Barack Obama became the Upper House's third black senator one hundred or more years after the Reconstruction Period.

Finally, Barack Obama took his turn in the Land o' Lincoln (Illinois) to revive our honor of keeping the mission alive and well. Obama's enthusiastic cry for needed change and encouragement of hope resonated among the diversity of throngs of supportive people who stood outside in the frigid, bitter coldness as they gathered in the warmth and wholeness of this new day, witnessing this electrifying candidate of promise, wrapping the depths and insulated covers of his dreams tightly around them, feeling the secure pride of being an American.

And Obama repeated the words of the first elected Republican president of the United States of America—Abraham Lincoln—who organized the forces against slavery, who once said:

> Of strange, discordant, and even hostile elements, we gathered from the four winds, and formed and fought to battle through. That is our purpose.[17]

Then, in his own words, this brave African American marching toward becoming president of the United States of America informed us by underscoring:

> That's why I'm in this race. Not just to hold an office, but, to gather with you to transform a nation. . . . And, if you will come join me in this improbable quest . . .
> Then I'm ready to take up the cause, and march with you, and work with you. Together, starting today, let us finish the work that needs to be done, and usher in a new birth of freedom on this Earth.[18]

Launching from the Prairie State of Illinois on the frontier of America in the nineteenth century, so did Abraham Lincoln's improbable quest and passion for civic politics commence. Although not born in Illinois, nearby, he drifted into Illinois (to be discussed in later chapters) and remained there for a quarter of a century (twenty-five years) until he departed as president-elect of the United States. Like Barack Obama, Abraham Lincoln's election to the presidency was stunning because he did not fit the standard profile of his fifteen predecessors (before him). No prestigious name, no military hero, no family wealth surrounded the sixteenth president of the United States, nor did Barack Obama lay claim to any such previous privileges of wealth, fame, or military honor. Conversely, Barack Obama announced his candidacy for president from the old Illinois state capitol building to crowds who gathered on a cold, clear, wintry day (February 10) in 2007 while approximately ten thousand people[19] stood to help launch this hopeful candidate of African descent and American origin to become their leader. President-elect Abraham Lincoln once bade farewell to a group of one thousand gathered friends and neighbors on a cold, rainy Saturday morning (February 11, 1861) at the Great Western Railroad Depot on the platform of his presidential train departing from his beloved Springfield bound for the White House and his inauguration in a few weeks (March 4). In sorrowful tones of departing, Lincoln expressed words of goodbye to his people/neighbors there:

> My friends, no one, not in my situation, can appreciate my feeling of sadness of this parting. To this place, and the kindness of these people, I owe everything. . . . Here my children have been born, and one is buried. I now leave, not knowing when, or whether ever, I may return, with a task before me greater than that which rested on [George] Washington.[20]

Ironically, when Barack Obama delivered his acceptance speech in Chicago at Grant Field (Tuesday, November 4, 2008), he expressed bittersweet memories of his grandmother who passed away in Honolulu, Hawaii, just two days before his election. President-elect Barack Obama paid tribute, too, as he reflected: "And, to my grandmother who is no longer with us and the family that made me who I am . . . I miss them tonight, my debt to them is beyond measure."[21] Both presidents-elect lifted up family departed as they began their journeys to deliver America from a growing crisis mounting and hopefully to heal a suffering/torn nation. When Abraham Lincoln became the sixteenth president of the United States, it was threatened by the very likelihood that he might be the final president of an authentic United States as the North and South signaled an ominous battle cry of a civil war testing whether two governments would divide the country or unite the country as one government. Therefore, the election of 1860 was as eventful and suspenseful while being anxiously awaited by blacks, enslaved, and white patriots alike as the election of 2008 unfurling majestically like the red, white, and blue stripes of Old Glory symbolically and proudly waving/heralding the spirit of its historic political significance. Lincoln's election to presidential executive political power could influence freedom for a people toiling to loosen the shackles of two hundred years in the clutches of a chattel slave system, combined with his shrewd and determined guidance of the Union

Army against the rebellious army of General Robert E. Lee. A mighty scourge battled on the soil of its own landscape from north to south, eventually ending the strife in a victory uniting America. Now, after twenty-seven presidents succeeding President Lincoln, America stood in line awaiting the election of the forty-fourth president of the United States of America. In the 2008 presidential election year, likely presidential nominees stood, such as Senator John McCain, the Republican nominee from Arizona and a Vietnam War hero, prisoner of war, and popular long-term senior senator in the House for over twenty-six distinguished years of service. On the other hand, an unlikely candidate hailed as the Democratic nominee from Illinois. There stood Senator Barack Obama, a junior senator in the House for a mere three years, the third African American elected senator since Reconstruction, currently the *only* African American senator in the House of Senate, who shocked the nation and world when he seized his party's nomination, posing another stunning question. Will the politics of racism deny him his turn to lead our country, or will the conscience of universal human rights lead us to elect him on the principle of "Turnabout is fair play. It's Obama's turn now in 2008"? It was granted. Indeed, in grand and unprecedented style, the forty-seven-year-old Barack Obama dramatically reached across the parameters of America, reversing division by heralding the clarion declaration of unity.

Barack Obama—elected as president of the United States of America—November 4, 2008! Indeed, he filled the consecutive count of numbers by becoming the forty-fourth, numerically speaking. Now, we ask, what are the paradoxes defining Barack Obama and Abraham Lincoln leading them on this strange odyssey to capture their turn or term and become the sixteenth and forty-fourth presidents of the United States of America?

Biographically, this book is organized into concisely six informative chapters covering the basics in profiling Obama and Lincoln's quest. Accordingly, chapters 1 and 2 discuss the beginning and developmental years of Barack Obama, with similar aspects given to Lincoln's early life in the parallel approach upon which this book mainly expresses itself. The educational process and intellectual paradigm of both presidents earmark the stark differences in academic achievement, but indicate how both understood the necessity for acquiring knowledge, although in similar and different ways, and considered education at the top in their philosophy of life.

Chapter 3 explores Barack Obama's career and how it crisscrossed the political path of President Lincoln by delving into their grassroots causes, eventually leading into law study, which promoted them into professional law so meaningful and influential in their political careers. Again, Obama and Lincoln may be characterized by their hunger to become distinguished in their professional/political fields because of their approach and goal-thinking directed toward the well-being of people and safeguarding/maintaining the honorability of this nation—especially during turbulent or unsteady times.

The first three opening chapters provide the foundation and introduce how each was raised, schooled, employed, and entered into political life. Yet the long wandering is unfinished, since other important aspects of the odyssey remain, such as religion, faith, governmental issues, and party affiliations, all of which take place before the presidential and campaign challenges.

At this point, I wish to acquaint you with a distinguishable brand featured in a section of my writing described as the Interlude. During the Interlude, I pause from chapter development and place an interlude in the middle evenly positioned between the first three opening chapters and the last three closing chapters. My rationale is to link the past with the present, in historical years in this case or for this presidential narrative. It is, indeed, a retrospection of the American experience as related to the presence of three iconic figures during the recent past of the turbulent sixties. It is like a part of the whole projected between the parts of a longer composition, drama, or service.

Next, chapter 4 continues the saga of Obama while incorporating pieces of Lincolnia within the odyssey because both presidents were interrogated about their faith and religion, basically in ways to degrade and penalize them as acceptable candidates. Their faith and religious perspectives are explored, from their stand on religion and interest. Of course, the subject of religion and faith can become critical and judgmental for those in prominent leadership positions such as a president.

Chapter 5 defines Obama's ties with the Democratic Party and reaches back to Lincoln's initial party affiliation. There are resemblances in their theories to governmental practices from pragmatist to constitutionalist, all culminating into servant leadership as their central goal. Liberation cannot be overlooked as a connecting power held by both presidents to heal the nation and unite with diplomacy. Liberation means peace and promise for a better world with opportunities for all.

Chapter 6 brings the personal odyssey within the quest of the White House by showing how Obama and his nineteenth-century predecessor attained the White House then remained incumbent, 2012 and 1864. All of the conventional protocol of campaigns, nominations, popular issues, stump speeches/orating, and rivalry, enveloped in the huge, challenging task of convincing the electorate that Obama should become the forty-fourth president of the United States . . . that Lincoln should be the sixteenth president of the United States.

The effects of the victory shared were both positively overwhelming and joyful, yet echoes of negative opposition still whisper *no* and nevermore.

Finally, expressed in more poetic prose, the conclusion is given at the end of this book. Upon writing the ending—A Conclusion and a Transition—I have presented in literary terms a version of a jeremiad. A jeremiad is when the author bitterly laments the state of society and its morals in a serious tone of sustained invective, which generally contains a prophecy of society's imminent downfall.[22] Such is my conclusion and a look at the transition from the forty-fourth to the forty-fifth.

This book chronicles the journey to the White House by the first African American elected president of the United States and presents a perspective on the making of a president who was never expected to be elected or even remain elected—should he win—since he was endangered by the historical barriers of race and heritage. Barack Obama's election is a case in phenomenal change, and as president he skillfully and heavily enabled transformation upon this nation. Yes, the presidential realm or place is the central theme in this book, which speaks of President Obama's political campaign and exercise in his hope to successfully reorder the American presidential institution with the aid of the electorate.

In addition, this is a study about the impact of presidential executive power, its meaning, and example of how two presidents (one white and only one black) at different times (forty-four and sixteen) felt about humanity on the basis of what is morally sound and right, about race, social justice, and the spirit of enlightened equitable economy.

NOTES

Introduction
Launching from Illinois as Political Seat

1. James McPherson, ed., *To the Best of My Ability: The American Presidents* (New York: Dorling Kindersley Publishing, Inc., 2001), 9.
2. In *Lincoln and Freedom: Slavery, Emancipation, and the Thirteenth Amendment*, Holzer and Gabbard, ed. Allen C. Guelzo, "Abraham Lincoln and the Doctrine of Necessity," *Journal of the Abraham Lincoln Association* 18, no. 1 (Winter 1997), 79.
3. John K. Wilson, *Barack Obama: This Improbable Quest* (Boulder, CO: Paradigm Publishers, 2008), 4.
4. David Herbert Donald, *Lincoln* (New York: Simon and Schuster, 1995), 111.
5. Donald, 111.
6. John K. Wilson, in *Barack Obama*, 54–55, Ted Kleine, "Is Bobby Rush in Trouble?" March 17, 2000, *Chicago Reader*.
7. Donald, *Lincoln*, 112.
8. Donald, 113.
9. Donald, 113.
10. Donald, 113.
11. Donald, 113.
12. William C. Harris, *Lincoln's Rise to the Presidency* (Lawrence, KS: University Press of Kansas, 2007), 23.
13. Harris, 18.
14. US Census Bureau, "Springfield Metro Statistical Area."
15. Steve Dougherty, *Hopes and Dreams: The Story of Barack Obama* (New York: Black Dog and Leventhal Publishers, Inc., 2008), 127.
16. McPherson, *To the Best of My Ability*, 124.

17. Dougherty, *Hopes and Dreams.*
18. Dougherty, *Hopes and Dreams.*
19. Dougherty, *Hopes and Dreams.*
20. Donald, *Lincoln*, 273.
21. Dougherty, *Hopes and Dreams.*
22. *English Oxford Living Dictionaries.*

CHAPTER ONE

FAMILY ORIGIN AND EARLY YEARS

HERITAGE AND BIRTH

I don't know who my grandfather was; I am much more concerned to know what his grandson will be.
— Abraham Lincoln

So that family get-togethers over Christmas take on the appearance of a UN General Assembly meeting, I've never had the option of restricting my loyalties on the basis of race, or measuring my worth on the basis of tribe.
— Barack Obama

One's heritage and family is the bloodline connecting and joining an individual with another in a common bond of kinship. No matter who we are, we understand that being comes from other beings, and that as a being, we are beyond just a being, but we are from the species of human beings. Yet it is not enough to define humans as the only group belonging to family. Plants do. Lower animals do. As humans, we classify as social beings according to variables in our families because family and heritage define, identify, and relate us. Heritage is our roots as the family tree grows from the solid root base while many branches spread forth from that baseline or root. Of course, it does not call for any degree of complexity to figure that out. It is quite a simple fact, but a useful one in relationship to family. In regard to family names, each carries historical meaning and origins when you delve into its origins. So it is with the Christian names of our sixteenth and forty-fourth presidents, namely Abraham and Barack—Lincoln and Obama.

At this point, let us delve into the origins and roots of these two very famous people. First of all, the etymology of the name Abraham means "father of many" in Hebrew, or else as a contraction of Abram and *hamon*, "many, multitude." The biblical Abraham was originally Abram, but God changed his name as found in the Book of Genesis: "No longer shall your name be called Abram, but your name shall be Abraham for I have made you a father of many nations" (KJV). Abraham then led his followers from Ur into Canaan, and is regarded by the Jews as being the founder of the Hebrews through his son Isaac and by the Muslims as being the founder of the Arabs through his son Ishmael. As an English Christian name, Abraham became common after the English Protestant Reformation during the sixteenth century, and the origin of the surname Lincoln is English. Its definition means "from the lake colony," or one who came from Lincoln, England, as derived from the Welsh element *lyn*, meaning "lake or pool," and the Latin element *colonia*, meaning colony. Lincoln's ancestor Samuel Lincoln had arrived in Hingham, Massachusetts, from England in the seventeenth century, but his descendants had gradually moved west from Pennsylvania to Virginia and then westward to the frontier.[1]

Second, Barack Obama's first name, Barack, is the anglicized version of Baraka, which means "blessing" in Kiswahili (a.k.a. Swahili), a language spoken by Barack Obama's Kenyan father. The word "Barack" is shared among several languages, and Baraka comes from the Arabic spoken by the Omani Arabs who lived and traded along the coast of East Africa. Though it came to Kiswahili from Arabic, it no longer has any sectarian connotations and is in common use amongst East Africans of all faiths. Furthermore, it is a common name for boys in Kenya and Tanzania, and the name Barak is also mentioned in the Bible in the book of Judges. Barak was part of the story of the prophetess Deborah. Regardless of how one spells the name, it gives two possible and not contradictory meanings. One is "a blessing from God," and another is "a blessing from God that the individual may pass on to others as a benefit to them."

Now, on the basis of Lincoln's heritage, Lincoln himself once quipped about anything associated with his beginnings in somewhat dismissive tones:

> Why Scripps [John Locke Scripps, editor of *Chicago Tribune* when Lincoln became president-elect], it is a great piece of folly to attempt to make anything out of my early life. It can be condensed into a single sentence and that sentence you will find in Gray's Elegy, the short and simple annals of the poor. That's my life, and that's all you or anyone else can make of it.[2]

Quite frankly, Lincoln considered himself a self-made man who did not really value his genealogy to the extent that it had not contributed any great effect on his life's progress, thus accounting for his impatient reply about autobiographical material on him from journalists when he became president-elect. Reconstructing the history of families can be difficult; historians have learned to mine certain sources that richly document the ways families and households functioned in the past: these include oral testimonies, mythologies, genealogies, life histories, legal codes, archaeological excavations, languages, and literature.[3]

Abraham Lincoln was born in a log cabin, according to legend, on a bed of poles covered with corn husks on February 12, 1809, in Kentucky, in the Appalachians near Hodgenville (Hardin County, now Laurens County) on the Sinking Springs Farm—a wilderness settlement. His parents were Thomas and Nancy Hanks Lincoln. He had one sister, Sarah, as a surviving sibling, and a younger brother, who died in infancy. Abraham was the middle child born to the Lincoln couple and would become the first president born outside the original thirteen colonies. He was named Abraham for his paternal grandfather. Lincoln's grandfather, Abraham Lincoln, served as a captain of Virginia troops in the American Revolutionary War.[4]

Actually, it was Thomas Lincoln's father, Abraham, who moved the Lincolns to Kentucky, and the elder Lincoln was a distant cousin of Daniel Boone; in addition, Lincoln's grandfather owned several thousand acres of virgin land in Kentucky, and while planting corn with his sons, Mordecai and Thomas, Lincoln's grandfather, Abraham, was slain by Indians. However, Lincoln himself took great pride in the fact that he was named for his grandfather, although he never knew either of his grandfathers.

Next, in speaking of Obama's origins, Obama was haunted by an article he found while in high school, published in the Honolulu Star-Bulletin upon his father's graduation from the university.

> It's a short piece, with a photograph of him. No mention is made of my mother or me, and I'm left to wonder whether the omission was intentional on my father's part.... I would not have known at the time, for I was too young to realize that I was supposed to have a live-in father, just as I was too young to know that I needed a race.[5]

Barack Hussein Obama II was born at the Kapi'olani Medical Center for Women and Children in Honolulu, Hawaii, on August 4, 1961. Hawaii is known as a world-famous tourist site, which is considered a resort paradise because of its beauty and comfortable climate on the Pacific Ocean. The natural beauty of Hawaii features deep-blue seas, flowing waterfalls, gorgeous flowers, swaying palm trees, and includes many nationalities/racial groups. What a wonderful setting in which to be born! Barack Hussein Obama Sr. and Stanley Ann Dunham (Obama) were not tourists here, for they were indeed the biological parents of Barack Obama II. In terms of natural birth, Abraham Lincoln, of course, was born to a white woman, Nancy; and Barack Obama was born to a white woman, Ann; however, Barack Obama's father was black, causing Obama to be of mixed heritage. Yet he is authentically of a contrast mixture of African and American bound in the truest sense by direct, intimate ties to Africa and

America. Ties that cling as close as his paternalism does in binding him to a Kenyan-born black father. Likewise, as any citizen born here, he (Obama) is as firmly an heir to America as anyone else born here while cradled within the maternal womb and bosom of his Kansas-born white mother, endorsing Barack's rightful place in this country. Within the historical origins of Obama's family, one of his maternal great-great-grandfathers, Christopher Columbus Clark, a decorated Union soldier, and Clark's wife's mother were rumored to have been a second cousin of Jefferson Davis, president of the Confederacy; and another distant ancestor had been a full-blooded Cherokee.[6] Furthermore, in growing up in the formative years from birth to his youthful years of adolescence, neither Obama nor Lincoln regularly came in close contact with massive amounts of black people or Negroes because of the environment where they lived, since Lincoln spent his early life in the remote backwoods of Kentucky and Indiana, and the parts of Illinois where he lived were not heavily populated with Negroes during that time. Of course, the real conditions were practically similar in Hawaii shortly after receiving statehood into the United States as the fiftieth state, August 21, 1959. It is the only state in the US located in the Oceania comprised entirely of islands.

For Lincoln, one who was raised in the backwoods of Kentucky and wilderness of Indiana until his adventure as a teen lad on the flatboat floating up the Mississippi River in voyage to New Orleans, legend has it that he encountered his first glimpse of Negroes and observed them being auctioned into bondage. Evidently, the unwarranted brute terror that Lincoln witnessed of the enforced harshness and scarred bruises of such cruelty must have pierced deeply like thorns into his white flesh. Although Barack Obama traveled beyond the borders of the United States, far from his home state of Hawaii, he did not frequently interact with other African Americans; therefore, his mother helped him face the issues of racism when as a boy Obama came across a picture in *Life* magazine of the black man who had tried to peel off his skin. Furthermore, his mother had warned Obama about "bigots—they were ignorant, uneducated people one should avoid."[7]

Additionally, Obama contemplated, "I noticed that there was nobody like me in the Sears, Roebuck Christmas catalog. . . . And that Santa was a white man."[8]

THE PROGENITORS

The seminal role of natural parents begins with the birthing process, followed by other related functions of parenthood. From birth to death, the child is on the spirit of the parent in heart, soul, and mind, creating internal feelings for his/her offspring. External primary traits by parents are demonstrated in provisions made for their child with specific social roles provided by mother and father. Progeny at the biological ancestral form simply means an ancestor in the direct line or to beget, dating back to the fourteenth-century etymology of Middle English. The progenitors of Abraham Lincoln and Barack Obama are listed and discussed here in the tradition of biological father and mother, including nonbiological relations defined as stepparents included among the supporting characters in this particular narrative. Objective narratives and biographical data are provided in an attempt to lend meaningful examples of depth about Abraham Lincoln's parents and stepmother, along with similar treatment of Barack Obama's parents and stepfather. The most intimate and basic social organizations are families and households. They are intersected and interacted with ideas, institutions, and communities from ancient times to about 1750 CE. But too often historians have ignored the private daily realm of human activity, instead in favor of large-scale political affairs and the actions of "great men."[9]

Yet with a recent approach to family, historians have viewed the familial structure differently as evidence of the variety and commonality of world history, such as models for ordering the world, as evidence of the dynamic nature of the past, and as a way to bring the ordinary and familiar into global perspective.[10] By a variety of interpretive accounts, the history of Lincoln's family has been written about including myth, oral testimony, and even legal codes.

Beginning with the closest patriarch that Lincoln knew in a personal perspective, the first progenitor is the father of Lincoln. Abraham Lincoln's father was Thomas Lincoln, of whom many controversial interpretations have been given concerning the elder Lincoln. As father of the sixteenth president, Thomas Lincoln never saw his son rise to the head of state, or the highest office in the land. Neither did the father of the forty-fourth president live to see his son become the first African American to be elected president of the United States of America.

Aside from that, Abraham Lincoln's father has been described as illiterate, crude, poor, lazy, and white trash, along with other unfavorable images conjured up about Thomas Lincoln; often suggesting that Thomas Lincoln mistreated his son and failed to appreciate Abraham's intellectual ability adds to the catalog of criticisms. Instead of his father showing pride in his apparently gifted son, Lincoln's father put him to work by hiring him out to do manual labor for the more prosperous farmers, but that was a tradition more or less during that period. The veracity of who Thomas Lincoln was and his relationship with his eldest son is not as jaded as given by some biographers. Separating facts from myth is important in the story of Lincoln and his father. It is a fact that Thomas Lincoln was not an educated man as was the highly educated senior Barack Obama—father of Barack Obama. To say that Thomas Lincoln did not appreciate learning is not a fact either, because he rarely interrupted Lincoln's love of reading and self-educating himself, indicating that the father, indeed, probably felt proud of his son's intellectual mind. He wanted Abraham to learn readin', writin', and cipherin' (arithmetic), even if Thomas had not. Perhaps he considered Abraham's learning ability and inquisitive mind as a fortunate thing. Although Thomas Lincoln was certainly not an elite Southern planter class, he was not shiftless and lazy, either. He worked hard at his trade of carpentry and his daily task of tilling the soil as any typical farmer on the American frontier. Unfortunately, Thomas Lincoln moved the family frequently, owning several hundreds of acres of land but always running into legal difficulties about titles of the land. As a result, Thomas Lincoln moved the family about on the basis of legal land problems and "partly on account of slavery,"[11] his father confided. Thomas Lincoln was a good-natured, jovial man who, surprisingly, enjoyed weaving stories to entertain his friends and neighbors who gathered about to hear "ol' Tom." He was morally good, and treated others well. Thomas Lincoln was a family man to the best of his ability according to the standards of the times for men of his status. As a family man, he followed the traditions of life in the sixteenth and seventeenth centuries as a man who provided for his wife and children, and to rule over his family.

And the wife was the "mother of the house," a position of high authority and equal respect.[12] On the part of some of the favorable narratives referencing Lincoln's father, according to historian Miller, his interpretation describes Thomas Lincoln more credibly:

> He did take the initiative to bring his family through two long and complicated moves, the second involving an entourage of thirteen people. He did take the initiative to return to Kentucky to find a woman he had known, Sarah Bush Johnston, to be a wife and mother to his children.[13]

Furthermore, Miller adds:

> One has sympathy for him when, in the Fall of 1818, he has to make a long series of pine coffins for folk who have died of the milk sickness, including his wife's cousins, the Sparrows and finally his wife herself; Abraham's mother.[14]

Young Abe Lincoln helped his father clear away the wooded areas, construct log cabins as their homes, till the soil, and plant corn and pumpkins, all of which are values of hard work and honesty instilled in the boy Abraham by his father. Biographically, Thomas Lincoln was born on January 6, 1778, to Bathsheba and Abraham Lincoln. He was born in Rockingham County, Virginia, the fourth of five siblings born to his parents. The Washington County Tax (1795) lists him as a white male between the ages of sixteen and twenty-one. In c. 1797, Thomas spent a year working as a hired hand for his Uncle Isaac on the Watauga River in Tennessee, moving to Hardin County, Kentucky, in 1802, where he purchased a 238-acre farm the next year. In 1806, he married Nancy Hanks and the couple had three children: Sarah, Abraham, and one child, Thomas, who died in infancy. As a farmer and a carpenter, Thomas Lincoln was a responsible citizen living on the frontier. At times, he served as a jury member, a petitioner for a road, and a guard for prisoners, and in terms of education, he lacked ambition because he never fully understood Abraham's desire to read and learn, but did not strongly interfere with his son's love of books.

Thomas and Nancy were members of the Little Mount Separate Baptist Church who had broken from the regular church over the issue of slavery. Lincoln's father stood approximately five foot nine or five foot ten and weighed about 190 pounds. His face was well-rounded with dark hazel eyes and coarse black hair; Thomas was compactly built and very strong physically, as was his son in strength. Temperate in his drinking habits and generally of an inoffensive personality characterizes Thomas Lincoln. Moving his family to southern Indiana in late 1816, a home site was chosen sixteen miles north of the Ohio River, about a mile from Little Pigeon Creek. By February 1817, Thomas built a new log cabin eighteen square feet with a packed dirt floor and a stone fireplace used for both cooking and heating. When his son, Abraham, was eight years old, his father handed him an ax and put his young son to work helping to clear fields, chop wood, and split rails for fences. After the death of his first wife, Thomas went to Elizabethtown, Kentucky, and proposed to Sarah Bush Johnston, a widow whom he had known for many years. On December 2, 1819, the two were married. Along with Sarah's three children by a previous marriage, the newlyweds and the children traveled back to the cabin in Pigeon Creek, Indiana, to join Abraham and Sarah Lincoln, the two motherless children of Thomas Lincoln.

By 1827, Thomas Lincoln became the owner of one hundred acres of land, and in 1829 began building a better cabin. Receiving news from John Hanks that Illinois had fertile soil and was free of the milk sickness that had claimed the life of his first wife, Thomas finished his new cabin, then decided to move again—this time to Illinois. In Illinois, he lived on three farms in Coles County, and he purchased his last one, the Goosenest Prairie Farm, in 1840. The Goosenest Prairie home was a double-room-style cabin, which was essentially two log cabins built close to each other with the space between boarded over. By 1845, eighteen people were living in the structure as an extended family arrangement. As a farmer, Thomas Lincoln raised corn, oats, and wheat, and his livestock included chickens, horses, hogs, milk cows, sheep, and geese. In 1848, he received twenty dollars from Abraham to save the rest of the land from forced sale. He is buried with his second wife, Sarah Bush Johnston, in Shiloh Cemetery located one mile west of the Lincoln Log Cabin State Historic Site between Charleston and Lerna, Illinois.

LINCOLN'S MOTHER

"God bless my mother; all that I am or ever hope to be I owe to her," Lincoln once shared with a friend about his mother.[15] How well did Lincoln know his mother, since she passed away when he was around eight or nine years old? As a result, Lincoln referred to her as his "angel mother." All that he owed to his mother perhaps indicates that Lincoln was speaking in terms of mental capacities inherited from her. The emotional attachment to his mother may mostly be speculated with the grief of a son over his deceased mother who was beloved, because it is quite unlikely that he had clear remembrance of her tucking him in at night or sitting down with him teaching him his alphabets or how to count; absolutely not any of those things associated with the instructs of academics occurred. So the social interactions are vague while strangely wrapped up in the psyche of nurturing ties binding him to his mother forever. Abraham Lincoln's mother did not live to raise her children up to maturity; it was common in the early eighteenth century for mothers to die in childbirth or other maladies due to the nonexistent or inaccessibility of medical care for the poor. Accordingly, Lincoln knew almost nothing about his mother's family, the Hanks.

It was at the Knob Creek Farm, a setting of ethereal beauty with a transparent, clear creek that ran through the property, where Lincoln held his earliest memories of his childhood, but few of them concerned his mother, who remained a shadowy image to him. It is not clear what she looked like since there are no pictures of her, only a recent painting. Of course, the science of photography was not available back then; however, many years later those who had known her described her variously as being tall or of average height, thin or stout, beautiful or plain. Most agreed that she was "brilliant" or "intellectual."[16]

According to tradition, Nancy Hanks was able to read, but like many other frontier women she did not know how to write and had to sign legal documents with an X. Abraham must have remembered how his mother set up housekeeping, cooked the family meals, washed and mended the scanty clothing that they wore, and perhaps helped in the farming. He recorded only that she gave birth to a third child, named Thomas, his brother, with whom Lincoln would never be able to interact because the child did not live beyond infancy, as stated earlier. Otherwise, again, Lincoln called her his "angel mother" in recognition of her loving affection, but partly to distinguish her from his stepmother, who was very much alive.[17]

The biography of Lincoln's mother comes from a small variety of sources. In short, however, Nancy Hanks Lincoln is the birth mother of Abraham Lincoln. She was born on February 5, 1784, in Hampshire County, in the west of Virginia. The birth occurred in a cabin along Mike's Run at the foot of New Creek Mountain in what is now Mineral County, West Virginia. Nancy's mother was Lucy Hanks, but nothing is really known for certain about Nancy's father. According to William Herndon (Abraham Lincoln's law partner), Lincoln gave the implication that his maternal grandfather was, perhaps, in the class of those considered as well-bred planters or farmers. Little is known of Nancy's early life. As a child, Nancy was taken by her mother along the Wilderness Road through the Cumberland Gap into Kentucky. There in Kentucky, Lucy Hanks married Henry Sparrow. Afterward, young Nancy went to live with Henry's brother, Thomas Sparrow, and Elizabeth Hanks Sparrow, a sister of Lucy. Soon Nancy began being called Nancy Sparrow because Elizabeth Hanks Sparrow became almost like a mother to Nancy. As Nancy grew up, she became skilled in the arts of needlework and she became an excellent seamstress. She was hired to sew anything from wedding gowns to funeral attire; meanwhile, Nancy became known for her work ethic, neatness, cheerfulness, and intelligence. She was deeply religious.

Her cousin, John Hanks, described Nancy as having dark hair, hazel eyes, five foot seven in height, a delicate frame, weighing, perhaps, a little over one hundred pounds, and evidently she was one who was admired and respected by those who knew her, as legend speaks of the mother of Lincoln. Nancy sometimes lived briefly with families for whom she was sewing; her services were in demand in Hardin, Mercer, and Washington Counties. It was during the time Nancy was working as a seamstress that she met Thomas Lincoln, a carpenter from Elizabethtown. Shortly after, a romance developed and the two decided to be married. So on June 12, 1806, Nancy Hanks and Thomas Lincoln were married; the Rev. Jesse Head presided over the ceremony. Nancy was a good and loving mother to her children. She was very ambitious for them and hoped they could have the opportunities in life that she and Thomas had missed; therefore, Nancy dutifully read to Sarah and Abraham from the Lincoln family Bible. But in 1818 an attack of milk sickness struck the Little Pigeon Creek community. Milk sickness is a disease contracted by drinking milk from cows that have grazed on poisonous white snakeroot, and such a disease was a mysterious ailment that caused dizziness, nausea, and stomach pains as the initial symptoms, followed by irregular respiration and pulse, prostration, then coma. Death came within seven days for both of the Sparrows who lived with the Lincolns, followed by Nancy taking ill also. For a week, sadly, she struggled, but she knew she was failing. Dennis Hanks, Nancy's cousin, recalled that she called the children to her bedside and asked them to be good and kind to their father, to each other, and to the world. On October 5, 1818, Nancy Hanks Lincoln passed away at the age of thirty-four years old. In later years, Abraham would recall helping to carve pegs for his mother's coffin wherein Thomas Lincoln hauled the coffin off made of green pine on a sled to the top of a thickly wooded hill to bury Nancy without a formal funeral service. The grave of Nancy Hanks Lincoln is located within the Lincoln Boyhood National Memorial in Lincoln City, Indiana.

> *If Nancy Hanks came back . . . Seeking news*
> *of what she loved most,*
> *She'd ask first "Where's my son?"*
> —Excerpts from poem entitled "Nancy Hanks" by
> Rosemary Benet[18]

From centuries past, the story of Abraham Lincoln has been recorded repeatedly. The progeny of Abraham Lincoln presents a tale woven from fabric of simplistic quality sewn and stitched together on the rugged pieces of American frontier in the aftermath of the Revolutionary days. When Lincoln was born (1809), Thomas Jefferson, one of the Founding Fathers, was completing his term as the third president of the United States; James Madison was president-elect to become the fourth president of the United States. Lincoln's father was born in 1778, before the first chief executive, George Washington 1789–1797, became president over the new republic, and before the First Congress (March 4, 1789) convened in the temporary federal capital of New York City.

Also, Lincoln's mother was born 1784, five years before the presidency of the first president, George Washington.

The frontier past separates the Lincolns and the Obamas, numerically. Nevertheless, the familial correlation is found in the natural biological factor of each family-tree tracing. Beginning somewhere and translating to someone becomes the common denominator and the hidden source distinguishing one family from another. Consequently in common, Lincoln and Obama have that standard universal factor, just as others have—heritage and origin—even though their times and lives present a new set of circumstances with modern times as we turn to the progeny of Barack Obama II.

***

His father was Barack Hussein Obama Sr. Unlike Abraham Lincoln, Barack Obama wrote a book about his father (*Dreams from My Father*) drawing on personal accounts as evidence, making it common knowledge that his father was not around in his formative years. Therefore, one concludes that Obama did not interact on a daily basis with his father as in the case of Lincoln and his father. On the other hand, the literature on Barack Obama Sr. has not made it down through the ages because he has not become as well-known as of yet in terms of historical narrative. In other words, the Obamas are recently inducted into the Hall of Fame—just a few brief years ago—so to speak. Speculations have been made about the man who is the father of Senator Barack Obama. The descriptions have ranged from he was smart, a foreigner, perhaps a polygamist, deserted his family, a divorced man, a lover, charming, charismatic, an intellect, recipient of the prestigious Phi Beta Kappa key, sophisticated, an academian, dignified, outgoing, strong, weak, successful, a failure, disappointing, or promising. Those are the descriptives given on behalf of Barack Obama Sr. Are they simply myths, as well? For certain, among the speculations, one descriptive fact is that Barack Obama's father was an absent father. And even more so, all of the above may very well be associated with this man of modern times.

Was he so different from many men during his times twentieth century? Perhaps not—or maybe so. It is Barack Obama Sr. was well educated, unlike Thomas Lincoln, Abraham Lincoln's father. Obama Sr. was a highly professional man, not a blue-collar worker nor common laborer by the standards of modern society in his adulthood. Additionally, Barack Obama Sr. was ambitious, unlike Abraham Lincoln's father, who did not really have too much use for going beyond his typical means or status. However, what the senior Obama had in common with the senior Lincoln, maybe, is that neither man connected emotionally with his son, causing a sense of estrangement between the father-and-son relationship. If not intentionally, the two fathers did not distinguish themselves in that parental role; as a result, each son gave his mother more credit for his success in life than to his father. Of course, that is common in families as well, although it is an unfortunate reality. Yet the resiliency of children generally rises above that flaw of behavior displayed by some fathers in the small diameter etched out in the compact role of biological relationship without extending father/son into the intensity of a full familial socialization. From a biographical point of view, accounts of the life of Barack Obama Sr. appear impressive in print. Barack Hussein Obama Sr. was born in 1936 (the month is not recorded) on the shores of Lake Victoria just outside Kendu Bay, Kenya (Eastern Africa), and raised in the village of Nyang'oma Kogelo, herding goats as a child. He was the son of Hussein Onyango Obama (c. 1895–1979) and his second wife, Akumu Habiba. His family are members of the Luo ethnic group. President-elect Obama states that his grandfather "had been a prominent farmer, and elder of the tribe and a medicine man with healing power."[19] Obama Sr. was raised as a Muslim, but later became an atheist. Before working as a cook for missionaries in Nairobi, Anyang (Barack Obama's paternal grandfather) had traveled widely, enlisting with the name Onyango Obama in the British colonial forces during World War I and visiting Europe, India, and Zanzibar, where he converted from Christianity to Islam. He had many wives, and Barack Obama's father was raised by his father's third wife, Sarah, after his own mother left her family and separated from her husband in 1945.

Now, Obama Sr. (Obama's father) married at the age of eighteen in a tribal ceremony to Kezia, with whom he had four children. His education was expansive. From 1950 to 1953, Obama Sr. studied at Maseno National School, an exclusive Christian boarding school that is run by the Anglican Church of Kenya. The head teacher, B. L. Bowers, described Obama Sr. in his records as "very keen, steady, trustworthy and friendly. Concentrates, reliable and outgoing."[20] He received a scholarship in economics through a program organized by nationalist leader Tom Mboya that offered Western educational opportunities to outstanding Kenyan students. At the age of twenty-three, Obama Sr. was the first African student to enroll at the University of Hawaii at Manoa in 1959, leaving behind an expecting wife, Kezia, and their infant son. He had already turned away from Islam and become an atheist by the time he moved to the United States. On February 21, 1961, Obama Sr. married fellow student Ann Dunham in Maui, Hawaii. Shortly thereafter, Obama Sr.'s and Dunham's son Barack was born. Evidently, Barack Obama Sr. did not bother to inform Ann Dunham that he had left behind a wife and child in Kenya with another on the way. Dunham left school to care for the baby, while Obama Sr. completed his degree, graduating from the University of Hawaii in June 1962. He left shortly thereafter to travel to Cambridge, Massachusetts, where he would begin graduate study at Harvard University in the fall.

In a matter of two years, his wife Ann Dunham (Obama) filed for a divorce in Honolulu on January 1964; nonetheless, Obama Sr. did not contest and the divorce was granted. While at Harvard, Obama Sr. met an American-born teacher named Ruth Nidesand, who followed him to Kenya when he returned there after receiving a master's degree in economics from Harvard in 1965 at the age of twenty-nine. Nidesand eventually became his third wife and had two children with him before they divorced.[21] Both the father and the son achieved success at young ages. Barack Obama Sr. often introduced himself as "Dr. Obama," although there is no record of him completing a doctorate degree.[22] At Harvard, Obama Sr. thrived in the academic setting and became a fixture in bars at Cambridge, chain-smoking in his signature black-rimmed glasses. Nearly thirty years later, his son would become the first African American president of the *Harvard Law Review*.[23]

After Harvard, Barack Obama's father returned to Africa to fulfill his mission. But he failed to take Barack's mother and his two-year-old son with him. Leaving his American family behind, the elder Obama left miles of distance between his son Barack and the child's formative years. Upon receiving sources of secondary commentaries on his father from his white maternal grandfather and mother, Barack tried to understand the mystique of this man. Eventually returning to Hawaii in 1971, Barack Obama's father visited his son, making the father's return a primary source of identity for his young son.

Within this unique scenario, previously at Punahou School, according to Barack, he had taken it upon himself to fantasize about his progeny by telling some of his classmates that his father was a prince and his grandfather a chief, insinuating that Obama himself came from royalty. He even stretched the tale more, making his classmates think that he could go back to his father's native land and become a prince upon his princely father's death. Questioning him, his friends inquired, "Will you go back and be a prince?" "Well . . . If I uh want to, I could. It's sort of complicated, see, 'cause the tribe is full of warriors like Obama . . . That means 'Burning Spear.' . . . So my father has to settle these feuds before I can come."[24]

Interestingly, Barack's story reflected his inner turmoil woven on the thin threads of the world of reality meeting the world of fantasy dreams. On his father's brief visit to Hawaii after ten years gone, he learned that his father had six other children in Kenya. Astonishingly, he had African sisters and brothers, and he was their

American brother, but they did not know each other. Additionally, Dr. Barack Obama Sr., who was frequently called "Doctor," by admiration, perhaps, not because of an authentic doctorate degree, had been hurt in a major car crash. After being hospitalized for an extensive time, his trip back to America was part of his recuperation regimen. Ten-year-old Barack Obama's tension increased, coupled with his mounting sense of wonderment while observing his father for the first time to remember in the junior Barack's tenth year of life.

"Well, Barry . . . It is a good thing to see you after so long. Very good," came his father's greeting to ten-year-old Barack.

Observantly, Barack recalled:

> I watched him carefully. . . . He was much thinner than I had expected, the bones in his knees cutting the legs of his trousers in sharp angles. . . . Beside him, a cane with a blunt ivory head leaned against the wall. . . . When he took off his horn-rimmed glasses to rub the bridge of his nose, I saw that they were slightly yellow, the eyes of someone who's had malaria more than once. There was a fragility about his frame, I thought, a caution when he lit a cigarette or reached for his beer.[25]

Another vivid memory about Obama Sr. was that his father emphasized preparation, study, and education above the trivial and nonsensical. Read, read, read, and more reading seemed to be the message enforced by Obama's father. When his father visited Punahou School, sharing his story about Kenya, Africa, Barack's teacher and classmates were overwhelmed, erasing Barack's previous doubts and feelings of shame or embarrassment about his black father coming to his school. "You've got a pretty impressive father," "Your dad is pretty cool," came his classmates' assessment of his father.[26]

Looking back, when Abraham Lincoln visited his son Robert Todd Lincoln at Harvard following Lincoln's successful Cooper

Union speech in New York, the senior Lincoln traveled to spend four days with Robert, wherein he made campaign addresses at Concord, Manchester, Dover, and Exeter. While at Exeter, many of the boys from the academy turned out, and he had an impressive audience of about five hundred people. The students who knew Bob (Lincoln's son) as "a gentleman in every sense of the word; quiet in manner with a certain dignity of his own" were astonished when Bob's father, Lincoln, came in to the hall: "Tall, lank, awkwardly dressed in a loose, ill-fitting black frock coat, with black trousers." They observed his rumpled hair, his necktie turned awry. "Isn't it too bad Bob's father is so homely?" they whispered to each other. "Don't you feel sorry for him?"[27]

But after Lincoln disentangled his legs, rose slowly from his chair, and began speaking, they forgot his appearance; they no longer pitied Bob but felt proud to know his father.[28] And now, Barack Obama could feel good about his father's visit to his school and the fine speech he made to the captive audience of fifth graders at Punahou in Hawaii.

The first reunion between the father and son lasted one month. "We may never meet again" echoes in regard to that once-memorable meeting between father and son back in 1971 in Honolulu, Hawaii, so long ago when Barack was just a *young boy* . . .

Consequently, his father was a stranger to him. Decades later, in 2006, upon traveling to Kenya as Senator Obama, he was in the Kenyatta International Airport. As he processed forms in efforts to locate his lost luggage from the States, interestingly, upon completion of the form and giving it back to the British Airways agent Miss Omoro, who was Kenyan like his father, she looked the forms over before returning them to him. The senator vividly remembered her inquiring, "You wouldn't be related to Dr. Obama, by any chance?" "Well, yes—he was my father." Accordingly, Barack Obama remembered how much that mention of recognition meant to him because . . .

> She had recognized my name. That had never happened before, I realized; not in Hawaii, amazingly not in Indonesia, not in L.A. or New York or Chicago. For the first time in my life, I felt the comfort, the firmness of identity that a name might provide, how it could carry an entire history in other people's memories, so that they might nod and say knowingly, "Oh, you are so and so's son."[29]

In reference to name and identity, as a boy, Abraham Lincoln wrote in his copy book: "Abraham Lincoln is my name, and with my pen I wrote the same, I wrote in both hast[e] and speed and left it here for fools to read."[30] For penmanship practice and a reinforcement of his identity, or partly in the self-indulgent fancy that that *name* would someday ring bells, a *name* that would fill all the nation and was not unknown even in foreign lands; actually, all would show the importance of name recognition and how both names have become so significantly recognizable and well-known.

On his own, Senator Barack Obama in politics is cerebral and cool, but he can become steely, and strong, behaviors acquired from the absence of his father, making President Obama a self-reliant man as was President Lincoln. After all these years, Barack Obama Sr. had not visited with his son whatsoever until Barack was ten years old, and what a contrast between the length of years before they reunited and the swiftness of time hurriedly ending those thirty days with his son before it was time for Barack's father to depart for his native country of Kenya after his month's holiday in America with his son. It is said that Barack Obama Sr. returned to Africa and bragged with pride to his fellow countrymen that he planned to bring his son to the continent.

As a result, on his return to Kenya, Obama Sr. was hired by an oil company and then served as an economist in the Ministry of Transport, and later became senior economist in the Kenyan Ministry of Finance. In 1965, Obama Sr. wrote a paper entitled "Problems Facing Our Socialism," published in the *East Africa Journal*, harshly criticizing the blueprint for national planning, "African Socialism and Its Applicability to Planning in Kenya," produced by Tom Mboya's Ministry of Economic Planning and Development.

Indeed, the elder Obama felt pride in his accomplishments in America and was eager to fulfill his duties to his fellow countrymen in Kenya as a governmental economist. Unfortunately, a crisis broke out in the government there as the nation's first president, Jomo Kenyatta, began rewarding members of his Kikuyu tribe with land tracts, loans, and lucrative jobs. For Kenyans schooled during the United States 1960s civil rights movement and expecting the birth of a new Africa, coming home was difficult. Unlike his son who would someday become a famous and shrewd politician, Obama Sr. did not exhibit political skills or interest in diplomacy in his interactions with others. In short, his interpersonal skills were not as sharp as his son's became as he took on negotiations with powerful governmental officials. His father publicly and openly contradicted superiors, belittled coworkers, and exposed fraud. He was labeled a troublemaker.

Once when Barack Obama visited his Kenyan family in 2000 (Nairobi, Kenya), Senator Barack Obama took time out from the festivities of his family, making an official visit to the Kenyan government boldly criticizing them for failing to abort corruption and tribalism. His uncle, Said (Sy-ēd) Obama, the younger brother to his father, observantly responded to his nephew's attack on the Kenyan government and considered that perhaps his nephew, Barack, merely shared one of the family traits of being direct in his criticisms on situations that were questionable or needed to be attacked. Yet upon keener observance of Senator Obama's similar attitude as Obama Sr. had been forty years ago when he took Kenya's elite to task about corruption and neglect of those below them, Said Obama (his uncle) expanded his observance contrary to his former analysis by describing Obama not quite his Kenyan father's son as he studied Senator Obama's use of self-control, steadiness in approach to stressful situations, and even temperament style. His uncle added, "But in many ways, the son is quite the opposite. The ambition is controlled. And, he has a more sober mind."³¹ Earlier when the senior Obama left for America, he was a role model. He was promising, intensified by his big, beautiful, baritone voice with a noticeable British accent, which created an essence of eloquence. So does his son's eloquence of speech captivate audiences, including his substance of context. Indeed, Obama Sr. was promising. And he was a free spirit, too, often resulting in his father Onyango Obama (the junior Obama's African grandfather) bringing down wrath upon the head of his disobedient son, threatening to seize Obama Sr.'s visa and revoke it.

Rising from the goat pastures of an eastern African village to the Ivy League academic halls of Harvard, eventually taking a coveted post among the nation's post-colonial government leaders in Kenya, Barack Obama Sr. ascended his flight as one of the prominent citizens of Kenya, but before he fully stretched his wings to glide upwardly, instead, like a fallen star, he descends into the night—the evenfall of his life's journey. "He was a brilliant guy, but in so many ways his life was a mess," Senator Obama concluded about his father.³²

On the basis of his character flaws, career problems, and rather ragged marital status, Barack Obama Sr.'s ambition has similarities to the tragic heroes found in the Shakespearean dramatic tragedies, no doubt. A disintegrating career broken because of complications associated with cronyism at his workplace in addition to his own internal weaknesses brought him down to levels of despair. Relying on drinking to resolve his problems turned him into an alcoholic, leading to poverty from which he never recovered. As President Barack Obama describes in his memoir, his father's conflict with President Kenyatta destroyed his career, and Obama Sr.'s friend Kenyan journalist Philip Ochieng describes Obama Sr.'s difficult personality and drinking problems in the Kenyan newspaper.³³ Prior to his death, Obama Sr. lost both legs in an automobile collision; he subsequently lost his job as well. Barack Obama Sr. is the father of eight children by four different wives. He is often remembered as the "Old Man" by his African children. The father of Barack Obama died in a car accident on November 24, 1982, at the age of forty-six in his homeland, Nairobi, Kenya, and he is buried in Alego at the village of Nyang'oma Kogelo, Siaya District, Kenya.

"Truly he was dead. He could no longer tell me how to live. . . . I now felt as if I had to make up for all of his mistakes," as expressed reflectively by his American son, Barack, in remembering his father fifteen years later in Kenya: a testimony by his son.[34]

OBAMA'S MOTHER

If Barack Obama felt estranged toward his father as did his long-ago predecessor, Abraham Lincoln, what was Obama's essay on his mother like? How did she impact her son's life? Chances are, assumingly, she played a major role in her only son's life on the basis that his father was absent from his life, except for the brevity of one month when he saw his child after ten years, living continents apart like their relationship with one another. It is said that Barack Obama II and his mother were very close, although often they were far away from each other on different physical continents, since his mother was a free-spirited wanderer whose life was unconventional in association with her career of assisting others to improve their lives. Indeed, she is the one who shaped her son's life most. Barack Obama reflected on his mom in words of endearment similar to Lincoln, his predecessor/presidential mentor. Barack Obama remarks about his mother:

> I know that she was the kindest, most generous spirit I have ever known, and that what is best in me I owe to her.[35]

Barack Obama's father and mother met at the University of Hawaii on the entrance of the 1960s when mainland America, especially its Southern regions, battled the conflict between segregation versus integration. Blacks and whites were not fully out of the darkness of blatant racism. A new version of freedom versus enslavement one hundred years ago when Lincoln became the sixteenth president in 1860 was like a replay. Now, in 1960, when Barack Obama Sr. and Ann Dunham married in Hawaii, their marriage was not the typical union, because the groom was black, an African, and the bride was white, an American. The vicissitudes of the times were paradoxical and provincial.

Obama's mother was Kansas born and had migrated to Hawaii with her parents when she was a teenager. Back in the late 1850s, Lincoln turned his attention to a burning issue at the time: the Kansas-Nebraska Act. Abraham Lincoln fought and debated the Kansas-Nebraska Act when it was uncompromised as he attempted to prevent the extension of slavery into Kansas, leading Lincoln to attack the issue hard and long. His aim was to ensure that Kansas was not omitted in the struggle to stop the spread of slavery into the federal territories. Kansas entered after "Bloody Kansas" violence as a free state. These events happened one hundred years earlier on the basis of attempts to prevent African slavery spread into Kansas.

And now, in 1960, a former Kansan white girl living in Hawaii joined hands in matrimony with an African black man. Interestingly, this marriage event was like a precursor to the popular movie *Guess Who's Coming to Dinner* in 1967. Ironically, the young white American woman Joanna and a man with whom she's had a whirlwind romance, Dr. Prentice (actor Sidney Poitier), an African American whom she met while on holiday in Hawaii, planned to marry and live in Switzerland, while they prepared to tell Joanna's parents about their upcoming marriage, played by actor Spencer Tracy (the father) and actress Katharine Hepburn (the mother). The senior Obamas' marriage echoed the theme of the popular MGM movie. Meanwhile, a recent observer's remarks were significant in 1997 about the movie: "But I can't help but think that the more things change in thirty years, sometimes they remain the same. Certainly there's more examples of interracial couples today than thirty years ago, and therefore a greater degree of tolerance, but for a lot of narrow-minded individuals, it's still as controversial or 'appalling' as it was thirty years ago."[36] Back in 1967, fifty-one years ago,

Guess Who's Coming to Dinner created quite a buzzing stir as people flocked to see the startling drama!

Regardless of his parents' rather episodic romance, the affection that Barack Obama had for his mother was obvious, as his frequent remembrances of his mother were configured into many of his campaign messages as he traveled the country as a politician. When promoting the universal healthcare package, the senator often related the huge need for healthcare for everyone by mentioning how his mother had to spend more time trying to convince the medical-care insurance bureaucracy to reimburse her than trying to concentrate on her illness while in the hospital. A photograph of her holding a young Obama is included in a thirty-second television advertisement called "Mother," in which Obama stated in the 2008 presidential campaign ad that his mother spent her final months "more worried about paying her medical bills than getting well."[37]

From the depths of his soul, he was sensitive of his mother's well-being and respected her strength of character and world view of life possessed by her and graciously passed on to him. His mother's influence shaped her son, Barack Obama, into what he was to become as she diligently inspired him with her high expectations and her ambitions for him. Although born in a different world from Abraham Lincoln's mother, the world for Barack Obama's mother became improved and broader in sophistication than the rural and remote limitations of the frontier in which Nancy Hanks Lincoln lived. However, like Lincoln's mother, who was, nonetheless, a skilled seamstress, which was considered as one of the highly marketable trades of the seventeenth and eighteenth centuries, on the other hand, the mother of Obama was an exceptionally skilled professional who cared about the core issues of the modern times in which she lived. His mother was enlightened and recognized the importance of uplifting Obama's father to him in favorable references, regardless of her divorcement from his father, or that Obama Sr. was not there for his son. Consequently, she toiled to make up the void of his absent father by seeking to fill the gap between father and son in abstract ways. For example, before Barack Obama met his own father back in 1971 to remember him, Obama's knowledge of his father's traits was garnered from his mother, primarily, with additional informs from "Gramps," his mother's father. Both of them gleaned out portraits of his father to Obama. Often his mother and grandfather chimed in on a litany of memorable scenes about the Kenyan, occasionally slanting them in favor of his father, even if they were not always facts. In summary, Barack heard his generous, spirited mother spin accolades and virtues about his father, trying to convince her son to understand the paternal source of his being from Barack Obama Sr.—his father. She hoped that her son would accept her praises about his daddy and move with confidence, competence, pride, and honesty in his stride toward life goals throughout this odyssey.

The honorable traits and virtues that his mother believed his father owned were those qualities that Obama's mother wanted Obama to embrace. Mr. Obama spoke of her as his single mother since she had divorced twice.

Lincoln's mother married only once in her short years of life. There were differences in the two women, but subtle similarities existed between them because both of them loved their sons—their only sons. What more can you say about a mother, since I am a single mother of an only child—an only son—who can relate vicariously to these two women extremely well.

Now, what's the jury out on one Ann Dunham? Her peers praised her highly. So does her only daughter, Ms. Maya Soetoro-Ng, Mr. Obama's half-sister. Accordingly, his sister said this about their mother:

> She felt that somehow, wandering through uncharted territory, we might stumble upon something that will, in an instant, seem to represent who we are at the core.... That was very much her philosophy of life—to not be limited by fear or narrow definitions, to not build walls around ourselves and to do our best to find kinship and beauty in unexpected places.[38]

Hers was an unconventional lifestyle whereby her friends said that Dunham was a very, very big thinker. According to Nancy Barry, a former president of Women's World Banking, an international network of microfinance providers where Obama's mother worked in New York City in the early 1990s, the coworker commented: "I think she was not at all personally ambitious, I think she cared about the core issues, and I think she was not afraid to speak truth to power."[39] Furthermore, on her dating habits, her peers stated that Ann never dated "the crew-cut white boys."[40] "She had a world view, even as a young girl. It was embracing the different, rather than that ethnocentric thing of shunning the different. That was where her mind took her."[41]

Stanley Ann Dunham was born November 29, 1942, on an army base at Fort Leavenworth, Kansas, to Stanley and Madelyn Dunham. Her father (who gave his only child his name) was a furniture salesman, and her mother a bank vice president. The family lived in Kansas, California, Texas, and in 1955 moved to Seattle, Washington. A year later they moved to nearby Mercer Island so that thirteen-year-old Ann could attend Mercer Island High School that had just opened. While at the school, she was on the debate team and graduated in 1960; afterward, her family moved to Hawaii; later, Ann attended the University of Hawaii at Manoa studying anthropology. Upon arrival in Hawaii, she was a full-fledged radical leftist and practitioner of "critical theory." As stated earlier, Ann Dunham married Barack Obama Sr. from Kenya, and a son was born—Barack Obama II. She did not complete school at the University of Hawaii, but some years later she returned and received her bachelor's degree from the university. Divorcing Barack Obama Sr. in 1964, citing "grievous mental suffering," Ann married the Indonesian Lolo Soetoro in 1967. He was an oil manager and practicing Muslim whom she also met at the University of Hawaii. They eventually moved to Jakarta, Indonesia, where she obtained a job at the American Embassy teaching English. Her second child was born in 1970—a daughter. Shortly thereafter, Obama's mother, Obama, and his little sister, Maya, moved back to Hawaii in 1974, whereby Ann attended the University of Hawaii to work on her master's degree in anthropology.

When she left to go back to Indonesia to complete her fieldwork for her master's degree, she took Maya, leaving Barack at home in Hawaii with her parents to be raised by them, and Barack preferred to remain in the States because here he found more stability with his maternal grandparents. His maternal grandparents were born and grew up in Kansas in very small-town USA in the solid, conservative, respectable family tradition. Their childhood was spent in the years of the Great Depression while coming from solid middle-class families. His grandfather, Stanley, had served in World War II and drifted about from one job to the other in Wichita. His grandmother, "Toot," was a high school graduate. While working as a furniture-store salesman, his grandfather was "informed by the manager there that a new store was opening in Honolulu, that business prospects seemed limitless there."[42] Hawaii was about to become the fiftieth state to enter the Union in 1959—that same Union that had become the United States of America almost one hundred years earlier when Abraham Lincoln (sixteenth president) preserved and enforced a more perfect union. Now, at the end of the decade of the 1950s, Dwight D. Eisenhower served as the thirty-fourth president in succession to Lincoln, who was the first elected Republican to be elected to the presidency. Although unknown at the time, a President-elect Barack Obama would become the tenth successor to President Eisenhower.

Now, at the eve of the Eisenhower years in this country, Obama's grandfather sold his home in Seattle and packed up his family, headed for Hawaii, the Aloha State (meaning "greetings"). It was in 1960 wherein Ann Dunham had recently finished high school. Their daughter, Stanley Ann, grew up as an only child with bouts of asthma as a child. She was somewhat of a loner because her family moving quite frequently, having little time to make enduring friendships. She was friendly and easy-tempered, but prone to bury her head in a book or wander off on solitary walks, often causing troubling concerns for her mother, Madelyn.[43] Barack

Obama adored his grandparents very much; indeed, they were his surrogate parents, causing his sentiments toward them to be of deepest affection. Finally, in 1980, Ann divorced her second husband and became a world traveler on a career mission in pursuit of rural development, taking her to Ghana, India, Thailand, Indonesia, Nepal, and Bangladesh. Being multilingual, speaking several languages fluently—French, Indonesian, Japanese, and some Urdu—made her articulate and able to communicate far beyond the norm. In 1986, Ann Dunham worked on a developmental project in Pakistan, and later that year, Ann and her daughter traveled the Silk Road in China. Then, in 1992, Barack Obama's mother earned a PhD in anthropology from the University of Hawaii. Her dissertation, "Peasant Blacksmithing in Indonesia: Surviving and Thriving Against All Odds," was 1,067 pages long.[44]

Dr. Stanley Ann Dunham was an American cultural anthropologist and social activist, exceptionally intelligent and well-educated. Conversely, Lincoln's mother was also intelligent, could read, especially the Bible, but she could not write, which posed limitations on her skills of communication or rhetoric. That is the extent to which the two mothers differ in educational preparation. Obama's mother was liberal and liberated, meaning that she was not the typical girl of the heartland spouting the conventional lifestyles of the conservative Kansan, but she was open-minded and enjoyed the company of the coffeehouse freethinkers in the Seattle area even during her young teenage years.

The critical theory–taught curriculum at the Mercer Island High School in Seattle included rejection of societal norms, attacks on Christianity and the traditional family, and assigned readings by Karl Marx. Ann Dunham was born during World War II, and her early childhood was spent during the New Deal Era of President Franklin Delano Roosevelt, the thirty-second president of the United States. Although she would not live to see her son become the first African American elected president of the United States because her health failed, and she died from ovarian cancer in 1995 at the age of fifty-three years old. Upon his mother's death,

Barack Obama was a mere thirty-four years old and recently married.

This is simply to say that the parents of Abraham Lincoln and the parents of Barack Obama died before either of their sons reached the high office of presidency. When the turn came for Lincoln and Obama to step up to the Oval Office, their parents' time of final transition came first. Ann Dunham (Obama) Soetoro was her son's prize keepsake because during his presidential campaign, Mr. Obama frequently made remembrance of such as speaking about how he treasured the photograph of the cliffs of the South Shore of Oahu in Hawaii where his mother's ashes were scattered.[45]

In retrospect, Mr. Obama reminisced: "I think sometimes that had I known my mother would not survive her illness, I might have written a different book—less a meditation on the absent parent, more a celebration of the one who was the single constant in my life."[46]

THE STEPPARENTS

After the death of young Abraham Lincoln's mother, Lincoln's father remarried about two years later. The parents of Barack Obama divorced when he was a child and his mother remarried, but so did his living father. As a result, in the early years of their lives, Lincoln and Obama were raised in a stepparent household. For Abraham Lincoln, his was a stepmother and for Barack Obama, his was a stepfather.

It was very fortunate for Lincoln that Sarah Bush Johnston married his widower father, because Lincoln and his stepmother related well, becoming an asset to him by treating him like her own biological son. Lincoln appreciated his stepmother and felt that she was a loving mother after he lost his beloved "angel mother" as a young lad. His stepmother was a widow and came with children of her own, blending the Lincoln household together while erasing the loneliness and depressing moments that Abraham and his sister endured after their mother died. Dennis Hanks, a cousin to Nancy

Hanks Lincoln, remembered that the new Mrs. Lincoln set to work at once, as she said, to making the children look "more human." "She soaped-rubbed and washed the children clean . . . so that they looked pretty neat—well and clean." His stepmother treated her own children and the Lincoln children with absolute impartiality, and she grew especially fond of Abraham; likewise, Lincoln expressed his warmth toward his stepmother equal to a son's endearment of his natural mother. He told a friend of the encouragement she had given him as a boy: "She had been his best friend in this world. . . . No man could love a mother more than I loved her." About her stepson, Abraham Lincoln, the second Mrs. Lincoln recalled, "Abe never gave me a cross word or look and never refused in fact, or even in appearance, to do anything I requested of him. His mind and mine . . . seemed to move together—move in the same channel."[47]

Sarah Bush Johnston Lincoln was born in Hardin County, Kentucky, on December 12, 1788, and was one of three daughters of Christopher and Hanna Bush of a family of nine children. By the time Sarah was two, the family moved to the Elizabethtown area where she grew up. Earlier, Sarah met young Thomas Lincoln in Elizabethtown, but she married a man named Daniel Johnston on March 13, 1806. Little is known about Johnston other than he was always in debt. The Johnston family had living quarters in the county jail, where Daniel Johnston worked as a jailer and Sarah cooked for the inmates there. In the summer of 1816, Daniel Johnston died. Afterward, Sarah purchased a cabin and was living there with three children when, late in 1819, Thomas Lincoln appeared at her door announcing that he had been a widower for more than a year. Quite respectfully, he paid off Sarah's debts and the two were married on December 2, 1819. Sarah was thirty-one years old and Thomas was age forty-one. When she left with Thomas Lincoln upon marrying him, she took all of her belongings with her to her new husband's home: furniture, dishes, and her children. Among other belongings, she brought several books, including *Webster's Speller* and *Robinson Crusoe*, that greatly motivated Lincoln's studious inclination. Quite beneficially, his stepmother had excellent motherly influence on Lincoln.

In appearance, Sarah stood straight and tall and had black, curly hair. Additionally, she was a hard worker who was charitable and kind-hearted, and those who knew her noted her strong moral character. When Abraham left his father's house and went out on his own in 1831, he continued to visit his stepmother periodically. When Thomas Lincoln died, Abraham retained land in his own name to provide a place for his Sarah Lincoln to live the rest of her lifetime if she so desired. After Abraham was elected president in 1860, he made one last visit to his stepmother before he left for Washington.

Similarly, a few days before Barack Obama became president-elect in 2008, he journeyed to the bedside of his beloved grandmother "Toot" in Hawaii before she passed away at the age of eighty-five. The stepmother of Abraham Lincoln, Sarah Johnston Lincoln, passed away at the age of eighty on April 12, 1869.[48]

Apparently Obama's feelings toward his stepfather carried a degree of respect that Lincoln felt for his stepparent. Although, it is understandable that such a bond of endearment existing between Barack and his stepfather was not as prevalent as in Lincoln's case, primarily because of the male factor. Yet the boy, Barack, displayed regard for his stepfather and interacted with him on a favorable basis. Indeed, there were no harsh feelings experienced between the two. Of course, young Barack realized that the Indonesian was not his biological father because his real father was African. Still, his new stepfather partially filled the place of Barack's absent father, although certainly not entirely. When his mother announced to him that her new male friend had proposed marriage to her, Barack was six years old. He had no objections and merely wanted to know if she loved him, according to Barack Obama in his memoir.[49]

To Obama, the man planning to marry his mother possessed good manners and easy grace with people. "His smile uncommonly even, and his temperament imperturbable."[50]

Although the stepmother of Lincoln traveled in a horse-drawn wagon from Elizabethtown, Kentucky, to Little Pigeon Creek, Indiana, it was quite different from little Barack and his mother, who boarded a Pan Am jet on an international flight across the globe to Jakarta to his stepfather's home in Indonesia, tremendously opposite though grounded in parallels.

Living in Jakarta was similar in its remoteness as Lincoln's backwoods upbringing. "There were small villages with unpaved roads and open sewers, shanties of mud brick and plywood and corrugated iron.... And families bathed and washed laundry in the murky river waters," recalled Barack.[51]

Further remembering that the house in which he lived on the outskirts of town was not fancy whatsoever and they were not well off—there was no car, no air-conditioning, refrigeration, or indoor plumbing—he speaks of his stepfather and their man-to-man talks. Shortly after Barack came home with a knot on his head, apparently from some bully at school, his stepfather advised him, "The first thing to remember is to protect yourself." So his stepfather showed him how to fight like a man, facing off in a boxing match in the backyard.[52] Soetoro, his stepfather, taught Barack how to eat small green chili peppers raw with dinner and plenty of rice at the table. But away from the dinner table and his mother's eyes, his stepfather also introduced him to tough dog meat, snake meat (tougher), and roasted grasshopper (crunchy), promising to bring home a piece of tiger meat for them to share.[53]

In Lincoln's early childhood in the wilderness of Little Pigeon Creek (southern Indiana) around 1816, he remembered the forests filled with bears and other threatening wild animals: "'Twas then the frontier lion: the panther's scream, filled the night with fear and bears preyed on the swine," Lincoln wrote about his childhood fears while living in this remote region. Here, Abraham and his family ate provisions of deer and bear meat products from the men hunting. Both future presidents had eaten wild game meat from the regions occupied by them during their youth. Such a tradition resembles a ritual of passage, supposedly. Additionally, Barack's stepfather advised him that one should not be weak: "Men take advantage of weakness in other men. They're just like countries in that way. The strong man takes the weak man's land.... If you can't be strong, be clever and make peace with someone who's strong. But always better to be strong yourself. Always."[54]

Just as Lincoln's stepmother treated her stepson with fairness, so did Obama's stepfather treat his stepson. His attention and care for his young stepson was solid, and he treated him as his own. Lolo Soetoro, also known as Lolo Soetoro Mangunharjo (new spelling: Lolo Sutoro), was born c. 1935 in Bandung. He was a native of Indonesia. Soetoro was the ninth of ten children of Martodihardjo, who hailed from Yogyakarta. During the Indonesian National Revolution (c. 1946) when Indonesia won independence from the Dutch, Soetoro's father and eldest brother were killed, after which the Dutch army burned down the family's home. Soetoro fled with his mother into the countryside to survive. He obtained his bachelor's degree in geography from Gadjah Mada University, Yogyakarta, later obtaining a scholarship from his workplace to study for a master's degree at the University of Hawaii, where he met Barack Obama's mother, Ann Dunham, also a student. Around 1966, Soetoro and Dunham married, and Soetoro returned to Indonesia when his native country called home its citizens who were studying abroad. About a year later, Barack and his mother followed, where the family took up residence in Menteng Dalam, Jakarta.

In 1970 Soetoro and Dunham had a daughter, Maya. After returning to Indonesia, Soetoro first worked for the army as a geologist and then took a job as a government relations consultant with Mobil Oil. After returning to Indonesia, Soetoro endured struggles there. His mother left Soetoro in 1972, which caused Soetoro and Dunham to see each other periodically in the 1970s, but never lived together again. Lolo Soetoro is the father of two other children other than Obama's half-sister, Maya, because he remarried. His stepfather's religious belief was that of Muslim. After his mother and Soetoro divorced, they remained cordial. Obama states that he saw his stepfather for the last time ten years later afterward when "my mother helped him travel to Los Angeles to treat a liver ailment."[55] His stepfather died on March 2, 1987, at the age of fifty-one in Jakarta, Indonesia.

ONE-PARENT HOUSEHOLD(S)

Family and household are generally used unanimously, although there is a distinction between the two. According to historians, the word family means shared kinship, whether by blood or adoption. They define the term household to mean shared residence, which is often an economic unit as well. These two definitions can overlap. Family and household structures vary across cultures and change over time. Indeed, families may be found in different structures. Since the Industrial Age began, a family has been defined as a heterosexual couple and their offspring, sharing a common dwelling and dividing work by gender. Yet with the inclusion of the recent gay rights movement, family structure may be defined as a partnership (male/male or female/female) couple and the children. However, in this particular context, emphasis is on the traditional family whereby in this definition, the woman takes care of the children inside the home and the man works outside the home. However, few of today's American families fit this definition. The nuclear family consists of both adults who are the biological or adoptive parents of the children. The blended families are generally created by divorce and remarriage. And in the single-parent family, there is only one parent in the home. Obviously, the single parent is referred to as a one-parent household and that parent is generally the mother, but it is not always a given because occasionally a father is the single parent in the household. No matter of what family members the structure may consist, the American family is our greatest resource, and families are better defined by what the people in them do for each other than by the way they are structured. Regardless of the diversity, various family structures deserve to be preserved and nurtured, according to Hare and Gray.[56] Based on the nontraditional or unconventional family structure, Barack Obama experienced living in a one-parent household with his mother, who remains the most important role model in shaping his life in a positive way. Sometimes, on the basis of circumstances, a woman has to make a choice for what she feels is best for her and her offspring; evidently that was the case with Ann Dunham when as a strong and independent woman she decided to live on her own together with her two children. The separation from her second husband and her return to Hawaii, near her parents, made her solely in charge of her life and her young son and baby daughter. There was a sense of social autonomy for women[57] critical for the independent nonconformist role of women, yet specifically involved in the internal household events related to raising their children as did Ann Dunham Obama Soetoro. Additionally, she understood that she must personally increase even more to enhance herself for this autonomous role as the family head; consequently, she pursued higher academic study. Her passion for anthropology and culture drove her to return to the University of Hawaii to begin working on her master's degree. Determined to broaden herself, Ann Dunham took advantage of educational opportunities to increase her, even more, for the challenges in her field of work and the significance of reaching out to the less fortunate to help them improve their lives. As with many women who find themselves in certain domestic circumstances, whether by their free will or not, a commonality exists that may be in comparison to the life of Gu Ruopu, a widow, who maintained her family. For example, in a letter to her two sons, she reports:

> Little did you know that your mother had to battle poverty, illness, and fatigue to keep the family from going adrift. Every fiber and every grain that this family owns are the fruits of my industry and hardship over several decades. Preserve and magnify them.[58]

Apparently, Ann wanted to expand her exercise in motherhood by being closer to her son and daughter so that she could play the huge role of mother and father to her children. Thus, the living arrangement for Barack and his sister became a one-parent household. Leaving the apartment of his grandparents, Barack came to live with his mother when she and his little sister returned to

Hawaii. Consequently, his mother and her two children were alone, resulting in a one-parent household at this juncture in his life. Separated from her second husband, Lolo, and back in Hawaii, Ann, Maya, and Barack lived together in a small apartment a block away from Punahou School while his mother's student grant money supported them, along with the food stamps. Perhaps it was during this time that Barack Obama experienced some degree of economic stress in the family of three with his mother heading the one-parent household.

On one occasion, his mother demonstrated her displeasure when some of Barack's more affluent classmates came over to Barack's tiny family apartment to visit him and, within the course of their visit, showed astonishment that Barry did not possess the comforts of their palatial and fashionable homes. Sometimes his mother would overhear them remark about the lack of food in the fridge or less-than-perfect housekeeping in the small apartment shared by Barack with his mother and small sister. Barack commented that his mother would "pull me aside and let me know that she was a single mother going to school again and raising two kids, so that baking cookies wasn't exactly at the top of her priority list; and while she appreciated the fine education I was receiving at Punahou she wasn't planning on putting up with any snotty attitudes from me or anyone else, was that understood?"[59] Without a doubt, as a teenager, Barack experienced some peer pressure, yet remained dutiful and close to his mother by assisting her with chores around the house, grocery shopping, and caring for his baby sister, Maya, while his mother studied. He seriously tried to step up and fill the man's place in this fatherless home. When it came time for his mother to return to Indonesia for her field study, Barack preferred to remain behind with his mother's parents, primarily because he did not want to change schools again. This time he lived in the grandparent-led home.

There is a difference here because Abraham Lincoln lived briefly in a one-parent household, and we know it to be based on the death of his mother. During the early eighteenth century, the traditional family consisted of the married family with the father as head of the household. Householder was a significant status, particularly because households were very important units of social and economic life in the pre-industrialized era. According to Daniel Scott Smith, householders served as the directors of the predominant institution of economic production. Since newlywed couples established households, becoming a head (and wives were considered co-heads, especially with respect to matters that were internal to the household) conveyed independence from the control of the couple's parents.[60]

Historians have agreed that the family of Lincoln is complicated and contradictory. In short, finding accurate and even adequate records about his family tree can be challenging. Even though it is a fact that Lincoln was a man on a mission to effect change even at the higher levels than one expected, which is one of the reasons why he wanted to be president, so that he could effect change at a time when the country was in great need for change and reform. Such was the case of Barack Obama, as well. According to historian Catherine Clinton, Lincoln learned during his formative years that he was very much on his own and had to rely on his own skills and wits. She further states:

> He was born into a fluid age, a time when families might separate and fragment, as so many did, dramatically, during the American Civil War.[61]

About his mother, Lincoln mentions her sparingly though affectionately. His mother's family origins were not so well-known, and the issue of illegitimacy was a dominant factor that suppressed lots of discussion from the son about his mother's father. The complexities of Lincoln may be traced back to his early years in his family. The theme of abandonment is clear in Lincoln's early life, causing him to be well-acquainted with being forsaken. Unfortunately, he had no control of being deprived of familial resources during his impressionable years. Moreover, historian Clinton writes that

Lincoln's life reflected the new directions of the antebellum generation defining anew their relationship to the past.[62] He realized that the natural order of circumstances in the family, such as mother's care and father's pride, could not be taken for granted.[63] He empathized with his mother, who had been cheated by circumstances; obviously she was less fortunate than others, one who did not enjoy privileges from birth. As a result, Lincoln embraced a strong ethic of charity.[64] Both Abraham (age nine) and his sister, Sarah (eleven), were devastated by their mother's death, believing Nancy irreplaceable. At this point in 1819, they were left motherless and found themselves in a one-parent household. Unlike Obama, Lincoln had no loving grandparents extending protective cushions of compassion to hold and support him and his sister Sarah, nor did he and his sister have caring adults to soothe and comfort the gaping wounds of grief felt by the children in the sudden loss of their young mother. After at least a year, their father, Thomas, left the squalid conditions of the household and sought a wife as a replacement for him, as well as a mother for his two little children, Abraham and Sarah. Theirs was a one-parent household brought on by the death of one of the parents, Nancy Lincoln. Of course, the one transient parent household in which Obama lived resulted from divorcement on the part of his mother.

Historian Clinton states that many narratives mention Nancy Lincoln's submission to her husband; she did not cross him. In contrast, Sarah Johnston Lincoln, the second wife of Lincoln's father, did make demands on her husband; one of the demands she made was championing Abraham's cause to Thomas on behalf of his enormous interest in books and building his cognitive skills.[65] Abraham was intensely sad during that time after his mother's recent death. His sister tried to perform the housekeeping duties, although not measuring up to her experienced beloved late mother. To add to the sadness and void of such a great loss, Thomas Lincoln left the children alone with Dennis Hanks, isolated and alone on his remote Indiana farm, for several months. This period sadly typified children "left behind," in every sense of the word.[66] It had been a severe trial for the young boy to have his beloved mother bid farewell, requiring such grown-up responsibilities to fall on his young shoulders. But Abraham seriously tried to take on the responsibilities that he felt his mother would want him to do. After a year or so of living in a one-parent household and brief abandonment by his father, the children were apparently relieved to see a mature, kindly female come into their household to fill the immediate void that Abraham and Sarah had endured. The new Mrs. Lincoln brought along "luxuries" to their rustic domain. The once one-parent household became a blended family with Sarah Johnston Lincoln's three children and Thomas Lincoln's two children all under one roof. In sum, the one-parent households for Lincoln and Obama as children were brief, temporary experiences. Nonetheless, both of them had only one biological parent whom they held in eternal esteem—their mothers. And both confronted and escaped whatever those barriers were that would fence them in, but on the contrary, expanded themselves beyond expectations simply on the powers and spirit of the will to "break free."

THE FATHER IMAGE

Conversely, Abraham Lincoln lived with his father as his major parental figure from birth to his young adulthood, and was familiar with his father to some extent because they lived in the same household during Abraham's formative years on the prairie. A sense of honesty became instilled in the boy by his father. For Barack Obama, his familiarity with his father did not exist in the way that Abraham Lincoln's did. Nevertheless, to the young Lincoln, his father was emotionally absent, even if he were present in a physical sense. Amazingly, parental bonds are powerful and extend beyond social dynamics and conventions exclusively, but tend to extend into the psyche domain as well. The bonding effect felt between a parent and child is huge, and its phenomenon is primal in nature, meaning that children have a natural instinct to connect with their mother and their father—whichever one is missing. One expects the mother to nurture and the father to protect, and the father often leads in the decision of religion that his children will follow. When one of the parents in the family is absent, the family experience becomes a broken-family syndrome. As a result, the child, by nature, misses that primal nature, meaning that children have a natural instinct to connect with their mother and their father. As a consequence, the human psyche will seek ways to fill this "family void." In that case, some children still seek that father image into adulthood that they longed for as a child. Barack Obama alludes to the fact by openly stating:

> Still, as I got older I came to realize how hard it had been for my mother and grandmother to raise us without a strong male presence in the house. I felt as well the mark that a father's absence can leave on a child. I determined that my father's irresponsibility toward his children, my stepfather's remoteness, and my grandfather's failures would all become object lessons for me, and that my own children would have a father they could count on.[67]

From a positive perspective, often boys who experience the missing father-and-son relationship within the primal familial ties substitute that basic family bond by becoming a strong leader himself over other people, or seek the head of hierarchy, and/or develop a great sense of family pride. Theoretically, Abraham Lincoln and Barack Obama's need to fill the void by choosing to become strong leaders and to show pride in their marriage and family as opposed to choosing destructive ways of life indicates the supportive family role of a father that their own fathers did not perform. Both Abraham Lincoln and Barack Obama headed the nation as presidents, providing them phenomenal fulfillment after missing the bonding found between father and son. In Obama's search for a father figure, the nearest person that he found was his maternal grandfather, who had his share of shortcomings in exhibiting a steadfast and practical approach to family and life.

By contrast, Lincoln had no living grandfathers and never knew them. In comparison, Lincoln had Anglo-American grandfathers. Obama has one Anglo-American grandfather. Their fathers lived until the sons were grown, and both had something in common about their fathers: the commonality is the emotional distances between father and son. No doubt, Abraham Lincoln and Barack Obama experienced an unfulfilling longing strangely mixed with feelings of resentment toward their fathers. Obviously, neither was close to his father, yet each bore a natural need or instinct to bond with his elder, uniquely nestled in a father-and-son relationship, as well as to be fully understood by the father. Upon the demise of Obama Sr., his son dreamed of his father, which is a common experience after the death of a loved one. And as dreams do recapture those longing places lingering there upon the soul of things that follow us and stay on our minds in reality, so it was with Barack. Upon awakening from the dream, he felt driven: "I needed to search for him . . . and talk with him again."[68] In the end, Lincoln and Obama found that both possessed an inner sense of peace and respect regardless of the extenuating estrangement hidden away long after their fathers were gone. Ironically, Abraham Lincoln lived with his father as his major parental figure from birth to his young adulthood, but underwent emotional estrangement. According to historian Clinton, Lincoln was a new man of the prairie who would not cling to the conventions of his father's generation, but pioneered a new path—one that comingled several generations.[69]

Although Barack Obama nor Abraham Lincoln hated his father, each son inherited circumstances beyond his control that hindered the bonding in which a father and son were expected to engage. One of the factors that Lincoln considered problematic about his father's life was the lack of education. Lincoln suggested that his father "grew up literally without education."[70] Thus, in reality, his father seemed to view his children as extensions to work and help him, causing Abraham and his sister to lack affectionate feelings toward him; feelings of disdain prevailed for their father instead.

As stated earlier, Barack did not interact in the same household with his Obama siblings, nor did he interact with his father in a household wherein he was the only child, because his father was truly absent. An absent father who still lives can be a disappointment and foster a feeling of abandonment in the child, as in Obama's case, causing some disdain, no doubt. The father image means support, by whatever means: a mentor, an aspirant, a leader, a counselor, a teacher, and a confidante. A father image is the epitome of family in the father-and-son relationship, helping the son transition from boyhood into manhood. It is an ancient ritual drilled into the depths of the traditional stones of family history concrete throughout mankind. When the transition is broken or missing because the abstract or concrete ceremonial father/son relationship is not there, it is like unto a leaking vessel or unfinished foundation. Neither Abraham nor Barack received fatherly affections over a sustained period of time. Because his father failed to reach out to him with a sustained fulfillment, Lincoln's happy years of boyhood were soon spent. David Donald Herbert inserts that Lincoln's relationship with his father began to deteriorate, perhaps because Thomas Lincoln was perceptibly aging. After an exceptional burst of energy at the time of his second marriage, his father began to slow down. He probably was not in good health, for one neighbor remembered that he became blind in one eye and lost sight in the other.[71] As Abraham became a teenager, he began to distance himself from his father. His sense of alienation may have originated at the time of his mother's death, when Abraham needed more support and compassion that his stolid father was unable to give, and it increased as the boy got older. Thomas Lincoln seemed to favor the stepson, John D. Johnston, more than he did his own son.[72]

Actually, Lincoln emancipated himself from his father as soon as he possibly could to find himself and rise above the confinements of farm life and the fate of his father. He wanted to overcome the challenges that his father, Thomas Lincoln, allowed to consume him. Abraham was not a chip off the old block, nor the spitting image of his father in mind and spirit.

Nor was Obama completely his father's son. Each escaped the fates of his father, which appeared to be failure in the son's eyes, and the emotional aspect was as distant as were the physical boundaries of Lincoln and Obama from their fathers. Although Lincoln shared external surroundings with his father, he did not share an internal satisfaction of his seemingly ambitionless father. After leaving his father's house in 1831, and putting space between them, he found in others not related to him the father figure that he sought. Historian Clinton writes that when "[Bowling Green, 1786–1842, a friend/mentor to young Lincoln] died in 1842, Lincoln was so choked up at the funeral that he was unable to finish the eulogy he was delivering."[73]

Small wonder, then, that each was notified by other family members about the death of his father. They were not in their father's presence when the final hour came. Moreover, Lincoln did not attend his father's funeral in 1851. Obama did not attend his father's funeral in 1982. As sons, each resided somewhere else with kilometers of miles between them and their fathers. Lincoln's father and stepmother lived in Coles County, Illinois; Obama's father lived a continent away in Kenya, East Africa. So when the news reached each son that the final hour had come for the men who were their biological fathers, Lincoln nor Obama reacted with tears and certainly did not put forth any effort to travel the distances to pay their last respects. At that time, Abraham Lincoln was a practicing lawyer in Illinois, but unfortunately, there was a case of illness in his own family causing Lincoln to conveniently excuse himself from attending his father's final services. Additionally, Lincoln's response about his father's death was thoughtfully phrased in a letter to his stepbrother, John D. Johnston. Though he had not been "uninterested," he "could write nothing which could do any good. You already know I desire that neither Father or [sic] Mother shall be in want of any comfort either in health or sickness while they live. My business is such, that I could hardly leave home, now, if it were not, as it is, that my own wife is sick-abed," expecting a baby (Willie).[74]

"Say to him," Lincoln wrote, "that if we could meet now, it is doubtful whether it would not be more painful than pleasant.... remember to call upon, and confide in, our great, and good, and merciful Maker; who will not turn away from you in an extremity."[75]

Moreover, in Lincoln's adulthood relationship to his father, Miller mentions that:

> For the twenty years after he left home, as he was rising in the world, Abraham would only very rarely go to see his father, who had moved to Coles County. Abraham's wife, Mary Todd, would never meet her father-in-law, and their sons would never meet their grandfather Lincoln.[76]

Nor did Mrs. Mary Lincoln or her sons meet Lincoln's stepmother, Sarah Lincoln. There was an aloofness between Lincoln and his father even into the son's adulthood. Although Obama's wife, Mrs. Michelle Obama, did not meet her late father-in-law, Obama Sr., nor did their two daughters meet their late grandfather Obama Sr., Barack Obama arranged a trip to Kenya so that his wife and daughters could meet his father's side of the family. For Lincoln, according to the historian David Herbert Donald, he wrote: "He [Lincoln] did not yet know who he was, or where he was heading, but was sure he did not want to be another Thomas Lincoln."[77]

Shortly, in some years after his father's death, in respect to his father, Lincoln named his last son Thomas after his own father. Lincoln was forty-two years old. On the other hand, Obama's father was killed in a car crash on the distant continent of Africa while the younger Obama resided in New York City (America). He was unmarried and twenty-one years old. The son remembered seeing his father once in his life when the boy was ten years old. The image and stories about his real father were told to him by "Gramps" and his beloved mother. While attempting to reach into the storehouse of memories about his father and successfully conjure up such images of him and the son, Barack Obama recalled:

> I'm left with mostly images that appear and die off in my mind like distant sounds: his head thrown back in laughter at one of Gramps' jokes as my mother and I hang Christmas ornaments... The stroking of his sparse goatee, as he reads his important books... Images, and his effect on other people.[78]

Further insight into the father-son relationship status as an aspect of his life may be revealed when Obama arrived in Manhattan after leaving Los Angeles. He reread a letter that his father had sent him four years earlier:

> I folded the letter along its seams and stuffed it back into my pocket. It hadn't been easy to write him; our correspondence had all but died over the past four years.[79]

In the letter, his father had given his son advice, saying, "The important thing is that you know your people, and also that you know where you belong."[80]

There had been sporadic communication between them through letters, but the father and the son had not met again. After Barack Obama Sr. left Hawaii back in 1971, returning to Kenya, his son, Barack Obama, experienced limited communication with him.

> My father's letters provided few clues. They would arrive sporadically. On a single blue page... He would report that everyone was fine, commend me on my progress in school, and insist that my mother, Maya, and I were welcome to take our rightful place beside him whenever we so desired.[81]

Now, eleven years later, his aunt called transatlantic informing Obama that the physical image of his father had expired—gone. After hanging up the phone, perhaps a sigh of bewilderment followed as Barack reflected alone, thinking deeply.

Penning a letter to a relative as condolence about Abraham's father—about Obama's father—each son shared in the letter-writing ritual at different times and different places, but all for the same purpose. And there came a time when each paused and reflected on the final and physical loss momentarily. Although the dimness of a father image had stretched over a period of years such as from birth and in between until adulthood, the death meant the loss of hope forever, and loss of nevermore connecting and relating as a father/son. *No more, no more . . .*

Coping with the death of a father by his son is complicated because there is sadness mixed with relief, lingering resentments, and sharp criticism.[82] Little emotion was displayed at the time, maybe later. Quietly thinking on the death of his father, Obama's reaction was:

> But, I felt no pain, only the vague sense of an opportunity lost, and I saw no reason to pretend otherwise. My plans to travel to Kenya were placed on indefinite hold.[83]

NOTES

Chapter One
Family Origin and Early Years

1. Wikipedia, "Lincoln name," retrieved November 21, 2008, www.en.wikipedia.org/wiki/Lincoln_name.
2. David Herbert Donald, *Lincoln* (New York: Simon and Schuster, 1995), 19.
3. Bridging World History website, retrieved November 26, 2008, www.learning.org/courses/worldhistory/unit_overview_13.html.
4. William C. Harris, *Lincoln's Rise to the Presidency* (Lawrence, KS: University Press of Kansas, 2007).
5. Barack Obama, *Dreams from My Father: A Story of Race and Inheritance* (Crown Publishers, 2004), 26–27.
6. Obama, 13.
7. Obama, 51.
8. Obama, 52.
9. Bridging World History website.
10. Bridging World History website.
11. Donald, *Lincoln*, 23.
12. Bridging World History website.
13. William Miller, *Lincoln's Virtues: An Ethical Biography* (New York: Vintage Books, 2008), 60.
14. Miller, 60.
15. Donald, *Lincoln*, 23.
16. Donald, 23.
17. Donald, 23.
18. See "Nancy Hanks," by Rosemary Benet.
19. Obama, *Dreams from My Father*, 9.
20. See www.revolvy.com/page/Barack-Obama-Sr., retrieved June 29, 2017.
21. Barack Obama Sr., www.revolvy.com.

22. Barack Obama Sr., www.revolvy.com.
23. *Los Angeles Times,* July 17, 2008.
24. Obama, *Dreams from My Father,* 63.
25. Obama, 65.
26. Obama, 70.
27. Donald, *Lincoln,* 240.
28. Donald, 240.
29. Obama, *Dreams from My Father,* 305.
30. Miller, *Lincoln's Virtues,* 67.
31. Edmund Sanders, "So Alike and Yet So Different," *Times,* July 17, 2008.
32. Sanders, "So Alike and Yet So Different."
33. Michael Dobbs, "The Nation," *Washington Post*, retrieved September 26, 2008.
34. Obama, *Dreams from My Father,* 221.
35. David Mendell, *Obama: From Promise to Power* (New York: Amistad Publishing, 2007), 14, 24.
36. See www.imdb.com/title/tt0061735, retrieved November 20, 2008.
37. See en.metapedia.org/wiki/Stanley_Ann_Dunham.
38. See en.metapedia.org/wiki/Stanley_Ann_Dunham.
39. Adam Na Gourney, "Barack Obama," *New York Times*, retrieved November 20, 2008.
40. Gourney, "Barack Obama."
41. Gourney, "Barack Obama."
42. Gourney, "Barack Obama."
43. Obama, *Dreams from My Father,* 16.
44. Dr. Stanley Ann Dunham (1942–1995); see http://www.geni.com/people/Dr.-Stanley-Dunham/6000000000240233401.
45. www.nytimes.com.
46. www.nytimes.com.
47. Donald, *Lincoln,* 28.
48. Mark Neely Jr., *The Abraham Lincoln Encyclopedia* (October 1982).

49. Obama, *Dreams from My Father*, 31.
50. Obama, 31.
51. Obama, *Audacity of Hope: Thoughts on Reclaiming the American Dream* (New York: Crown Publishers, 2006), 273.
52. Obama, *Dreams from My Father*, 35.
53. Obama, 37.
54. Obama, 41.
55. Obama, 47.
56. Jan Hare and Lizbeth A. Gray, in "All Kinds of Families: A Guide for Parents," University of Wisconsin, Stout, and Oregon State University, www.kogermasters.weebly.com/families.html.
57. Daniel Smith, "Female Householding in Late 18th Century America and the Problem of Poverty," *Journal of Social History* (Fall 1994), 1.
58. Susan Mann and Yu-Yin Cheng, eds., *Under Confucian Eyes: Writings on Gender in Chinese History* (Berkeley and Los Angeles: University of California Press, 2001), 1551–2.
59. Obama, *Dreams from My Father*, 75.
60. Smith, "Female Householding."
61. Catherine Clinton, "Abraham Lincoln: The Family That Made Him, The Family He Made," in *Our Lincoln*, Eric Foner (2008), 250.
62. Clinton, 251–52.
63. Clinton, 252.
64. Clinton, 252.
65. Clinton, 256.
66. Clinton, 255.
67. Obama, *The Audacity of Hope*, 346.
68. Obama, *Dreams from My Father*, 129.
69. Clinton, "Abraham Lincoln," 249.
70. Donald, *Lincoln*, 32–33.
71. Donald, 32–33.

72. Donald, 33.
73. Clinton, "Abraham Lincoln," 258.
74. Entry for January 26, 1857, *Lincoln Day by Day: A Chronology, 1809–1865*, 2:189, ed. Miers, in *Lincoln's Rise to the Presidency*, William Harris (2007), 59.
75. Entry for January 26, 1857, *Lincoln Day by Day*, 59.
76. Miller, *Lincoln's Virtues*, 62.
77. Donald, *Lincoln*, quoted in Miller, *Lincoln's Virtues*, 62.
78. Obama, *Dreams from My Father*, 66.
79. Obama, 114.
80. Obama, 114.
81. Obama, 76.
82. See www.webmd.com/men/features/death-my-father#1, retrieved June 29, 2018.
83. Obama, *Dreams from My Father*, 128.

CHAPTER TWO

EDUCATION DEFECTIVE AND EDUCATION PAR EXCELLENCE

> *Upon the subject of education, not presuming to dictate any plan or system respecting it, I can only say that I view it as the most important subject which we as a people can be engaged in.*
> —Lincoln: Essential Wisdom

> *If we want America to lead in the twenty-first century, nothing is more important than giving everyone the best education possible.*
> —Barack Obama

If Abraham Lincoln were to complete a job application or write his résumé to compete for a job vacancy, it would not include high school graduation or mention matriculation at any college/undergraduate school nor graduate/university by him. His formal school years would only cover his early childhood to a limited extent and then stop. Abraham Lincoln remembered going for two brief periods to an ABC school, some two miles from the Lincoln's cabin. Here he was sent, according to a relative, "More as company for his sister than with the expectation that he would learn much."[1] How much they misjudged his mental capabilities. In contrast to Lincoln's sporadic sum of one year of formal education of brief school days spent in the rugged frontier schools, Barack Obama experienced his education in the ivy-covered walls of Harvard and Columbia, which are institutions of highest standards in academia. Their educational roads are markedly different in terms of clock hours spent in school, but comparably alike in terms of developmental domains such as intellectual and cognitive abilities.

According to Piaget, there are mainly four stages of cognitive development, two of which will be centered around Lincoln and Obama in this narrative. They are stages three and four, known as concrete operations stage three and formal operations stage four, using Piaget's developmental stages. Stage three, concrete operations, occurs between ages seven to twelve years. During this stage—characterized by conservation of number, length, liquid, mass, weight, area, volume—intelligence is increasingly demonstrated through logical and systematic manipulation of symbols relating to concrete objects; thinking is operational, reversible, and less egocentric. The fourth stage is the final stage of cognitive development (from ages twelve and beyond). Emotional development is another integral part of a child's period of development. Emotional development concerns children's increasing awareness and control of their feelings and how they react to these feelings in a given situation.

Evidence of emotional development of young Lincoln and Obama is prevalent throughout their developmental formative years in family and school life. The education of two of America's eminently outstanding civic-minded political figures is ebbed in a cast of differences; one is labeled as inadequate or defective while the other is extraordinaire or par excellence as related to his formative schooling. The beginning school years of both Obama and Lincoln are defined as early childhood education, which according to NAEYC (National Association for the Education of Young Children), spans the human life from birth to age eight. Early childhood education regards education in early childhood as the most vulnerable stages in a person's life. Researchers in the field and early childhood educators both view the parents and/or families as an integral part of the early childhood–education process.[2]

Quite appropriately, their families were involved in the early school years of Lincoln and Obama; however, the degree of the involvement differs. Of course, for Abraham Lincoln, the involvement was much less than for Obama. Lincoln's birth mother and later his stepmother influenced his early years of school by providing books for him and complimented his love for learning. Likewise, Obama's own mother prompted him to achieve basic literacy and numeracy as well as establishing his foundations in social studies, geography, and natural sciences. Of course, pre-K and kindergarten were not available in the nineteenth-century frontier towns of Indiana for Abraham Lincoln. Nor had universal pre-K caught the attention of politicians and educational leaders in many states.[3] But, being the enlightened personalities and intellectuals Obama and Lincoln became, both presidents no doubt were capable of considering universal pre-K or examining its pros and cons before making a decision, although this educational benefit arrived after their early school days. However, tuition-free college (Obama) and land-grant colleges (Lincoln) have been heralded by each during his term of office.

EARLY CHILDHOOD EDUCATION

"Abraham probably mastered the alphabet, but he did not yet know how to write when the family left Kentucky,"[4] according to historians. After the family moved to Indiana, his parents (father and stepmother) enrolled him, along with the other children, in the school that Andrew Crawford had opened in a cabin about a mile from the Lincoln house. Crawford, a justice of the peace and man of some importance in the area, ran a subscription school, where parents paid their children's tuition in cash or in commodities. Though his parents were illiterate, each accepted the value of education or love of basic knowledge that education was important, and Thomas Lincoln wanted his son to at least learn how to read and cipher.[5]

Sarah Lincoln, the stepmother, understood better than anyone and recognized his need fully to master what he read or heard. She remembered:

> He must understand everything—even to the smallest thing—minutely and exactly. He would then repeat it over to himself again and again—sometimes in one form and then in another and when it was sometimes in one form and then in another and when it was fixed in his mind to suit him he ... Never lost that fact or his understanding of it.[6]

Lincoln attended Crawford's school for one term, maybe three months. Ungraded, it was a "blab" school where students recited their lessons aloud, and the schoolmaster listened through the din (noise) for errors. For a year, the Lincoln children did not attend any school because going to the nearest school was such a distance away that Abraham could not attend regularly and spent most of his school time attending to farm chores. After a year, he attended a school taught by Azel W. Dorsey in the same cabin that Crawford had used. With that term, at the age of fifteen, his formal education ended. Summarizing his education as "the aggregate of all his schooling did not amount to one year."[7] No qualification was required of a teacher beyond readin', writin', and cipherin', to the rule of three (i.e. ratio and proportions).[8] On the basis of what his teachers had taught him, Abraham was able to master the basic tools so that in later years he could educate himself. Although he attended school sporadically in one-room rural pioneer schoolhouses that lacked the sophistication of modern suburban school buildings as we know it in this century, the school Lincoln attended was typical of the late-eighteenth-century education and learning.

> *Abraham Lincoln*
> *His hand & pen*
> *He will be good but*
> *[God] knows When.*[9]

These are the words Lincoln wrote in his schoolbook when he was a young boy, because his teachers in the pioneer schools in

Indiana did not have any arithmetic textbooks, so Lincoln found some paper, which was hard to come by, tied it together, and created his own "sum book." Such an endeavor on the part of young Lincoln demonstrates his need to develop his cognitive skills, thus improvising a book for himself to function as a tool for learning his arithmetic. In the primitive settings of the pioneer schools, Lincoln began his long search for knowledge, and legend has it that he would walk miles to borrow a book from a neighbor. For young Abraham, reading was placed above hunting or participating in the other manual traditions of the male group living on the frontier; he simply had no interest in farm work, hunting, fishing, etc. True, he assisted his father in manual labor, but it was only from necessity, not by choice; instead, he preferred to read books and newspapers.

For his one-room schoolhouse years that he briefly spent during his early education, when Lincoln became a man of the public, he refused to romanticize the rustic, below-standards conditions of the schools for the less privileged, such as the realization that such school settings needed improvement at every angle.

Early childhood education, which was the equivalent of a few years in elementary school, was the extent of his attendance in a physical school environment at Pigeon Creek in Indiana. As a result, Lincoln did not speak very highly of his limited school surroundings because to him it was backward rather than progressive or inspirational. A place such as Pigeon Creek raised no idealistic outlook on his quest for knowledge, for it contributed very little to the formal operative stage four of his development. The boy became his own teacher. As Miller points out, Lincoln frequently wrote of himself in third person in his longer autobiographical sketches, or about his education in general, stating: "He studied with no one,"[10] meaning that he was self-taught and did not give credit to a teacher or some scholar who mentored him. Instead his steadfast claim was, indeed, "I studied with no one, but myself," of course. Additionally, as related to his early culture or lack of it, Lincoln somewhat scorned Little Pigeon Creek's lack of academic enlightenment by saying: "There was absolutely nothing to excite ambition for education."[11] Although the backwoods veneer environment and limited social surroundings did not evoke a thirst for knowledge or academia, Abraham Lincoln's reactions toward education loomed in contrast to this meager access to knowledge, and he sought to improve himself in spite of the lack of available quality education for him and others during that time. Strongly realizing the importance of education, Lincoln determinedly created his own study venue wherever it may be: in the fields, under the tree, or by the candlelight in the cabin, he pored over his few books. Consequently, he considered the deficiencies in his education and proposed to improve himself regardless of the shortcomings of his circumstances in this rural, remote, and less-opportune frontier village. Many years afterward, when Lincoln was well establishing himself in politics, he was once asked for a thumbnail biography for a *Directory of Congressmen*, at which time, Lincoln took one of six short lines to state with stunning succinctness: "Education defective,"[12] describing himself.

On the other hand, the education of Barack Obama was par excellence according to the standards of education today or even during the eighteenth-century times of Lincoln. Obama received a formal education and spent many years in school attaining diplomas and degrees. Unlike Lincoln's parents, Obama's parents were well educated; however, both families possessed an affinity for education and wanted their children to learn, although the females in their families were more adamant and instrumental about academic preparation for the sons than their male figures demonstrated on a consistent basis. Known as "Barry," Barack Obama began kindergarten at Noelani Elementary School in Honolulu, Hawaii, in America. By the time he was ready for first grade at six years old, he and his mother were living in another country upon her remarriage. As a result, Barack entered the first grade at Saint Francis of Assisi Catholic School in Jakarta, Indonesia, remaining at the school until third grade. Obama speaks of his early school years in Indonesia in relationship to their economic status there.

He explains:

> Without money to go to the International School that most expatriate children attended, I went to local Indonesian schools and ran the streets with the children of farmers, servants, tailors, and clerks.[13]

Barack was enrolled in the State Elementary School in Menteng for fourth grade in Jakarta. Regardless of the fact that he did not attend the International School, his mother's strong interest in her son's education during his developmental years prompted her to arrange for a United States correspondence course to supplement and enhance Barack's early education upon arriving in Indonesia. Obama recalls how she awoke him early each day (in Indonesia) at four o'clock in the morning to teach him English three hours before he left for school. On his part, young Barack tried many tricks to avoid doing lessons that interrupted his sleep; even so, he remembers his mother's uncompromising determination to teach him regardless of his childish antic resistance, and would remind him that he was not alone in this inconvenient time of coaching her son, no doubt, bluntly informing him that "this is no picnic for me either, Buster."[14]

On the basis of education in Indonesia, education is the responsibility of the Ministry of National Education of Indonesia (Departemen Pendidikan Nasional Republik Indonesia/Depdiknas). In Indonesia, currently, every citizen has to have nine years of education: six years at elementary and three in middle. Historically, the Dutch introduced a system of formal education for the local population of Indonesia, although this was restricted to certain privileged children. By the 1930s, the Dutch had introduced limited formal education to nearly every province of the Dutch East Indies.

To his advantage, Barack's mother looked beyond the limitations of the Indonesian schools and continued to ply education onto the brain of her precocious young son. She would say to him, "You have me to thank for your eyebrows.... Your father has these wispy eyebrows that don't amount to much. But your brains, your character, you got from him."[15] She educated him as much as she could about black people, his other side of the family tree, by telling him about Thurgood Marshall, Dr. Martin Luther King Jr., music of Mahalia Jackson, and other great black leaders, even including his own father's struggle from a poor country in Africa to his impressive education in American universities. His father was a high achiever, in spite of the negatives, and his mother wanted to emphasize that quality to her impressionable young son, Barack Obama. And she talked about the history of the Deep South and how blacks were "forced to read books handed down from wealthier white schools but that those blacks went on to become doctors and lawyers and scientists, and the marches of freedom by children no older than he was."[16]

Parental interest and involvement play a significant role in a child's developmental years, socially and cognitively. Sensing that her son needed to attend an American school, as he reached his stage-four formal operations of cognitive development, his mother decided that her young son needed an American education. As he reached this stage, considered as the final stage of cognitive development, wherein intelligence is demonstrated through the logical use of symbols related to abstract concepts, thinking is abstract, hypothetical, and early on quite egocentric; it is commonly held that the majority of people never complete this stage. As evidence of reaching stage four cognitively, Barack had accelerated in his English-correspondence courses serving as an assessment for his mother to send him back to America to improve the quality of his education during those vulnerable early years. He was ready for the fifth grade. Upon arriving in the United States and back in Hawaii with his grandparents, "Toot" and "Gramps," ten-year-old Barack was faced with entering another new school and settling in Honolulu, far from Jakarta. Enrolling in fifth grade at Punahou Academy, Barack Obama learned that the school had a reputation for excellence as a prep school for the island elites. He knew that he gained admission primarily on the basis of his grandfather's boss, an alumnus, who had interceded on his behalf as a favor to "Gramps." In short, it was not easy to gain admission to such an elitist school, although Punahou was started by missionaries in 1841. Back during 1841, Lincoln was an Illinois state legislator. And Hawaii had not been admitted to the Union, nor was there any consideration of it becoming a state during the mid-nineteenth century, for it was looked upon as a remote island on the Pacific.

There was no comparison between Punahou Academy and the one-room pioneer "blab" school in Little Pigeon Creek, Indiana, that Lincoln probably would have felt just as unsettled in such a "high fer lootin" school. Nevertheless, the stuff of books immersed in the study of academics would have been incredibly engaging for Lincoln, and he probably would have overlooked the fancy buildings, manicured campus green, and additional amenities of Punahou by setting his sights on the printed word and so forth. But Lincoln never entered such a school. Obama did, and he overcame the uncomfortable feelings that arose within him at first. He learned to fit in, so to speak, and become another student at Punahou. By the time he reached high school, he was on the basketball team there. Playing basketball provided him with an outlet beyond Punahou. Basketball was an extracurricular learning experience. Socially, he and Ray became friends. Ray attended Punahou, and he was black like him. Indeed, Ray was like his passage into the otherwise black experience. In 1979, Obama graduated from high school, ending his academic tenure at Punahou, and completing his schooling from kindergarten, primary grades, elementary, and middle through high school at different schools, and even outside of the United States in some instances.

The next phase of his formal training would begin at the higher educational level: college. Lincoln never entered college; he was a self-taught man. At this time in Obama's life he, like Lincoln, was ready to move beyond parental boundaries as a young man wanting to make it on his own. Indeed, he had had his ups and downs in school toward the senior year in high school. Hanging out, peer pressure, and trying to find himself, grades dropping, definitely not because he lacked the ability to master the academics—after all, Barack was academically talented—but because he was drifting, not focusing, using slick, elusive responses to his mother's inquiries about his indifference to his future. What was he doing? What about his destiny? His mother had questions and she wanted to know. "Are you going to be a good-time Charlie? A loafer?"[17]

College. That was the big question confronting him, and his mother wanted answers. So he told her that his grandfather never went to college, so maybe I'll just follow in his footsteps. His mother's quick response: "You're already much better educated than your grandfather."[18] *This too shall pass*, and fortunately Barack did not let his mother down, nor himself. He set his eyes on the prize and headed toward college with a host of letters of acceptance from a number of outstanding colleges. Going off to college caused Barack to reflect and no doubt appraise what his grandfather's old black friend Frank had called college: an advanced degree in compromise.[19] And old Frank told him that "you're not going to college to get educated. You're going there to be trained."[20]

SELF-TAUGHT VS. FORMAL TRAINING

Barack Obama continued his formal education by entering Occidental College in Los Angeles, California, in 1979. Here he would matriculate during his freshman and sophomore years before transferring to Columbia University in New York City for his junior and senior years. At Columbia University, he majored in political science with an international relations focus, graduating in 1983 with a bachelor of arts degree. Next, he worked at Business International Corporation and New York Public Interest Research Group before moving to Chicago in 1985. In Chicago, he worked as a community organizer. After about two years in Chicago, he returned to formal education to become a lawyer entering Harvard Law School (Cambridge, Massachusetts) in 1988. In 1990, the *New York Times* reported his election as the first black president of the *Harvard Law Review*. He was enrolled in a three-year program at Harvard. Obama graduated with a JD magna cum laude from Harvard in 1991. He wrote his first book, *Dreams from My Father*, a memoir published in 1995. Obama taught constitutional law part time at the University of Chicago Law School from 1993 until his election to the US Senate in 2004.

In sum, that is the extent of his formal training. Perhaps, one may interpret that Frank's version of training was that they will feed you book knowledge insisting that you believe what you read in the book and believe, in a verbatim way, what the professor tells you to memorize or write. Then, when you get through with the packaged deal of training, you'll be stuffed away in some office cubicle and become programmed to the routines expected in job performance and regurgitate policies made by someone else while being patronized because you're the kind of token black whom they need for your canned, compromised behavior; they will let you mingle with them to show you off as their little robot with wages that compensate for your bowing down and letting them lead you around. That's *training*. You are not allowed to think for yourself or create ideas connected to making decisions that you coordinate into implementation for the good of the industry. Oh yes, that's *training for sure*.

According to Carter McNamara, formal training is training that follows some designed form. Systematic, formal training includes careful assessments and attention to determining training goals, designing and building methods and material that are directly aligned (and often pretested) to achieve the goals, implementing training, and careful evaluation to ensure that training is carried out effectively and that training goals were reached. In systematic, formal training, each phase of the process produces results directly needed by the next phase.[21]

By definition of formal training, Barack Obama received training that followed a designed form on the basis of the curriculum and pedagogy of the college and universities where he matriculated. Additionally, he was a part of the system/institution of higher education in America. Again, his formal training included all those dynamics of the systematic/institutional formal training that McNamara described. The definitive contrast in formal training between Lincoln and Obama appears different from an external point of view. Ironically, parallels exist within their quest for knowledge, to be discussed later in the context.

Abraham Lincoln's inquisitive mind refused to be stifled by the inadequacies of the meager rural early schoolhouse with teachers who were transient and poorly trained themselves. Instead, Abraham Lincoln read avidly by candlelight, while plowing or resting after his many chores. He seized books and read to educate himself. The *Dilworth's Spelling Book* used by his sister and him in Kentucky provided his introduction to grammar and spelling. Of course, books were not in an abundance on the frontier during Lincoln's youth. Other than classroom textbooks, his first books were the family Bible, followed by *The Pilgrim's Progress*, *Aesop's Fables*, *Lessons in Elocution* by William Scott, William Shakespeare, and he was fascinated by history. He read *History of the United States* by William Grimshaw. Other nonfiction interested him such as biographies. In fact, he was the most well-read among his peers as a youth. Even though his father, Thomas, thought him strange to show more interest in books than manual labor, his father did not interfere with his son's fascination with book learning. Nonetheless, Lincoln was strong and skillful in manual labor, demonstrated in his splitting rails and laboring hard in the fields and surrounding areas; clearly physical labor was not an objective of his goals, indeed not. His schooling, meager as it was, empowered Abraham with the self-confidence needed to stand up in intellectual capacity against men who achieved high formal training above his "defective education," or his lack of formal years in school. To his credit, his foresight of the necessity of studying on his own serves as a significant substitute for being taught by well-trained teachers. But this did not erase the fact that Abraham Lincoln felt that in comparison to his contemporaries' formal study, his education remained defective.

Lincoln declared himself a self-made man. Obama matriculated in the academy. Yet both approached the world critically, analytically, probing for answers, truth, and possessed the proclivity for success by pressing on with driving ambitions. Each man may be categorized as compelling men who set their ambitions on the road to find a sizeable place in the world and America. Commencing with their formative years in different places and centuries apart, each rose above the ordinary and the likely by embracing his vision, and even the unlikely, making each phenomenal studies in the world universe.

The education that each received significantly represented the times in which he lived—the former in the nineteenth century and the latter in the twentieth century, which was ironically unusual because of race and class. On the basis of the privileged among the American Anglican families, education was par excellence, like President John Adams and his son John Quincy Adams, along with other aristocratic families who attended prestigious universities. But Lincoln did not hail from aristocracy nor high societal circles; rather, his origin comes from humble beginnings, or the "annals of the poor." Access to Harvard was not readily in reach for him, even though he was white.

On the basis of race, the African American families' education was defective during the nineteenth century and earlier, although in some instances even today. Often learning to read and write were not accessible to the enslaved or even to free Negroes; slipping to learn to decode the printed word and alphabet could erupt into cruel punishment, even for the "house Negro." Barack Obama attained an education "second to none" and was able to attend top universities in the land regardless of his black ancestry.

Of course, the civil rights movement of the 1960s had been responsible for blacks' emergence into quality education at major schools and institutions, whereas Barack Obama, like other African Americans born in this period known for its relentless move for social justice, reaped the benefits of this historical movement, one hundred years later since the Civil War period. So, quite understandably, Obama and Lincoln represented different times, yet specifically underwent some similar personal episodic experiences in their developmental lives, which may affirm that America has grown and progressed toward its true destiny of democracy and opportunity for all.

In looking back, one can say that the contrasts of Lincoln's education and Obama's are sharply divided into uneven parts, yet each is similar in each man's thirst for knowledge and inquiry complemented by his innate intellectual strength while honored with spiritual insight, producing a holistic balance held by each of them.

THIRST-FOR-KNOWLEDGE PARALLELS

We suppose ourselves to possess unqualified scientific knowledge of a thing, as opposed to knowing it in the accidental way in which the sophist knows, when we think that we know the cause on which the fact depends, as the cause of that fact and of no other than it is. . . . Consequently the proper object of unqualified scientific knowledge is something which cannot be other than it is.

—Aristotle

No matter what the formal education or training may be, the search and desire to acquire more information, analyze truth, or delve into the innermost centers of logic/reasoning describe elements of the need to gain more knowledge. The sage approach means appreciating wisdom, learning, and truth combined with cognitive components of belief, theory, and concepts that embody the broad spectrum of knowledge and understanding. The definition of knowledge is a matter of ongoing debate among philosophers in the field of epistemology. The classical definition, described but not ultimately endorsed by Plato, has it that in order for there to be knowledge, at least three criteria must be fulfilled: that in order to count as knowledge, a statement must be justified, true, and believed. Basically, knowledge is defined (*Oxford English Dictionary*) variously as (i) expertise and skills acquired by a person through experience or education, the theoretical or practical understanding of a subject; (ii) what is known in a particular field or in total, facts and information; or (iii) awareness or familiarity gained by experience of a fact or situation.

Again, philosophical debates in general start with Plato's formulation of knowledge as "justified true belief" (the JTB analysis of knowledge). There is no one agreed-upon definition of knowledge; a number of concepts of knowledge exist. Knowledge acquisition involves complex cognitive processes: perception, learning, communication, association, and reasoning. The term knowledge is used to mean the confident understanding of a subject with the ability to use it for a specific purpose, if appropriate. Considering the thirst-for-knowledge parallels includes the need for gathering facts, constructing theories, using inductive and deductive reasoning, investigating, and looking for evidence as Lincoln and Obama enhanced themselves in their ambitious quests. Epistemology is, broadly speaking, the study of what knowledge is and how one comes to have knowledge. Knowledge carries several properties. For Abraham Lincoln and Barack Obama, knowledge was invaluable and highly respected, thus leading to their quest for knowledge beyond the walls of the schoolhouse; but knowledge that enriched them as self-made men actually presents evidence of their thirst to seek truth for application and evaluation purposes.

Considering that Lincoln and Obama possessed knowledge in the cognitive domain and processed what they learned from experience and/or training shows how they came to earn knowledge. First, they gained knowledge because of their innate high regard for it, leading and motivating them to embrace knowledge at the sacrifice of mundane things. What tasks did they perform to acquire knowledge? Why did they actually thirst for knowledge, which means to be wise, skilled, knowledgeable, aware, and sagacious? All of those agents parallel the significance of Lincoln and Obama's thirst for knowledge. The most common parallel in which they engaged in the acquisition of knowledge came through print or the printed page. Both were cognizant of the benefits of reading to increase self. Lincoln once said:

> A capacity, and taste, for reading, gives access to whatever has already been discovered by others. It is

the key, or one of the keys, to the already solved problems. And not only so. It gives a relish, and facility, for successfully pursuing the [yet] unsolved one.

Lincoln further commented on his favorite style of reading:

> When I read aloud two senses catch the idea: first, I see what I read; second, I hear it, therefore I can remember it better.[22]

With Barack Obama, his desire for knowledge was to improve himself as well. When Obama arrived in New York City and was asked by his immigrant friend Sadik why he had come to New York, Obama reminisced:

> I had spent the summer brooding over a misspent youth ... And the state of the world and the state of my soul. I want to make amends. Make myself of some use.[23]

Furthermore, in his move to New York to further his education at Columbia University, he claimed that the city changed him, making him want to improve himself in spite of the attractions that a city such as New York City held. Instead, his thirst was not for recreational pleasures whatsoever, but for just the opposite. His description of his new image follows:

> I stopped getting high. I ran three miles a day and fasted on Sundays. For the first time in years, I applied myself to my studies and started keeping a journal of daily reflections and very bad poetry. I'd beg off hitting the bar, I'd give some excuse, too much work or not enough cash.

Sadik called him a "bore."[24] Lincoln writes that:

He was never in a college or academy as a student; and never inside a college or academy building till since he had a law license. What he was in the way of education, he picked up. . . . He regrets his lack of education, and does what he can to supply the want.[25]

Again, the theme of self-improvement serves as a parallel in the quest for both of them in their studious capacity to reshape themselves to higher levels through self-preparation, self-actualization, and dedication to knowledge and learning.

The education of two of America's arguably greatest political figures is marked by bold contrast between their formative schooling, such as from the rugged frontier school equipped, perhaps, with the sum of one year of instruction, which wrapped up the school-day experience for Abe Lincoln, in contrast to the ivy-covered walls of Harvard—one of the world's premiere standards in academia. Again, Barack Obama achieved distinction as the first black editor of the prestigious *Harvard Law Review*.

NOTES

Chapter Two
Education Defective and Education Par Excellence

1. David Herbert Donald, *Lincoln* (New York: Simon and Schuster, 1995), 23.
2. *Encyclopedia Britannica*, s.v. "Early Childhood Education," accessed December 3, 2008.
3. David McKay Wilson, "When Worlds Collide," *Harvard Education Letter* (Nov./Dec. 2008), 1.
4. Donald, *Lincoln*, 23.
5. Donald, 23.
6. Donald, 23.
7. Donald, 29.
8. Donald, 23.
9. William Miller, *Lincoln's Virtues: An Ethical Biography* (New York: Vintage Books, 2008), 67.
10. Miller, 57.
11. Miller, 57.
12. Miller, 57.
13. Barack Obama, *The Audacity of Hope: Thoughts on Reclaiming the American Dream* (New York: Crown Publishers, 2006), 274.
14. Barack Obama, *Dreams from My Father: A Story of Race and Inheritance* (Crown Publishers, 2004), 48.
15. Obama, 50.
16. Obama, 50.
17. Obama, 95.
18. Obama, 96.
19. Obama, 91.
20. Obama, 97.
21. Formal, Carter McNamara, ed., [Not Necessarily Systematic] Training and Development Processes, Authenticity Consulting, LLC (1997–2008), 1.

22. In *Abraham Lincoln: His Essential Wisdom*, Address before the Wisconsin State Agricultural Society, Milwaukee, WI, September 30, 1859; remark to William H. Herndon about Lincoln's habit of reading aloud, from *Abraham Lincoln: The True Story of a Great Life*, William H. Herndon and Jesse W. A. Weik.
23. Obama, *Dreams from My Father*, 119.
24. Obama, 119.
25. Miller, *Lincoln's Virtues*, 45.

CHAPTER THREE

CROSSING CAREER PATHS

If you love and serve man, you cannot, by any hiding or stratagem, escape remuneration.
— Ralph Waldo Emerson

To work for the common good is the greatest creed.
— Albert Schweitzer

They never met. They never came face to face. They would never know each other personally; however, professionally and historically their career paths intersected as both grew from the nurturing grassroots to towering crests of dedicated careers immersed in total service to the country of their birthplace—America—producing dividends that stretch into diverse domestic and global domains. At the crossroads of the frontier yesteryears and traversing through the cyberspace of the new technology age, two paths did crisscross, moving and blending into images of professional likeness and dynamics, although constructed across different times but not altogether at different places. From the remote hamlet of New Salem to the inner-city blight of Southside Chicago (geographically located at least a half hour apart in modern times, although perhaps a day apart in earlier times), both places physically interwoven in the Prairie State of Illinois sent forth two preservers of an American democracy, reformers/change agents sustaining the principle of a new birth of liberty and the audacity to hope amidst troubling times of conflict in this land of promise and prospects. Each man came from different eras in United States history, one from the early nineteenth to the mid-nineteenth centuries, the other from the mid-twentieth to the early twenty-first centuries. One became a leading Whig transformed Republican, and the other became one of the leading Democrats of his time. One man's heritage was Anglo-American (white), the other man's heritage, African and American (black); still, each had professional beginnings at the grassroots levels.

Upon completing college (Columbia) in New York, Obama moved to Chicago in 1985 at the age of twenty-four to work for a church-based group seeking to improve living conditions in poor neighborhoods plagued with crime and high unemployment. He remained at this job where he was first a community organizer until he left to further his par excellence education.

Basically, grassroots begins at the local and popular level of society, especially in rural areas as distinguished from the centers of political leadership. Did Obama or Lincoln work at the local level, whether rural or urban society? What was their motivation?

Barack Obama had idealistic views about starting at the grassroots as a community organizer. In fact, he somewhat romanticized it as the ideal job. At twenty-four years old, he commented on his idealistic future job, stating:

> Change won't come from the top, I would say. Change will come from a mobilized grassroots. That's what I'll do. I'll organize black folks at the grassroots for change. Obama further increased his idealism in which he would go to organize the capital of the African American community in the country, (Chicago).[1]

After all, Harold Washington—Chicago's first black mayor—had actually won out over Richard J. Daley, the dominant political machine. Well-known and outstanding African Americans were inspiring young Obama in his aspirations. According to Lizza from the *New Republic,* Obama found Chicago an ideal place for an "identity-starved Kenyan-Kansan to engage himself in a more typical black American experience."[2] Conversely, this Illinois son Abraham Lincoln's key to his motivation illustrated itself through his desire to move forth on more rugged terms while launching his career.

During the young adulthood of Abraham Lincoln, he too found himself opening a new life for himself, starting out on his own. His voyage took him to the little village of New Salem on the Sangamon River in Illinois. The change for young Lincoln all began when he, his stepbrother, and cousin John Hanks took a cargo of goods to New Orleans for a trader, Denton Offutt. Since Offutt had become impressed with Lincoln's ability and dexterity in moving a flat boat over a mill dome, he employed the promising lad to perform the task for him; and at the same time, Offutt was as equally impressed with the prospects of New Salem and had arranged to open a store and rent the mill. Later, Offutt offered Lincoln the job as clerk and handyman at his store.

In July 1831, New Salem enjoyed what proved to be a short-lived boom based on a local conviction that the Sangamon River would be made manageable for steamboats, transforming the New Salem village into a trading center for the surrounding area. From a cultural sense, the people were from the South, though a number of Yankees had also drifted into New Salem while community pastimes were similar to those Lincoln had once known, only somewhat more advanced.

While in New Salem, Lincoln immersed himself into the community life, including his becoming a member of the debating society. In addition, Lincoln enlisted in the Black Hawk War when it broke out (April 1832) in Illinois. Notably, it was in New Salem that Lincoln began his political advocacy in this small community around the Sangamon River.

As stated earlier, the people of New Salem believed that the Sangamon River would make the town a navigation town with steamships rolling in and out developing commerce and trade around New Salem. However, the promises were short lived; the possibility failed.

Nonetheless, community life in New Salem during its height of trade appeared promising, and Lincoln advanced himself to the forefront among the locals there. Even among the rough crowd in the community such as the Clary's Grove boys, Lincoln found himself tackling one of them in a wrestling match, which he won, to the surprise of the tough Clary boys, resulting in them and the townspeople holding Lincoln in high esteem there, causing Lincoln to become an insider even more than an outsider here in New Salem. His association with the common folk endeared him to them. In fact, Lincoln gained popularity among the people of New Salem on the basis of his honesty and kindness toward them. Additionally, Lincoln's drive for self-improvement impressed the business men and working class at New Salem. Indeed, Lincoln increased himself even more by enlisting in the Black Hawk War, primarily for political reasons, then he returned to New Salem, directing his attention to politics and law.

When he engaged in running for one of the open political offices, it is noted that he won almost all of the votes in his own community, but lost the election because he was not known throughout the county. He held several jobs in New Salem, one in partnership with William Berry by purchasing a store on credit that failed shortly thereafter. As a result, Lincoln incurred the debt from this entrepreneurial venture; following the store episode, Lincoln's series of jobs were deputy surveyor, appointed postmaster, and simply odd jobs to help him make a meager living.

Unlike Obama's opportunities to grow and develop in his job as a community organizer on the South Side of Chicago in 1985, when Chicago was a full-fledged modern city, Lincoln chose to leave New Salem for more opportunities. By 1836, as a result of lack of commerce and economics, New Salem began experiencing a population decline and would soon become a ghost town. During such time, Lincoln moved to Springfield, Illinois, on April 15, 1837, to become John Todd Stuart's law partner. Of course, New Salem has since been restored as a state park in Illinois.

Comparative to a modern industrial city like Chicago to the declining small hamlet of New Salem in the 1800s, very little appears in common; however, it is not completely true, because Lincoln's small community of New Salem around the Sangamon River (where he began his political advocacy) diminished, the community where Obama began his political community organizing shares similarities of decline. Speaking of the Altgeld Gardens Public Housing Project at the far southern end of Chicago west of the Calumet River, a serious approach to improving conditions was warranted and badly needed for implementation during the mid-1980s. And to this issue, Barack Obama arrived and advocated on behalf of the needs of this poor black neighborhood where he connected through his grassroots involvement as a community organizer.

What, then, is community organizing, one may ask? Accordingly, it is a process by which people are brought together to act in common self-interest. ACORN (Association of Community Organizations for Reform Now) is one of the community-organizing groups in the United States for which Obama later wrote legislative support while in the Senate. Advocates like Barack Obama, Cesar Chavez, Saul Alinsky, Jesse Jackson, Martin Luther King Jr., and John Lewis, among a host of others, have served as notable community organizers.[3]

Many groups seek populist goals and the ideal of participatory democracy. Organized community groups seek accountability from elected officials and corporations/institutions, as well as increased direct representation within decision-making bodies and social reform.

Pressure on decision makers through a variety of means such as picketing, petitioning, boycotting, and electoral politics is practiced. Organizing is empowering all community members, often with the end goal of distributing power equally throughout the community.

Grassroots is only one of the three types of community organizing of which Obama is noted. Coalition and faith-based are the other two. Likewise, Lincoln was a part of both, grassroots and coalition organizing. Lincoln, in later years of his political career, took leadership in organizing a coalition for the existing group of the new Republican political party in the Midwest (Illinois). Coalition-building efforts seek instead to motivate existing groups to more effectively pursue a common agenda. Thus, Lincoln's leadership qualified him as a coalition builder among the existing 1856 New Republican Party after the former Whigs became defunct.

The ideal of grassroots organizing is to build community groups from scratch, develop new leadership where none existed, and otherwise organize the unorganized. It is a values-based process where people are brought together to act in the interest of their communities and the common good. Grassroots is a strategy that revitalizes communities and allows the individuals to participate and incite social change. Sometimes those outside the grassroots organizing or movements refer to such organizers as "agitators."

Briefly, Lincoln's concept of improving one's condition is similar to what Obama sought in changing the condition of the urban poor in Altgeld Gardens. Many years ago in 1861, President Lincoln spoke to a Cincinnati audience uplifting his vision of individual economic opportunity:

> Whatever is calculated to advance the condition of the honest, struggling laboring man, I am for that thing.[4]

Or, as he sympathetically told a delegation of striking workers who visited the White House in 1863, "I know the trials and woes of working men. I have always felt for them."[5]

According to Garfinkle and Holzer, Lincoln understood that the purpose of the United States was to "clear the path for the individual to labor and get ahead."[6] Moreover, Lincoln understood that this purpose was challenged by the slave-based, aristocratic, economic, and social system of the Southern states. To Lincoln, the economic, moral, and political elements were inextricably intertwined. Together they represented what is distinctively American about our economy and democracy.[7] Furthermore, Lincoln viewed liberty as—above all—the right of individuals to the fruits of their own labor, seen as a path to prosperity.[8] "To (secure) each laborer, the whole product of his labor, or as nearly as possible," he wrote, "is a most worthy object of any good government."[9]

The slave system created a denial of this economic right. Lincoln insisted that "African Americans were entitled to the same economic rights as all other Americans." The universal promise of opportunity was for Lincoln the philosophical core of America, according to Garfinkle and Holzer.[10] To Lincoln, liberty to all was a principle that clears the path for all—gives hope to all—and, by consequence, enterprise and industry to all.[11]

Barack Obama is a Democrat and he states in his prologue his concerns about policies that consistently "favor the wealthy and powerful over average Americans," and insists that government has an important role in opening up opportunity to all.[12]

According to Obama, after "clearing the path" over a century ago, where are we now? He continues that America feels less deeply divided. Illinois, for example, is no longer considered a bellwether state. For more than a decade now, it's become more and more Democratic, partly because of increased urbanization, partly because the social conservatism of today's GOP doesn't wear well in the "Land of Lincoln." But Illinois remains a microcosm of the country, a rough stew of North and South, East and West, urban and rural, black, white, and everything in between.[13]

Obama credits Lincoln, in *Audacity of Hope*, as one of a kind in his understanding and grasp of liberty. After probing and searching, Obama concludes:

> I'm left then with Lincoln, who like no man before or since understood both the deliberative function of our democracy and the limits of such deliberation. We remember him for the firmness and depth of his convictions—his unyielding opposition to slavery and his determination that a house divided couldn't stand.... I like to believe that for Lincoln, it was never a matter of abandoning conviction for the sake of expediency. Rather, it was a matter of maintaining within himself the

balance between two contradictory ideas—while we must talk and reach for common understandings.[14]

Furthermore, Barack Obama gives far-reaching credit to Lincoln and reflects on the qualities of the sixteenth president. He states:

> Self-awareness combined with that humility led Lincoln to advance his principles through the framework of our democracy as expressed in his speeches and his positions in debates in the reasoned arguments that might appeal to the "better angels" of our nature. It was in this same humility that allowed him, once the conversation between North and South broke down and war became inevitable realizing that resisting the temptation to demonize the fathers and sons who did battle on the other side, or to diminish the horrors of war, no matter how just it might be could no longer suffice. The blood of the enslaved reminds us that our pragmatism can sometimes be moral cowardice. Lincoln, and those buried at Gettysburg, remind us that we should pursue our own absolute truths only if we acknowledge those may be a terrible price to pay.[15]

After giving his sister a tour of the South Side of Chicago, Auma, his Kenyan sister, asked her brother, "Are you doing this for them, Barack? This organizing business, I mean?"[16]

He continued to implement and advocate for "them" before leaving for Harvard Law School in 1988, and receiving his JD degree in 1991, Obama dutifully returned to Chicago to continue his work in organizing among his people. In 1992, Obama directed Illinois Project VOTE, registering 150,000 new voters.

> We hold these truths to be self-evident. In those words, the struggles of Martin and Malcolm and unheralded marchers to bring these words to life. Douglass and

Delany, as well as Jefferson and Lincoln, I hear the voice of Japanese families interned behind barbed wire; young Russian Jews cutting patterns in Lower East Side sweat shops; dust-bowl farmers loading up their trucks with the remains of shattered lives. I hear the voices of the people in Altgeld Gardens.[17]

In Obama's return to Chicago, the work remained unfinished as he saw the "signs of decay accelerated throughout the Southside—the neighborhoods shabbier, the children edgier and less restrained; more middle class families heading out to the suburbs, the jails bursting with glowering youth, my brothers without prospects," he reports in his advocacy.[18]

In summary, in Lincoln's times, some of the issues and challenges that face Obama and the United States today have not changed in many ways.

The bicentennial celebration of Lincoln in February 2009 causes us to remember that the historical election of President-elect Obama's inauguration January 2009 indicates preservation and promise of an American democracy that stands as a beacon of hope for economic opportunity and the liberty and right of upward mobility for all.[19] The people must support the American dream.

Is there balm in Gilead? Could Obama become that balm?

Indeed, many successive American presidents have reflected on the sixteenth president, Abraham Lincoln—have been inspired by him, identified with him, and even imitated him on the basis of his speeches—and compared the dynamics of contemporary crisis with the major historic crisis that Lincoln withstood. This has been a bipartisan practice among contemporary Democrat and Republican presidents, including Theodore Roosevelt, Franklin Delano Roosevelt, Harry Truman, John F. Kennedy, Richard Nixon, Ronald Reagan, George Bush, and Bill Clinton.

When the Democratic presidential nominee Barack Obama reached far across the aisle in terms of a century or so connecting with the sixteenth president, Abraham Lincoln, when Obama launched his campaign in Springfield at the old statehouse where Lincoln delivered his "House Divided" speech, his admiration for aspects of the ideologies of Lincoln is frequently mirrored in Obama's own theories and aims on politics, society, and economics.

Barack Obama comes as another adopted son of Illinois, like Abraham Lincoln, who adopted the Prairie State as his home, although each was born elsewhere: Kentucky (Lincoln) and Hawaii (Obama). The question is, why did Obama and Lincoln choose Illinois? Did their early ideology blend? Is it true that "great minds think alike"? Indeed, it is imperative to examine their thoughts and actions more closely as an effort to answer the questions presented.

First, let us review Lincoln's reasons for moving to Illinois. Actually, growing up and developing into young adulthood, Abraham Lincoln moved with his father to Indiana (the Hoosier State) in 1816, which is in close proximity to Illinois. But it was actually Abraham Lincoln's father who chose Illinois because the elder Lincoln found the land in central Illinois more fertile and conducive to growing crops; consequently, the Lincoln family settled on the banks of the Sangamon River in Macon County, near Decatur, Illinois. However, there are a number of controversial biographical reasons written about Thomas Lincoln's real motive of moving so often in relationship to many poor white men like him who were hard pressed or hopeless about improving their condition and were in opposition to having to work beside the Negro enslaved men, so to speak. However, slavery had been prohibited by the Northwest Ordinance in the state of Indiana, and as a result, perhaps, did not pose a competitive threat to Lincoln's father.

Nevertheless, at this time, Lincoln was twenty-one years old and eager to broaden his experience beyond wilderness communities of sowing, planting, and splitting rails. So, in March 1830, upon assisting his father Thomas Lincoln in moving the family from Indiana to Illinois[20] by spring of next year, Lincoln left his father's household and landed in New Salem to improve himself and embark upon a new life.

Becoming involved professionally in politics and law, combined with developing his skills as a stump speaker, Lincoln left for Springfield, Illinois, in 1837. Headed to Springfield, after his time was spent in New Salem, he left carrying all of his possessions: only two saddlebags of his personal goods/clothing. Truth is that he borrowed a horse for his transportation and threw his two saddlebags of belongings over his horse's back and rode off to the horizons of Springfield, Illinois.[21]

Here he roomed with Joshua Speed above the general store, and it was here his political interest deepened as the young, gangly man filled with ambition to make a difference in society, which included collaborating with the press in support of him while making friends with young journalists in the *Sangamon Journal* and appealing to the growing society in the new frontier town of Springfield. In 1821, his choice of Springfield became a resourceful base for Lincoln because it was a growing and thriving community, unlike New Salem that had dried up for lack of commerce/trade. Regardless of its infancy, just over ten years old, Springfield may be described as the town, other than Chicago, as one of the more cosmopolitan and sophisticated during that time. In Springfield, he could participate intellectually and politically as he increased his political aspirations for the good of the people.

There is some nuance in Obama's need to move somewhat similar to Lincoln's reason. After leaving the Waikiki islands of Hawaii, as a youth, Obama left for Occidental College in Los Angeles, California. Growing restless to embrace the African American experience to help him resolve his identification problem, he followed his instinct to move from the West Coast to the East Coast in New York City. After learning about the Occidental University transfer program with Columbia University, Barack seized the opportunity to transfer from Occidental.

In New York at Columbia, Barack concluded that he could partially meet his desire to connect with black America:

> I figured that if there weren't any more black students at Columbia than there were at Oxy, I'd at least be in the

heart of a true city, with black neighborhoods in close proximity.[22]

Traveling from Hawaii to the mainland, Obama's odyssey really began. Barack Obama's journey to Illinois was long: all the way from the Pacific to the Atlantic Ocean (West to East) and middle of America known as the heartland—crossing from the West Coast. He traversed to the East Coast to find a new beginning for himself, truly in search of belonging to a community, a union with his people. He deepened his search for fulfillment. Barack's circle toward belonging drew him into the middle and heart of America—the midwestern state of Illinois—initially settling into the South Side of Chicago before heading to Springfield, Illinois—Springfield, the grounds that Lincoln frequented over one hundred years earlier.

Yet here in Illinois, two young men came at different epochs in time, but each raising the torch of ambition and the desire to lift it meriting historical legacies and universal appeal. Both gangly in stature, accompanied by protruding ears standing out broadly marked their physical resemblance, imaging sharpness in appearance. Each believing in self-improvement. Both politically oriented and intellectually driven, Barack Obama confided that his quest focused on "what I needed was a community . . . a place where I could put down stakes and test my commitments."[23]

On the other hand, at this time in his life, Abraham Lincoln described his current sense of restlessness in terms of identifying himself as "a piece of floating driftwood."[24]

With the growing need to establish themselves, both attached themselves to their interests in public life in the domain of servant leadership meant to uplift and change the status quo. Their quality traits depict each as the deep thinker, philosophical, ethical, heroic, results oriented, masterful public speakers, reflective, thought led, visionaries, diplomatic, serious, influential problem solvers, and reformist by nature.

Notwithstanding that people in various careers often share similar traits, like those of Obama and Lincoln, what causes them to be so different from their peers? The answer is simple. Each has utilized his abilities/skills in applicable ways. Of course. But others have done so as well. Perhaps we cannot give a definitive answer that provides a direct reason about Obama's or Lincoln's quality traits as unique to other achievers. But what can be said is that each rose above the odds combined with a sense of greatness and aspiration attributed to hard work and perseverance. Again, many have achieved such. But amidst crisis, doubts, and the odds, still Obama prevails, and so does Lincoln.

The objective of Barack Obama's idealistic agenda was to change: "Change will come from a mobilized grass roots."[25]

On Lincoln's agenda, his objectives of community for the "economically hard strapped people of New Salem (Illinois)" were similar to the grassroots approach that sought to facilitate in the best interest of the community on basis of the needs of the people. He wrote that he believed that it was honorable "to do for a community of people, whatever they need to have done, but cannot do, at all or cannot do so well for themselves."[26]

The framework of those statements came before either achieved a political status or a professional law position. In his early twenties, while in college in New York, Barack Obama later moved to Chicago to really take a job as a community organizer. Abraham Lincoln, in his midtwenties, after the defeat of running for the second time as an Illinois state representative as a Whig, found his mind on community.

When Barack Obama left New York for Chicago, he simply loaded up his used car with his meager belongings and drove down to Illinois. After some defeat in trying to find a job as an organizer upon writing letters of application resulting in zero response, Obama found himself rather broke money-wise, combined with being broken in spirit. He left his conventional job as a research assistant in a Mid-Manhattan office and headed to Chicago to capture his dream. Just as Lincoln had visited New Salem, Illinois, before he settled there (by accident), so had Obama visited Chicago, Illinois, before he went there. Ronald Reagan, a Republican, served as president when Obama arrived in Chicago, Illinois, to fulfill his idealism of a community organizer. Back in 1831, Andrew Jackson, a Democrat, served as the president when Lincoln arrived in New Salem, Illinois, to shape his future.

PROFESSION: LEGAL PRACTICE

The leading rule for the lawyer as for the man of every calling is diligence.
—Lincoln, 1850

We need to recognize that the situation in Ferguson speaks to broader challenges that we still face as a nation. The fact is, in too many parts of this country, a deep distrust exists between law enforcement and communities of color.
—Obama, 2015

We have talked long enough in this country about equal rights. It is time now to write the next chapter—and to write it in the books of law.
—Lyndon B. Johnson, 1965

By profession, Lincoln was a lawyer. So is Obama. Both pursued law. Lincoln read law books to pass the bar, and he was admitted into law in 1837. There was no formal law school experience for Lincoln, simply reading and interacting with other experienced figures in the profession during his day. Unlike Lincoln, Obama studied law by actually attending classes and pursuing a prescribed course of study at Harvard University School of Law in Cambridge, Massachusetts. In looking at their professional pursuits, we find that parallels and differences exist.

"During the legislative campaign of 1834, John Todd Stuart, the leading Whig in Sangamon County and a candidate for the State House, urged Lincoln to become a lawyer, a thought that had already occurred to him."[27] Borrowing books from Stuart after the Legislature met,

Lincoln afterward wrote, "When the Legislature met, the law books were dropped, but were taken up again at the end of the session."[28]

What did Lincoln study to equip him for the profession of law? Displaying self-discipline and motivation, Lincoln studied and comprehended Sir William Blackstone's *Commentaries on the Laws of England* (1765). He read other legal treatises in addition to the statutes of the state. In 1836, at the age of twenty-seven, Abraham Lincoln received a license to practice law. He sought the profession by means of motivation, self-discipline, and ambition, and becoming self-educated. In measuring their preparation in educational professional practices, the substance is authentic on the basis of the needs of each man and what each hoped to gain.

In addition, Obama was distinct and studious in his studies and finished near the top of his Harvard Law class.[29] Obama began his career in law as an intern in 1988 at the Chicago law firm of Sidley and Austin three months shortly after he entered Harvard Law School. Obama worked as an associate attorney with Davis, Miner, Barnhill, and Gallard from 1993 to 2002. Just as Lincoln borrowed law books to study from Stuart after the Illinois legislature met, likewise Obama worked at the law firm only during the summer when the Illinois Senate was not in session.

According to Lincoln, he informs us of his scholarship in law: "From 1849–1854, both inclusive, I practiced law more assiduously than ever before," Lincoln wrote in an 1859 autobiographical sketch. During this time, Lincoln had taken a break from politics after his brief period of congressional work in Washington. Upon resuming his law practice with William Herndon in Springfield, Lincoln became a full-time lawyer. "His profession had almost superseded the thought of politics in his mind."[30]

Notably, each had turned down more lucrative job offers from Chicago law firms to lend their talents toward his own preferred choice of service by giving up top salaries that in reality each could command. Lincoln developed a sizeable law practice before the Illinois Supreme Court. Additionally, Lincoln built a large practice before the US circuit and district courts in Illinois.

Abraham Lincoln handled almost every kind of proceeding in federal courts as well. Yet the essence of his law practice was in the circuit courts, as Lincoln and Herndon practiced the majority of its business in the Sangamon County Circuit Court. His law practice increased sizably, causing him to move to a larger facility on the Illinois Capital Square. Lincoln supported railroads (Illinois Central Railroad) as a key agent for economic growth. Of course, in the nineteenth century, the law profession and political aspirations coincided and continues into the twenty-first century.

Unlike Lincoln, in Obama's period of law development, his work mostly involved drawing up briefs, contracts, and other legal documents, generally as a junior associate on legal teams. Obama's law practice involved real estate, representing community organizers, discrimination claims, and on voting-rights cases. One successful lawsuit in which Obama participated was the Association of Community Organizations for Reform Now (ACORN) forcing Illinois to implement the Motor Voter Act. Obama taught constitutional law as an adjunct professor at the University of Chicago Law School from 1993 until his election to the United States Senate in 2004.[31]

In comparison, both men immersed themselves in the importance of the Constitution. Each was a constitutionalist. Constitutional interpretation and its application were crucial frameworks for Lincoln in his deliberations and decisions of the Civil War and slavery.

Lincoln and Obama recognized that the Constitution as a legal document drawn up by the Founding Fathers (two hundred years ago) continued to maintain its relevancy. The Declaration of Independence, the Federalist Papers, and the Constitution guided Lincoln in his ideas and decision-making on the issues of the time. Likewise, as a civil rights lawyer, Obama governed his actions and based his arguments on those founding documents as well as taught constitutional law. The principle of the right to individual liberties and other rights of human beings/people were considered basic, justifiable human conditions for a quality of life. Consequently, Lincoln and Obama sought to pursue and maintain significant universal freedom of rights for all people with the empowerment of unity, integrity, and change toward a more perfect union.

Like Lincoln, Obama subscribed to the Founding Fathers' principles as outlined in the Constitution and the Declaration of Independence: inalienable rights that all men are created equal. Democracy—the great experiment of a democratic government of freedom and order of a republic state of elected representative government—gained exquisite meaning for each of them in the nineteenth century and later in the twenty-first century. Theoretically, the Constitution and Declaration of Independence served as standards in best practices of law implementation.

POLITICAL: RISING POLITICIANS

In conjunction with the law profession, the clarion call to politics summoned Obama and Lincoln to provide service to their government in the role of an elected public official, from the state legislature of Illinois to the congressional halls of Washington, DC.

Each man rose to leadership in his party, starting from practically unknowns to the highest ranks of membership in the political arena. Ironically, each waited his turn while making giant steps toward his goal on the world stage.

Lincoln's rise to a prominent politician chronicles interactive work within his party, beginning with the Whig Party, and Lincoln's admiration for the principles and vision of Henry Clay, the founder of the party. Eventually, he served as a presidential elector for Clay in 1844 and increased his standing as a Whig with an extensive speaking campaign for the party.[32]

Forming alliances and interacting with lawyers in the state capital (Springfield) who assisted him in cementing political alliances,[33] Lincoln utilized his enterprising skills here. Indeed, Lincoln initiated his rise to politics at least twenty years before the activation of the Civil War. The Eighth Judicial Circuit Court (Central and Eastern Illinois), which seriously influenced his success in politics, began with the Whig Party, which later evolved into the Republican

Party years later. In 1834, Lincoln was elected to the Illinois General Assembly for the Whig Party, representing Sangamon County.

Becoming a leader in the Whig Party afforded Lincoln numerous opportunities to campaign and speak on behalf of Whig candidates; meanwhile, Lincoln served as a Whig floor leader in the Illinois General Assembly. By 1845, Lincoln made an unsuccessful bid for the Whig nomination for United States Congress, but the following year (May 1846) Lincoln won the congressional nomination of the Whig Party and was elected to the US House of Representatives on August 3, 1846, taking his seat in the US House of Representatives on December 6, 1847, in Washington, DC.

In 1849, Lincoln voted to exclude slavery from federal territories and end the slave trade in the District of Columbia, yet he avoided participating in the congressional debates on slavery. On January 22, 1848, one of the highlight moments for Lincoln, by his own standards, came when he gave a speech in opposition to President Polk's policy regarding Mexico. Lincoln left the United States Congress without seeking reelection in 1849 and returned to Springfield on March 31; he resumed his law practice by devoting his time to law, removing himself from any dealings with politics.

He did not renew his interest in politics until Congress passed the Kansas-Nebraska Act on May 30 appealing the anti-slavery restriction in the Missouri Compromise, and without hesitation, he spoke out against the act at Bloomington, Springfield, and Peoria, appearing either before or after Senator Stephen A. Douglas, the principal author of the act. Next, Lincoln became elected to the legislature, but declined instead to run for a seat in the Senate. However, he lost the bid for a Senate seat.

Lincoln lost the Senate seat to Douglas by a vote of 54 to 46; still his increased popularity, fueled by the Lincoln–Douglas Debates, prompted major attention on Lincoln's behalf regardless of his loss of the Senate seat. Consequently, from August to October in 1856, Lincoln made speeches for Republican candidates in Iowa, Ohio, and Wisconsin. Eventually, the name of Lincoln gained notoriety as a possible presidential candidate.

Later, in 1856 (May), Lincoln helped to establish the Republican Party of Illinois, and at the first Republican Convention in Philadelphia in June, Lincoln received 110 votes for the vice-presidential nomination, giving him national recognition and a significant brand.

As a result of Lincoln's leadership in his party, he became well-sought-after on the speech circuit, delivering speeches on the issues confronting the nineteenth-century times, yet speaking enduring and empowering words that have withstood the test of time for their sagacity and purpose.

Lincoln spoke against the Dred Scott decision by the Supreme Court (June 26, 1857). Lincoln's "House Divided" speech at the State Convention in Springfield led to the seven debates between Stephen Douglas and him (Lincoln–Douglas Debates), and was attended enthusiastically by major crowds of people all over the Springfield area. He accepted endorsement on June 16, 1858, by the Republican State Convention for Senate seat, opposing Democrat Stephen A. Douglas.

On the other hand, Barack Obama's prominence in politics, like Lincoln, began with interactive work and forming alliances among his colleagues. From lawyer to an outstanding political figure, Obama moved in influential circles, providing him opportunities in legislature experiences and submitting while purveying his ideas/theories on the key issues of the twenty-first century. Within this odyssey of rise to political prominence, Obama, like Lincoln, became an unexpected presidential candidate.

Barack Obama's record consists of important speeches that shaped his political potential toward significant promise among major national Democrat forums. As a result, his visibility and speeches catapulted him to the forefront in the Democratic Party as far back as the 1990s to the present.

Obama's political run included success and failures at bids for seats as well. From a state senator in Illinois for eight years, Obama was a minority. Similarly, he was a pragmatic progressive like Lincoln, believing that an idea is to be sought in its practical bearings and that the function of their thoughts should guide their actions, while that truth is to be tested by the practical consequences of belief. Small wonder, then, that Barack Obama's legislative record in the Illinois Thirteenth District reflected such pragmatic progress by showing the people and community that their interest was his interest as well. He continued to work and develop alliances with other political forces.[34]

He participated in cosponsoring a bipartisan package of reform legislation in 1998 that included the Gift Ban, overhauling ethics laws in a state full of corruption.[35]

Principled and active, Obama spoke up for progressive and enlightened policies in the State Senate and the United States Senate in Washington. Of course, he achieved senatorship, unlike Lincoln, who lost in his bid for such an esteemed seat in US government. Both were equally equipped with deep clarity on the issue of attaining the support/partnership of Europe (Middle East) to ensure strategic, positive movements internationally.

As commander in chief, the question of performance in this role pressed each man to demonstrate his strength, logistics, knowledge, and application in foreign policy and to sustain its effect upon war—wars that would mark their effectiveness as commanders in chief. Of course, Lincoln faced the challenges of a civil war fought on his own interior, forcing destructive division between the North and South for four years (1861–1865). Opposite from a war fought on its own geographical territory or land, Obama faced the challenge of the aftermath of an external war fought overseas—the Iraqi War—in addition to domestic displeasure and wrath among pundits and divisive groups attacking his performance and race.

However, the unpopularity of both wars fought centuries apart caused massive criticism, confusion, dissatisfaction with the incumbent administration, and hopes and cries for an end to each of the wars resonated. Assessment of the commander in chief was high during both periods of time—for Lincoln, late nineteenth century; Obama as twenty-first-century presumptive nominee (Democrat Party)—while attesting to the fact that human nature does not change for peoples of the world, just names.

After engaging in dual roles of law and political community organizer and voter drive registration, Obama's career turned in the direction of fulfilling the calling of an elected political figure. As a result, the young idealist began at the state legislature in Illinois, as did Lincoln. Beginning in July 1995, Obama challenged incumbents by announcing plans to run for the Illinois Senate from Chicago's Thirteenth District (heavily Democrat, which represented Chicago's South Side). In 2000, he unsuccessfully ran against incumbent Bobby Rush for the US House of Representatives, receiving 30 percent of the vote to Rush's 61 percent.

Reelected to the Illinois Senate in 1998 and 2002, Obama, then, served in the state legislature quite well. While there, the young senator from Illinois was appointed by the new majority leader, Emil Jones, to serve as the sponsor of important legislation previously under development.

As a rising politician, Barack Obama sponsored many bills in the Illinois state legislature, gaining bipartisan support for legislating reform ethics and healthcare laws, enhancing tax credits for low-income workers, negotiating welfare reform, and promoting increased subsidies for children.

As an Illinois state senator, he led the passage of legislation mandating videotaping of homicide interrogations, and a law to monitor racial profiling by requiring police to record the race of drivers they stopped. Customarily looking ahead, in mid-2002, Obama began considering a run for the United States Senate by forming a strong campaign and supporting team headed by political strategist David Axelrod that fall, formally announcing his candidacy in January 2003.

Similarly, in August 2004, with less than three months to go before Election Day, Alan Keyes, an African American, accepted the Illinois Republican Party's nomination, replacing Jack Ryan, who withdrew from the race in June 2004. By November 2004, Obama resigned from the Illinois Senate following his election to the United States Senate. Although Keyes' residency was established in Maryland, he established legal residency in Illinois with his nomination.

Similar to Lincoln and Douglas running for Senate seats, followed by seven debates, primarily with opposing views on slavery, states' rights, and expanding slavery throughout central towns in Illinois in 1858, Obama and Keyes held three televised debates expressing opposing views on stem-cell research, abortion, gun control, school vouchers, and tax cuts. In the November 2004 General Election, the noted results were 70 percent for Obama and 27 percent for Keyes, the largest electoral victory in Illinois history. Like Lincoln, after the Lincoln–Douglas Debates in his run for Senate, Lincoln's fame rose and he was widely sought and considered as a seriously strong politician moving toward statesmanship.

Likewise, Barack Obama's popularity grew widely, and while in the State Senate, he was tapped by John Kerry, the 2004 Democratic presidential nominee, to write and deliver the keynote address at the 2004 Democratic National Convention in Boston, Massachusetts, gaining attention and launching his national political figure as an interesting figure among media.

Sworn in as a United States senator on January 4, 2005, he is listed by the United States Senate Historical Office as the fifth African American senator in United States history, the third to have been popularly elected, and he became the only African American currently serving in the Senate.

In his Democratic National Convention keynote speech, Obama resounded his beliefs of an America that can find unity in diversity, proclaiming, "There is not a liberal America and a conservative America. There's the United States of America."[36]

Contemporarily echoing Abraham Lincoln's view of one unified nation and magnifying his role and his unbending will to preserve the Union, "A House divided cannot stand."[37]

In the 110th Democratic-controlled Congress, the junior Senator Barack Obama collaborated with several of the seasoned key congressional members to cosponsor significant bills in the interest of reform ethics, such as eliminating gifts of travel on corporate jets by lobbyists to members of Congress.

Meanwhile, in February 2007, Barack Obama announced his

candidacy for president of the United States for the 2008 United States presidential election. This momentous and historical occasion took place at none other than the Old State Capitol building in Springfield, Illinois.

Describing his working life in Illinois while symbolically linking his presidential campaign to Abraham Lincoln's 1858 "House Divided" speech, Obama said:

> That is why, in the shadow of the Old State Capitol, where Lincoln once called on a house divided to stand together, where common hopes and common dreams still live . . .

Similar to Lincoln speaking out against the Mexican War in his "Spot Resolution" speech in Congress and severely criticized for so doing, Obama spoke out against the Iraqi War and did not vote for its continuation. Obama introduced the Iraq War De-Escalation Act of 2007. He was criticized by Senate Republicans such as 2008 presidential candidate John McCain (R-AZ), his Republican opponent.

A career can make or break you depending on one's readiness, skill, or clarity of purpose, among other critical variables that substantiate effective and sustainable progress in a particular field or calling. Indeed, the career experience of Obama remains as a politician, but more as a successful servant leader who will impact future generations, even though they may never meet the forty-fourth president face to face.

NOTES

Chapter Three
Crossing Career Paths

1. Ryan Lizza, "The Agitator," *The New Republic,* March 19, 2007.
2. Lizza, "The Agitator."
3. Barack Obama's Rules for Resolution. See *The Alinsky Model* by David Horowitz.
4. William C. Harris, *Lincoln's Rise to the Presidency* (Lawrence, KS: University Press of Kansas, 2007), 214.
5. Norton Garfinkle and Harold Holzer, *A Just and Generous Nation: Abraham Lincoln and the Fight for American Opportunity* (Barry Press), 9.
6. Garfinkle and Holzer, 9.
7. Garfinkle and Holzer, 8.
8. Garfinkle and Holzer, 8.
9. Garfinkle and Holzer, 8.
10. Garfinkle and Holzer, 8.
11. Garfinkle and Holzer, 8.
12. Barack Obama, *The Audacity of Hope: Thoughts on Reclaiming the American Dream* (New York: Crown Publishers, 2006), 10.
13. Obama, 48.
14. Obama, 98.
15. Obama, 98.
16. Obama, *Dreams from My Father: A Story of Race and Inheritance* (Crown Publishers, 2004), 209.
17. Obama, 437.
18. Obama, 438.
19. Garfinkle and Holzer, *A Just and Generous Nation,* 9.
20. Harris, *Lincoln's Rise to the Presidency,* 10–11.
21. Harris, 18.

22. Obama, *Dreams from My Father*, 115.
23. Obama, 115.
24. David Herbert Donald, *Lincoln* (New York: Simon and Schuster, 1995), 38.
25. Obama, *Dreams from My Father*, 113.
26. Carol Kelly-Gangi, ed., *Abraham Lincoln: His Essential Wisdom* (n.p.: Fall River, 2007), 19.
27. Harris, *Lincoln's Rise to the Presidency*, 16.
28. Harris, 16.
29. "Obama Rises from Political Obscurity," Politics News, www.comcast.net.articles/newspolitics/5October200 80510/Obama.Odyssey.
30. Donald, *Lincoln*, 142.
31. See Robert Fisher and Peter Romanofsky, "Community Organizing for Urban Social Change: A Historical Perspective," Greenwood Press, 1981.
32. Harris, *Lincoln's Rise to the Presidency*, 37.
33. Harris, 36.
34. John K. Wilson, *Barack Obama: This Improbable Quest* (Boulder, CO: Paradigm Publishers, 2008), 147.
35. Wilson, 145.
36. Steve Dougherty, *Hopes and Dreams: The Story of Barack Obama* (New York: Black Dog and Leventhal Publishers, Inc., 2008), 10.
37. Donald, *Lincoln*, 206.

IN RETROSPECT—ON THE ICONIC 1960S POLITICAL AND SOCIAL FIGURES OF CHANGE: JFK/MLK/RFK

I've always felt a curious relationship to the sixties. In a sense, I'm a pure product of that era.
—Barack Obama

A sense of change sweeps over the vastness of the social and political landscape swerving into intervals of calm, contentment, and the ordinary, one might say after the turmoil of the 1860s disappeared. Then, one hundred years later, a change evolved, placing America on a new course of direction and demands fueling unrest in a revolutionary sort of way. Indeed, it was the moving panorama of the 1960s that would leave its mark on the domestic issues of America, punctuated by a dramatic intervention that heralded the promises of a twenty-first century and highlighted by the dawning decade of the 2000s.

A separation from the old past resembled an interlude dividing the former way of life and its political and social structure toward another destiny of its own. Each historical epoch pauses after its course of actions or major causes exit the stage, generally followed by interventions sequestered amidst the centuries of time, creating interludes that release the long compositions of history necessitating a retrospective glance on iconic figures who conducted episodic influence during that respective period of time. After each era of history, the indelible footprints of iconic leadership have effected meaning and significance in the domain of change at critical times in the social and political composition of American life. "There are moments in our country—the 1960s was one of them—when people were looking for more and are willing to take a chance on [a candidate's potential for greatness]."[1] Meaning the possibility or potentiality is significant enough to merit the trust of the people in them as opposed to the previous establishment. Such icons initiate and define the profound changes or movements, signaling the major/minor key signatures in which to play. They leave guiding landmarks in the scope and sequence of time pressed with measurable timing between each iconic figure like an interlude in an operatic opus. Within the grand stage of American history during each interlude, reflections are called upon as we pass from one part to the other part. We reflect, review, reevaluate, and recapitulate on the progress of this country at the break of each historical period.

Even in recent times, such a factor is necessary between acts within big events as we take time to look back thoughtfully and review/recapture the ideas or regroup events before moving on to the next grand act: that is the PURPOSE of the interlude. Traveling on the road to the presidency during an era preceding Barack Obama's birth, and on the dawn of the civil rights movement while embracing the New Frontier that galvanized the nation from the post–World War II years, John Fitzgerald Kennedy, thirty-fifth president of the United States (1961–1963), led the country toward promising horizons. The year of Barack Obama's birth, 1961, John F. Kennedy engaged in his first presidential term, although it was cut short by an assassin's bullet in 1963 when Obama was a mere child of two years old. Meanwhile, ninety-eight years earlier (1865), Abraham Lincoln, the sixteenth president, was assassinated.

According to essayist Reeves, John F. Kennedy was the first of those identified as self-selected presidents in modern times. He did not wait his turn, because that turn might never come.[2] He, too, was one unlikely to be selected based on the establishment and the well-trenched national Democratic convention because Kennedy did not meet the norm. He was young, only forty-three years old, and a Roman Catholic; no Catholic had been president before.

Yet John Kennedy, a Harvard graduate as well, was determined to carve out new roads in the American political structure regardless of the formed conventional dynamics. Kennedy did not conform to the status quo but took on the challenge of change. His charismatic personality, good looks, and his presentation of himself as the people's choice armored him with the greatness of promise that the country needed and gripped. "The New Generation offers a Leader" with personal control of enough delegates—men and women committed not to political party or to ideology but to him—to roll over the old leaders and old ways.[3]

Of course, Kennedy's opponent was Vice President Richard Nixon, forty-seven years old and a navy veteran, but he was an old man's idea of what a young man should be.[4] Nixon was stiff and formal; Kennedy appeared warm and youthful. John F. Kennedy was one of the older brothers of the surviving Kennedy sons: Senator Edward M. Kennedy of Massachusetts and Robert Francis Kennedy. Winning votes on the basis of lifting the people to heights of honorable pride with a new fervor of hope and belief by the people of America transformed Kennedy into a presidential victory at the beginning of the decade of the 1960s as recorded in the annals of time. One hundred years earlier, the 1860 election transported another unlikely presidential candidate into America's political spotlight: Abraham Lincoln. Surprisingly and above all a stunning victory, so unexpected as never before when Barack Obama snatched a victory in the Iowa caucus—a predominantly white state, of course. This win became as equally striking as the two previous victories of Kennedy and Lincoln during the mid-eighteenth and twentieth centuries. Truly defining moments in American history, Kennedy urged America to follow his new frontier, impressing upon them that "America is ready for a new set of challenges. This is our time. A new generation is prepared to lead."[5]

And some decades later in the 2000s, Obama reflected that "one thing I'm convinced of is that people want something now," after Kennedy's rallying call for "a new generation of leadership," forty-three years later.[6]

Faced with the challenge to strengthen America, John F.

Kennedy met that need during a post-war era crowned with the honor of a people and their long-awaited cry to gain their basic human rights promised to them for over two hundred years—far too long.

Heeding the call to finish the job started back in 1865 with the Thirteenth Amendment, Kennedy was finally persuaded to support the cause of equality and justice for all with the passing of the civil rights legislation, joining hands with the civil rights movement led by another spirit whose courageous crusade marched throughout the land/country. Since the 1955 Montgomery bus boycott, Dr. Martin Luther King Jr. (1929–1968) waged his movement of discontent with Jim Crowism, denial of fundamental civil rights to people of color, and challenged Plessy v. Ferguson 1857 (separate-but-equal doctrine). Yet King did this so masterfully, without violence and hatred, using the philosophical theme of Mahatma Gandhi's nonviolence and love philosophy. From the Deep South, Dr. King, the young black Baptist minister, led a civil rights movement to unite rather than divide; he saw all men and women as sisters and brothers consisting of one universal race of humanity. In common protest as an anti-war advocate, he spoke out against the Vietnam War during the 1960s. Memorably, while at the foot of the Lincoln Memorial in Washington, DC, on one hot summer day, August 28, 1963, Dr. King's "I Have a Dream" speech reverberated to the masses while the world paused to listen.

He too spoke of generations to come who would benefit from the dream, such as Barack Obama and other children who belonged to that new generation that John F. Kennedy and Martin Luther King Jr. imagined in their promise and hopes for a new America. There was the hope of a new America that would provide all children opportunities and accessibility to a world-class education, a chance to work, study, and achieve their dreams, pursue happiness, and rise, believing that they could really fly!

Of the new frontiers and dreams stood the possibility of attaining the goal, the prize, floating up the mainstream as citizens whose rights and privileges will not be tampered with by bias, disenfranchisement, or the injustice of white supremacy ever! And if, just if, any child got the idea to dream big dreams, they could responsibly pursue those dreams and turn them into realities, even if it meant dreaming of occupying the highest office in the land—the presidency. Even if you were black or whatever color/gender! Why not?

Small wonder, then, that on August 28, 2008, forty-five years after Dr. King's famous "I Have a Dream" speech, standing at the foot of Lincoln's Monument during the mid-twentieth century, and moving forward to the early twenty-first century (2007) standing at the podium in Denver, Colorado, Barack Obama, an African American, stepped forth to accept the nomination of the president of the United States of America (from a major political party).

Quite compelling, then, that Robert F. Kennedy (1925–1968), brother of President John Kennedy, once voiced a prediction about the progress and elevation of African Americans during the turmoil of the civil rights movement when he spoke of future decades on the horizon.

Without hesitation, back in 1968, Senator Robert F. Kennedy, a civil rights advocate, suggested strongly that he could imagine that in forty years an African American could be nominated to become president of the United States of America. Senator Kennedy reflected: "Things are moving so fast in race relations. A Negro could be President in forty years. There is no question about it. In the next forty years, a Negro can achieve the same position that my brother [John F. Kennedy] has," said RFK, according to the Washington Post. "Prejudice exists and probably will continue to ... but we have tried to make progress and we are making progress. We are not going to accept the status quo."[7]

Barack Obama—the first African American to accept the presidential nomination at the powerful Democratic National Convention—confirms America's status as a beacon of hope and as a signature of change that uplifts democracy for all the world to view. True to Robert Kennedy's predilection and prophecy, the reality has come to pass forty years later. Although the younger brother of John and Robert Kennedy, Senator Edward M. Kennedy, lived to see his brother's prophecy fulfilled, the senator died (2009) a few months after President Obama began his presidential term, or "turn."

However, Senator Edward Kennedy was an encouraging and empowering mentor for the brilliant young African American who took his turn as the forty-fourth in the successive line of presidents of the United States, yet number one in line to take his "turn" as an African American elected president of the United States.

The 1860 and 1960 eras are descriptive of disturbing times of unrest, tremendous conflict, and dangerous sectional/partisan divide rooted in the selfish indulgence of racial supremacy waging hostile war against the civility of human rights and justice for all people. Historically, the 1860s and 1960s are separated by an interlude of one hundred or more years swept up in tumultuous struggles to achieve necessary harmonious relationships combined with open windows of possibilities as the core principles of America in its ultimate answer toward true and worthy progress rising in the millennium.

The interlude is over. It ceases. The curtain opens for the next act to begin or measure to be written, commencing with another revelation in chapters to be finished or scores to be orchestrated/played.

Tell me, tell me, Is there—Is there really balm in Gilead?
—Traditional African American Spiritual

NOTES

Interlude
In Retrospect—On the Iconic 1960s Political and Social Figures of Change: JFK/MLK/RFK

1. Steve Dougherty, *Hopes and Dreams: The Story of Barack Obama* (New York: Black Dog and Leventhal Publishers, Inc., 2007), 23.
2. Richard Reeves, "John F. Kennedy," quoted in James McPherson, ed., *To the Best of My Ability: The American Presidents* (New York: DK Publishing, Inc., 2001), 250.
3. Reeves, in McPherson, *To the Best of My Ability*, 250.
4. Reeves, 250.
5. Dougherty, *Hopes and Dreams*, 23.
6. Dougherty, 23.
7. Terry Shropshire, December 25, 2008, *Rolling Out*, Executive Suite.

CHAPTER FOUR

FAITH AND RELIGION

I have been many times driven to my knees by the overwhelming conviction that I had nowhere else to go. My own wisdom, and that of all about me, seemed insufficient for that day.

—Lincoln

Obviously as an African American politician rooted in the African American community, I spend a lot of time in the black church. I have no qualms in those settings in participating fully in those services and celebrating my God in that wonderful community that is the black church.

—Obama

So when I read Gandhi or I read King or I read certain passages of Abraham Lincoln and I think about those times where people's values are tested, I think those inspire me.

—Obama

In relationship to Lincoln and Obama, some controversy registers on issues of faith and religion since each man has been questioned on his position on the topic. Notwithstanding that either really disdained religious/philosophical aspects or persuasions, each of them has been accused of being non-Christians during his campaign for office. For example, when Lincoln ran for congressional election in 1846, he was opposed by Democrat Peter Cartwright, a circuit-riding Methodist minister who had served in the state legislature.[1] Cartwright implicated that Lincoln was an "infidel" and "an open scoffer at Christianity."[2]

Similar to Lincoln, critics of Obama have challenged his religious faith by questioning whether he was Christian or Muslim. Both defended themselves on the truth of their faith/religion.

Originally, Lincoln's parents belonged to an orthodox Baptist church in Kentucky that opposed slavery. In fact, the Lincolns joined that church because of its stand against slavery. Within the course of time, Abraham Lincoln did not affiliate himself with an organized religion. He did not join a church; however, later in life he attended the Presbyterian Church in Springfield with his wife and children, frequently. In his early years, Barack Obama was not raised up in the traditions of the black church, nor did he grow up in a religious household. His mother internalized some of the religious skepticism of her mother and father, Barack's grandparents, who helped in raising him.

Barack Obama's mother shunned organized religion such as joining a particular denomination, Baptist or Methodist, among others. However, she did instill in Barack's mind the "working knowledge of the world's great religions as a necessary part of any well-rounded education." As he grew up, religious documents were available in Obama's home: the Bible, Koran, Bhagavad Gita, and books of Greek and Norse/African mythology. Obama states that his mother, on occasion, carried him to Christian churches on special times like Christmas and Easter with a balancing attempt to expose him. As a result, they visited the Buddhist temple, the Chinese New Year celebration shrine, and the ancient Hawaiian burial sites.[3] "Religion was viewed by his mother as an expression of human culture wherein man attempted to control the unknown and understand the deeper truths of life,"[4] according to Barack Obama.

His mother was an anthropologist. On the other hand, his father had been raised as a Muslim in Africa. According to Obama, his father, by the time his parents met, had become a confirmed atheist and looked upon religion more or less as a superstition based on the strange rituals and practices of witch doctors in the villages of his homeland, Kenya, when Obama Sr. was a child. It was through his mother that Obama understood the central doctrines of various moral characteristics.

Later, Barack Obama gave his view on his mother's influence as related to her practice of faith, but did not define it as religious. According to Obama:

> My mother's confidence in virtues depended on a faith I didn't possess, a faith that she would refuse to describe as religious; that in fact, her experience told her was sacrilegious; a faith that rational, thoughtful people should shape their own destiny. In a land where fatalism remained a necessary tool for enduring hardships, where ultimate truths were kept separate from day to day realities; she was a lonely witness for secular humanism a soldier for New Deal Peace Corps.[5]

Furthermore, Obama recognized that his mother wanted him to understand black people's struggle and their strength above all amidst the injustices hurled upon their backs and thrown at them. Again, Barack Obama credits his mother's values that influenced him. He writes:

> Her message came to embrace black people generally. She would come home with books on the civil rights movement, the recordings of gospel singer Mahalia Jackson and the speeches of Rev. Dr. Martin Luther King, Jr. . . . To be black was to be the beneficiary of a great inheritance, a special destiny, glorious burdens that only we were strong enough to bear.[6]

On the basis of the attacks hurled at Lincoln and tossed at Obama on religion and faith, each had to defend where he stood—especially on the most practiced religion in America, which is Christianity. First, Lincoln's rebuttal to Peter Cartwright's accusation about him being against Christianity forced Lincoln to publish a formal denial, stating:

> That I am not a member of any Christian Church, is true; but, I have never denied the truth of the scriptures, and I have never spoken with intentional disrespect of religion in general or of any denomination of Christians in particular. It is true that in early development, I was inclined to believe in what I understand is called the "Doctrine of Necessity"—that is that the human mind is impelled to action, or held in rest by some power over which the mind itself has no control and I have sometimes (with one, two or three but never publicly, tried to maintain this opinion in argument).[7]

Parallel to using religion against opponent Barack Obama, the Republican Alan Keyes taunted his Democrat contender, arguing: "Mr. Obama says he's a Christian . . . yet he supports a lifestyle that the Bible calls an abomination."[8]

Obama responded in defense of such threatening attacks on his faith/religion rationally:

> I answered with the usual literal response in such debates—that we live in a pluralistic society, that I can't impose my religious views on another and that I was running to be a United States Senator from Illinois and not the minister of Illinois.[9]

In discussing his faith, Obama wrote that what our deliberative, pluralistic democracy does demand is that the religiously motivated translate their concerns into universal rather than religion-specific values.[10]

Different from Lincoln, who did not join a church or an organized religion, despite Obama's challenges surrounding his specific choice and the fact that he was not raised in a household of churchgoers, eventually as a politician and community activist he joined a Christian church.

In reference to the many allegations about Obama being Muslim rather than Christian, some of the misinformation leads back to his early life in Indonesia with his mother and stepfather. Yet the truth, however, is that Obama only attended schools of specific religious denominations in his early years of education, but those schools did not have any bearing on his religious choice. Initially, he went to a Catholic school, followed by enrollment in a predominantly Muslim school, although it was in interest of pursuing academics and not religion. Thus, he did not embrace either religion, but merely was sent there to learn the academics of math, reading, and writing in the process of education, nor did his mother emphasize or promote his "learning the catechism or the meaning of the muezzins call to evening prayer as she was with whether he learned his multiplication tables."[11]

Furthermore, he was nurtured in his mother's spirituality manifested through her outpouring of love, kindness, and other charitable endeavors as she reached out to others, embracing universal truths of right and good above evil and wrong, justice over injustice, and love over hatred. Those values and morals were instilled by her to the son, Barack, as well. Practical application based on faith and his values of justice and community inspired Obama to embrace the faith of Christianity. He accepted the Christian faith by understanding the significance of the historical African American religious tradition in such effects and movements for social change that Rev. Martin Luther King Jr. and other visionary clergy led. For example, on the subject of religion and faith, he commented favorably in this regard:

> I think Gandhi is a great example of a profoundly spiritual man who acted and risked everything on behalf of those values but never slipped into intolerance or dogma. He seemed to always maintain an air of doubt about him. I think Dr. King, and Lincoln, those three are good examples for me of people who applied their faith to a larger canvas without allowing that faith to metastasize into something that is hurtful.[12]

By no means did Barack Obama dismiss rational thinking to take on purely emotional casting into religion or evangelical behaviors when he became a member of the Christian church. He states that it was by "choice not an epiphany; no the questions I had did not magically disappear."[13] He joined and was baptized at the Trinity United Church of Christ on the South Side of Chicago, pastored by the Reverend Jeremiah Wright.

In Lincoln's case, according to Miller, who wrote on the ethical virtues of Lincoln, the explanation given on Lincoln and church concludes that "Lincoln long since old enough to have professed his faith and had been baptized and taken into the church abstained from joining even though his parents Thomas and stepmother Sarah Bush Johnston, along with Lincoln's sister Sarah, joined the Indiana Pigeon Creek Baptist Church in 1826."[14]

Lincoln did not join in Pigeon Creek; he did not join a church in New Salem (where there was not yet a building); and he would not join a church in Springfield—or in Washington, DC, either.

In sum, both men possess an incredible sense of spirituality and moral authority implicated in their progressive and moral application to humanity and devotion to their nation. As great leaders, both have inserted principles and beliefs of faith/religion in truths characterized in the rhetoric of their speeches. For example, Lincoln refers to the Founding Fathers while Obama leans on Dr. King by frequently referencing or invoking deity as a need for higher-being intervention on behalf of the universal common good of the world/nation.

Speeches like Lincoln's Farewell Address to Springfield upon boarding the train as president-elect on his way to Washington, DC (February 1861), and his second inaugural address, "With Malice toward None," and "The Almighty Has His Purposes," all portray moral and ethical evidence.

> Without the assistance of that Divine Being, who ever attended him, I cannot succeed. With that assistance I cannot fail . . . let us confidently hope that all will yet be

well. To His care commending you, as I hope in your prayers you will commend me, I bid you an affectionate farewell.[15]

Even Obama's name has spiritual overtones from his father's Swahili language: Barack means "blessing" or "blessing from God." In Hebrew, it means "flash of lightning."

And Lincoln's given name is biblical; Abraham comes from meaning "father" of Israel.

Senator Obama announced his presidential candidacy on February 2007 at the Old State Capitol in Springfield, where Abraham Lincoln delivered his "House Divided" speech in 1858, 150 years before the candidacy of Obama.

Speeches given by Obama likewise include allegiance to values of faith and religion wherein he was inspired by *The Audacity of Hope*, originating from a sermon by his pastor, Rev. Jeremiah Wright.

The Gettysburg Address includes rhetorical antitheses; in the context of rural cemetery rituals, contrasts are those mediated by nature—life springing again from death, from the soil, and in the circle of seasons.[16] The ceremony dedicating the National Cemetery at Gettysburg symbolized ancient Greece and the culture of death during the nineteenth century, according to Wills' study of Lincoln at Gettysburg.

> The old graveyard was set apart from life, a narrow confine cut off from communication with its surroundings ... walled in only to preserve them from violation. The new cemetery would be a place of frequent resort for the living, who could commune with nature as a way of finding life in death. ... The place of the dead must be made a school for the living—a paideia, as Pericles might have said: Our cemeteries, rightly selected and properly arranged may be made subservient to some of the highest purposes of religion and human duty ... .[17]

In the Gettysburg Address, Lincoln used language resembling religious overtones. Don Fehrenbacher traced the form of Lincoln's opening words back to an 1861 speech in the House of Representatives, in which Galusha Grow said, "Four score and five years ago." But all such uses echo the "four score and ten" years allotted to mankind in Psalm 90. Lincoln's fertility language of conception and rebirth is made especially resonant for his audience by its scripted echoes.[18]

Noting the Greek Revival Oratory during the nineteenth century was known for public rhetoric in style and tone.[19] Small wonder, then, that Edward Everett was promptly invited as keynote speaker or orator at the dedication of the National Cemetery in Gettysburg. Everett was a Greek scholar who knew the state funeral oration. It was certainly not by accident that Edward Everett (president of Harvard) was called upon to pay tribute to the fallen soldiers' newly made burial ground in Gettysburg, because Everett was a "celebrant of American battlefields" and connoisseur of American cemeteries. He participated in the creation of the Maine, Auburn, the Cambridge cemetery that became one of the principal cultural institutions of the nineteenth century.[20]

"The rituals of dedication for such cemeteries included the procession of dignitaries, opening prayer, an ode for the occasion, formal address, the formula of dedication, a closing prayer, and the recessional."[21] As a result, the format was preserved at Gettysburg; Lincoln was familiar with it from the Springfield opening. Wills points out that the dedication of Gettysburg represents the nineteenth century's fascination with death in general and with cemeteries in particular, which actually goes beyond its connection with the Civil War and military ceremonies. The closing lines of the Gettysburg Address invoke theological terms: "That this nation under God shall have a new birth of freedom."

Again, Lincoln's use of "God" and "new birth" indicates themes of religion spoken in Lincoln's own words. Finally, "new birth" continues the deity theme of mortal—immortality, life, and death (*limina*) in nature, meeting of the sky and earth.

Additionally, the second inaugural address reveals Lincoln's deep political and theological understanding. When President Abraham Lincoln stood to deliver his inaugural speech, the sun burst forth, changing the earlier cloudy day to an uncloudy one; the powerful moment conveyed the pathos of a recovering nation. It was March 4, 1865, yet Lincoln stood in the shadows of eternity. Within a month, he would be gone to belong to the ages!

Throughout the address, though shorter than the first inaugural, Lincoln's theological understanding is spread in the context by phrases like those in reference to the immorality of slavery:

> Both [North and South] read the same Bible and pray to the same God; and each invokes His aid against the other. It may seem strange that any men should dare to ask a just God's assistance in wringing their bread from the sweat of other men's faces; but let us judge not that we be judged. The prayers of both could not be answered; that of neither has been answered fully. The Almighty has his own purposes. . . . If we shall suppose that American slavery is one of those offences, which in the providence to God, must needs come but which having continued through his appointed time, He now wills to remove, and that He gives to both North and South, this terrible war, as the woe due to those by whom the offence came, shall we discern therein any departure from those divine attributes which the believers in a Living God always ascribe to Him? Fondly do we hope—fervently do we pray—that this mighty scourge of war may speedily pass away.

Aspects of faith and theology seem to run full course in the speech as Lincoln addresses "slavery, the war and the judgments of the Lord" in relationship to the crisis of those moral and divisive issues that threaten the nation.

Lincoln closed the speech to the nation by lifting up thoughtful rhetoric of reconciliation and love to the nation to see God's right forgiveness in order for the nation to overcome the wrath of war and the shackles of the enslaved—"With malice toward none, with charity for all."

Barack Obama's presidential announcement (2007) in Springfield reveals his commitment to a higher being and his belief in God's guidance to sustain him as he began the awesome journey in the presidential race. The discourse consistently parallels Lincoln's "House Divided" speech, whose origin comes from among three of the gospels.

Obama spoke:

> In the face of war, you believe there can be peace. In the face of despair, you believe there can be hope. In the face of a politics that's shut you out, that's told you to settle, that's divided up for too long, you believe we can be one people, reaching for what's possible, building the more perfect union.... It was in these neighborhoods (Chicago's poorest neighborhoods)... where I learned the true meaning of my Christian faith...
>
> For that is our unyielding faith—that in the face of impossible odds, people who love their country can change it.... That's what Abraham Lincoln understood.... But, through his will and his words, he moved a nation and helped free a people.

In the keynote address at the Call to Renewal's Building a Covenant for a New America conference (June 28, 2006), Barack Obama began by airing his knowledge of the controversies of referring to religion and politics as an underscore to his experience of being bashed about his relationship to religion, if any.

In developing his speech, he began:

> But today, I'd like to talk about the connection between religion and politics and perhaps offer some thoughts

about how we can sort through some of the often bitter arguments that we've been seeing over the last several years. I do so because, as you all know, we can affirm the importance of poverty in the Bible . . .

And so forth, the argument or controversy of religion practiced or not practiced by these two presidents indicates public reaction that questions the moral aspect of Lincoln and Obama. But one may conclude that their works speak for them on the basis of humanitarian acts executed while each served in the Oval Office as well as even before then.

While spiritually and socially connected in the tradition of the black church, being moved by the charisma of its gospel singing, earnest praying, exultant preaching, and glorious faith celebrating, President Obama easily blended into that aura, such as his eulogizing South Carolina State Senator Clementa Pinckney, slain pastor of Mother Emanuel African Methodist Episcopal (AME) Church, in Charleston, South Carolina, in June 2015. Using the metaphor of *grace* as his inspiration in remembering Rev. Pinckney and the eight other souls murdered in that massacre, President Obama so effortlessly and timely broke into song by calling on the need for "Amazing Grace," stirring the church's ready response in harmonious chorus with the president.

Indeed, benevolent grace overcomes malevolent disgrace. Grace is salvation to a suffering people. At such a moment, singing about grace as amazing confirms President Obama's faith and religion, and affirms his place in the black church experience as he stood participating among the elders, AME bishops, and thousands of mourners who embraced the bereaved families and suffering Charlestonians in the aftermath of the tragedy.

Obama typified the plaintive cry for grace as the amazing unifier and balm amidst the turmoil and languish of a people who still need God to shed His grace on the United States of America.

NOTES

Chapter Four
Faith and Religion

1. William C. Harris, *Lincoln's Rise to the Presidency* (Lawrence, KS: University Press of Kansas, 2007), 39.
2. Harris, 39.
3. Barack Obama, *The Audacity of Hope: Thoughts on Reclaiming the American Dream* (New York: Crown Publishers, 2006), 203–204.
4. Obama, 203–204.
5. Barack Obama, *Dreams from My Father: A Story of Race and Inheritance* (Crown Publishers, 2004), 50.
6. Obama, 50–51.
7. David Herbert Donald, *Lincoln* (New York: Simon and Schuster, 1995), 48.
8. Obama, *The Audacity of Hope*, 212.
9. Obama, 212.
10. Obama, 212.
11. Obama, 204.
12. Obama on Faith, the Executive Interview (March 2004).
13. Obama, *The Audacity of Hope*, 208.
14. William Miller, *Lincoln's Virtues: An Ethical Biography* (New York: Vintage Books, 2008), 42.
15. Donald, *Lincoln*, 273.
16. Garry Wills, *Lincoln At Gettysburg: The Words That Remade America* (New York: Simon and Schuster, 1992), 77.
17. Wills, 77.
18. Wills, 77.
19. Wills, 77.
20. Wills, 77.
21. Wills, 77.

CHAPTER FIVE

ON POLITICS AND GOVERNMENT

The legitimate object of government, is to do for a community of people, whatever they need to have done, but cannot do at all, or cannot so well do, for themselves—in their separate, and individual capacities.
—Lincoln

If the people cannot trust their government to do the job for which it exists—to protect them and to promote their common welfare—all else is lost.
—Obama

The common knowledge that Abraham Lincoln became the foremost leader of the Republican Party while his name is famously associated with established membership in the Republican Party is never questioned. It is general knowledge that Abraham Lincoln was a Republican, and in contemporary times the majority of Republicans are proud to point to him as their standard-bearer leader. No one even doubts the allegiance or loyalty that he had for his party as a Republican. In short, as Americans, we simply accept "Abraham Lincoln's super affiliation" to the Republican Party (GOP), and it is not a matter of consideration. Just acceptance. However, Lincoln actually is considered as one of the original Republicans as that party existed in the politics of the nineteenth century; more specifically, 1860, when Lincoln presided as the first Republican president. The Republican Party has changed from what it was then and what it is now. Accordingly, the Republican Party of Lincoln's time may be characterized as a party that was more inclined to sustain an America where the "individual is master and the government is servant." David W. Blight candidly asks, "Does anyone really believe that the Republican Party from 1964 to 2004 was the party of Abraham Lincoln?"[1] And today in 2018, with added amazement, the question looms: Does anyone remotely recognize any similarities to the original Republican party of Abraham Lincoln?

Conversely, Lincoln did not belong to the Republican Party when he began his political career, nor did he grow up in a Republican Party household. Thomas Lincoln, his father, was not a Republican. Like his father, Abraham Lincoln was "always a Whig."[2]

A Whig from youth to a mature adult characterizes Lincoln. The Whig Party was formed in the winter of 1833–1834 by former National Republicans such as Henry Clay and John Quincy Adams, and by the Southern states' "rights" supporters such as W. P. Mangum.

In its early form, the Whig Party was united only by opposition to the policies of President Andrew Jackson, especially his removal of the deposits from the Bank of the United States without the consent of Congress. As a result, the Whigs pledged themselves to congressional supremacy, as opposed to "King Andrew's" executive actions.[3] The Whigs saw President Andrew Jackson as a dangerous maverick on horseback with a reactionary opposition to the forces of social, economic, and moral modernization.

The Whigs united around Clay's vision of the "American System," which favored government support for a more modern, industrial economy in which education and commerce would equal physical labor or land ownership as a means of productive wealth. The Whigs promoted domestic manufacturing through protective tariffs (as had Alexander Hamilton forty years prior), a growth-oriented monetary policy with a new Bank of the United States, and a vigorous program of "internal improvements"—especially to roads, canal systems, and railroads, funded by the proceeds of public land sales. The Whigs also promoted public schools, private colleges, charities, and cultural institutions.[4]

In the early years of the Whig Party, the party was not yet sufficiently organized to run one nationwide candidate. By 1839, the Whigs had their first national convention and nominated William Henry Harrison as their presidential candidate. He was the first president of the United States elected from the Whig Party and became the ninth president, though he died in office after serving one month.

In 1850, led by Henry Clay, the Compromise of 1850 was first proposed in hopes of ending the controversies over slavery. But in 1852, the Whig Party began its decline after the deaths of its leaders, Henry Clay and Daniel Webster, causing the party to weaken.

The American Whigs of 1776 fought for independence, and because "Whig" was then a widely recognized label of choice for people who saw themselves as opposing autocratic rule, it was in existence over two decades. Abraham Lincoln became a Whig leader in frontier Illinois. The party was ultimately destroyed by the question of whether to allow the expansion of slavery into the territories.

Lincoln was surrounded by Whigs in his family: his father, Thomas Lincoln; his wife, Mary Todd Lincoln; and her father had been an influential Whig in Kentucky. Even as the Whig Party began disintegrating on the basis of policy, Lincoln labored relentlessly to salvage the crumbling party, wherein as late as 1859, Lincoln's support remained with the Whigs as he held on to the party even during its decline—characterizing himself as "always a Whig in politics."

From the beginning of his political years, Abraham Lincoln affiliated himself with the new Whig Party that Clay started in 1833–1834 with John Quincy Adams in opposition to President Andrew Jackson's Democratic policies. To Lincoln, his interest in Whig politics went beyond political issues, and he had sound belief in their principles of upward mobility for the people of America. "Clay's American System, as promoted by the Whigs, sought to link the manufacturing of the Northeast with the grain production of the West and the cotton and tobacco crops of the South, so that the nation's economy would become one vast interdependent web."[5] In Lincoln's election to the Thirtieth Congress, 1847, he represented the Whig Party from Illinois, not the Republican Party District of

Sangamon County. In fact, he was the only Whig representative from Illinois during the time. A Democratic administration led by Democrat President James K. Polk, number eleven, held the office of presidency during that time.

As a Whig, while in Congress, he spoke out against the Mexican War in the infamous "Spots" speech. This issue will be explained later. As a Whig, he was instrumental in leading a coalition to move the state capital to Springfield from Vandalia. Lincoln was a conservative Whig. After returning to Springfield at the end of his two years in office as US Representative in Congress, he devoted his time to his law practice, placing politics on hold. The issue of slavery hewed larger and larger sectional dimensions as Lincoln simply sat back and observed, retreating from active involvement in politics. But his mind was actively concentrating on issues of pro-slavery and anti-slavery. The pro-slavery argument troubled Lincoln. "Although volumes upon volume is written to prove slavery a very good thing," he noted, "we never hear of the man who wishes to take the good of it by being a slave himself," Lincoln contemplated.[6]

By 1855, as a Whig, Lincoln wrote a Kentucky friend that decades of experience had demonstrated:

> That there is no peaceful extinction of slavery in prospect for us.... The condition of the Negro slave in America ... is now as fixed and hopeless of change for the better, as that of the lost souls of the finally impenitent. The autocrat of all the Russians will resign his crown, and proclaim his subjects free republicans sooner than will our American masters voluntarily give up their slaves. With voluntary emancipation nowhere in sight, the US had to face up to reality. Can we, as a nation, continue together permanently—forever half slave, and half free? The problem is too mighty for me. May God in his mercy, superintend the solution.[7]

Although Lincoln's sentiments were anti-slavery, he was not an abolitionist, because abolition shaped itself in more radical terms/actions. Instead, Lincoln believed in using more effective means such as politics. At this time, in 1855, Lincoln realized that the economic programs of the Whig Party were becoming obsolete as prosperity grew, resulting in the 1848 California gold rush. Next, the appeal of the Kansas–Nebraska Act opened up slavery to the territories. Lincoln's fury over the Kansas issue rose as he emphasized its danger. "There could not have been a more apt invention to bring about collision and violence, on the slavery question" than the Kansas–Nebraska Act. "It was conceived in violence, passed in violence, is maintained in violence, and is executed in violence," according to Lincoln.[8]

Interestingly, the nineteenth-century Lincoln spoke of injustices and race problems in terms of violence; Dr. Martin Luther King Jr. voiced his unfavorable attitude toward denial of civil rights in twentieth century in his nonviolence campaign against racism. Ironically, Barack Obama's grandparents and mother came from Kansas.

Kansas was in turmoil during the time (1850s) that Lincoln brooded over the question of slavery.

The Whig Party's conflicts grew and weakened the party after the endorsement of the 1850 Compromise. The slave issue and other issues divided the Whigs; loyalties dissipated as the Whig Party fell apart. No one really knew on what position of policy they stood as a Whig. Even Lincoln became doubtful about what the Whigs represented this time. Disenchantment arose among strong Whigs as the issues of slavery, compromise, immigrants, and economic conflicts grew. Lincoln once confronted the question of his remaining with the Whigs or whether he had moved on. In response, he answered: "That is a disputed point. I think I am a Whig, but others say there are no Whigs, and that I am an abolitionist." He resented efforts to "unwhig" him since he was doing no more than oppose "the extension of slavery," which had long been the position of most Northern Whigs.[9]

In January 1856, Lincoln took the lead in a fusion of all the opponents to the extension of slavery in a new political party.[10]

Abraham Lincoln joined the noble goal to eliminate slavery by using his own strategies, analysis, observation, and evaluation. He broke publicly with the Whig Party on May 29, 1855, and the Illinois Republican Party was organized.

The forty-seven-year-old Lincoln ensured that he would be in attendance as a delegate at that eventful Bloomington, Illinois, Anti-Slavery Party Convention in May and was recognized for his role in creating the new party by giving him the privilege to deliver the last major speech before the convention closed. Historians claim that Lincoln gave the best speech of his life at this anti-slavery/anti-Kansas–Nebraska convention of the new coalition of Republicans.

It was this public forum that formally ended Lincoln's long years of affiliation with the now-defunct Whig Party. So at forty-seven years old, he became a Republican in 1855.

Gaining inspiration for the moment, his closing words came by urging a "union of all who opposed the expansion of slavery," pledging that he was "ready to fuse with anyone who would unite with him to oppose slave power." If the united opposition of the North caused Southerners to raise "the question of disunion they should be told bluntly, the union must be preserved in the purity of its principles as well as in the integrity of its territorial parts. . . . Liberty and Union, now and forever, one and inseparable,"[11] remind us of other nobles who echoed Lincoln's sentiments.

The Republican Party dates back to the strong anti-slavery opposition to the Kansas-Nebraska Bill of 1854 advocated by Abraham Lincoln. By the late 1800s the party had become a firm alliance of the agricultural West and the industrial East. In the 1920s, the Republican Party became known as the "prosperity party."

The Republicans were defeated in the 1856 presidential election with John Calhoun Frémont as their candidate. The party leaders, such as Lincoln, realized that they could not win the presidency on just the slave issue. Consequently, they broadened their policy to include the endorsement of construction of a transcontinental railroad system and federal aid to improve harbors, rivers, and the modernization of America.

The Democratic Party traces its beginnings back to the Democratic-Republican Party that Thomas Jefferson created around the 1790s. Most historians, however, regard Andrew Jackson's presidential campaign organization, formed in 1828, as the beginning of the modern Democratic Party. After 1816, the Democratic-Republican Party began to split into several groups and fell apart as a national organization. Jackson became the favorite of one of these groups and gained tremendous popularity; consequently, by the late 1830s, the Jacksonian Democrats had turned Jackson's loose organization into an effective national political party: the Democratic Party, which is the oldest political party in continuous operation in the United States, and one of the oldest parties in the world.

Since the division of the Republican Party in the election of 1912, it has consistently positioned itself to the left of the Republican Party in economics and libertarian on some social matters. The economically activist philosophy of Franklin Delano Roosevelt, which has strongly influenced American liberalism, shaped much of the party's economic agenda since 1932. Roosevelt's New Deal Coalition generally controlled the national government until the 1970s.

In terms of comparison of politics of the two major contemporary parties in the US, the political ideologies of the Republicans versus the Democrats historically differ, somewhat. The historical political ideology of Democrat is that of classical liberalism and states' rights wherein the historical political ideology of Republican is abolition, classical liberalism/progressivism. Modern Republican political ideology is manifested in conservatism, social and fiscal conservatism. On the other hand, modern Democrats' political ideology is center left, social liberalism, and progressivism.

In the twenty-first century, the Republican Party is defined by social conservatism, an aggressive foreign policy to defeat terrorism and promote global democracy, a more powerful executive branch, tax cuts, and deregulation and subsidization of industry.[12]

On the other hand, the civil rights movement of the 1960s has continued to inspire the Democratic Party's liberal principles. In unequal democracy, the political economy of the new gilded age,

Princeton political scientist Larry Bartels presents his research findings that modern Democratic presidents have generally been more successful in both spurring overall income growth and creating a more equitable distribution of income since World War II.[13]

Barack Obama once said, "I do think there are moments in American history where there are opportunities to change the language of politics or set the country's sights in a different place, and I think we're in one of those moments."[14] Yet, Barack Obama believes that modern politics, since the Reagan days, indicate that lines have been drawn more sharply between the Republicans and Democrats, liberal and conservative. As stated:

> Our leaders in Washington seem incapable of working together in a practical, common-sense way. Politics has become so bitter and partisan, so gummed up by money and influence, that we can't tackle the big problems that demand solutions.[15]

Barack Obama's affiliation with the party noted for its American liberalism ideology—progressivism as opposed to the modern Republican's conservatism, a party whose political spectrum favored legal abortion that Republicans opposed—had mixed reactions about universal healthcare, which Republicans defiantly opposed. Democrats further demonstrated their liberalism by opposing state-sanctioned school prayer that Republicans generally favored, and as Democrats opposed taxpayers' funding of private schools while Republicans favored the funding of private schools by taxpayers. The Democratic Party presidential contention is more center left, and the Republicans are the opposite, being center right.

The attitude of partisan rigidity between the two major parties exists in cutting divides that significantly reduce national renewal needed for the people. To Barack Obama, such existence is problematic politically; therefore, putting aside party differences and divides is more or less championed by Obama. He steadfastly believes in reaching across the aisle to accomplish or get the job done in interest of the people, while politics should not reduce itself to a game of winning only, but a platform to work for the good of the people by way of its government: to listen to the people, observe their real needs, and offer workable solutions to fix the problems, or better still, prevent many of the conflicting profusions that the people may face. In essence, Barack Obama felt that his party needed an overhaul, but so did the opposite major party. He chose the Democratic Party on the basis of its liberal/progressive ideology from the 1930s New Deal of Roosevelt that his mother idolized.

The party that embraced the civil rights movement of the 1960s into which his parents were incumbents resulted in uniting themselves that would provide new opportunities for humans beyond race. Embedded, then, in the liberal and progressive elements of the principle of democracy, equality and such, small wonder, then, that Barack Obama moved in this political arena. After all, he was a child of civil liberties, humanitarian tolerance, and standing up for the disadvantaged. Unlike his predecessor, Abraham Lincoln, Barack Obama did not change from a former party, but remained in the same party.

Other examples of Obama and Lincoln from a comparative view on each other's ideology may be revealed in varied political and personal descriptive contexts of each man, such as philosophical doctrine, legislative issues, self-improvement, the knowledge and choice of communicative applications and messages conveyed, and their understanding of America and its people, including their leadership styles. Their philosophical doctrines expressed progressive pragmatism characterized by each of the individuals. As pragmatists, each believed that he must allow his thoughts to guide actions to find truth on the basis of testing his practical consequences of belief.

Speaking about Obama's political analysis and how he approaches issues of the nation and world becomes significant. First of all, he rises above party or partisan perspective. He can balance his views with a bipartisan approach when appropriate and timely. Obama took pride in activating legislature by "reaching across the aisle" to achieve the best results for the country.

Just as Abraham Lincoln rose above party denominations, the use of pragmatism and principle is crucial and is more beneficial when balanced according to a symposium member on this topic. According to "Learning from Lincoln—Principle and Pragmatism: Getting the Balance Right," Barack Obama proposed to translate his idealism into actions or to get results based on his ideas. The argument dealt with when to stand on principle alone or when it is necessary to search for choices/decisions whereby the results are beneficial for the good of the people or find ways that will achieve the best results on the basis of legal principles/law and morals. In short, one must be able to accept different or diverse views or the pragmatic willingness to consider differing perspectives, according to David Allen.[16]

Standing on principle for one's actions is decisive and insightful. Acting pragmatically to achieve the best results for the good of the whole rather than just self or the select few individuals is significantly relevant to any servant leader, such as the president.

According to David Allen, standing on principle demonstrates an arrogance that should be carefully asserted. Standing on principle is insisting that I am right and you are wrong. The consequences of standing on principle can be as severe as dividing a nation or starting a war. Wisely discerning the rare time when it is necessary to assert the moral superiority of a stand on principle is one of the defining marks of an effective leader or advocate.[17]

Barack Obama's position on Iran and Syria focused on achieving results. He does not adhere to being overly tough in speaking to the Iranians and Syrians, nor Russia or North Korea, but he urges engaging in diplomacy talks with them. Likewise, he advocates similar strategies for stabilizing Afghanistan to ensure pursuit of Al-Qaeda and Taliban militants in the border area of Pakistan.

Moreover, Obama understands the significance of engaging in pragmatic dialogue in order to attain results, rather than an arrogant position of assertion on his alone by attacking the enemies on the principle of defense and peace. About military and international affairs, Senator Obama once said, "We must understand that the might of our military has to be matched by the strength of our diplomacy."[18]

Similarly, as Lincoln presided over the country during its greatest turmoil when the Civil War cut and divided on the abolitionist principle of freedom from slavery and preserving the Union, Lincoln did not just act on the perspective of principle, but acted from a pragmatic perspective. This is not to say that Lincoln or Obama simply abandon principle, either. But to attain the results, they realize the key to solving the problem or conflict resolution is gained by pragmatic perspectives of persuasion rather than rugged coercion.

Barack Obama, currently, favors former President George H. W. Bush's approach to ending the Cold War, observantly stating: "They didn't overreach. . . . They understood that you couldn't spook the Russians or be unnecessarily provocative. . . . You have to coax them into permitting more freedom and not acting rashly. They understood the absolute priority of securing those nuclear weapons." Obama's perspective on President George W. Bush and Senator John McCain's approach to the 2003 Iraq invasion was "overreaching."[19]

In retrospect, Lincoln acted in a consistent manner and used the consistency rationale in the majority of his management/leadership as president, lawyer, and legislator, often using the phrase "If it can consistently be done." And he was flexible as well when necessary, demonstrating another balance of principles in correlation with flexible pragmatism.

For instance, in a letter to editor Horace Greeley in 1862, President Lincoln described his view of this "official duty" thusly:

> I shall do less whenever I shall believe what I am doing hurts the cause, and I shall do more whenever I shall believe doing more will help the cause. I shall try to correct errors when shown to be errors; and I shall adopt new views so fast as they shall appear to be true views.[20]

Senator Obama governed with a professional calmness, demonstrated sturdy consistency and thoughtful deliberations, and did not break under mounting ruthless pressure, but remained calm, cool, and prevails wrapped in a guarded demeanor—although pleasantly strong, he cannot be easily brushed aside.

Obama's pragmatist world view and even temperament are illustrated in his thoughtful, deliberative thinking and speaking during his candidacy. The senator criticized Russia's actions and called for reconstruction aid for Georgia, but believes kicking Russia out of the Group of Eight (G8 Club of Rich Nations) would do little good and harm United States efforts to work with Russia on other issues.

Even though the editor Horace Greeley often disagreed with Lincoln for not moving faster on the slave issue, later Greeley admiringly understood the president's deliberative efforts, judgment, and even temperament. Greeley praised the president because he was open to all impressions and influences and gladly profited by the teachings of events and circumstances, no matter how adverse or unwelcome.

"There was probably no year of his life when he was not a wiser, cooler, and better man than he had been the year preceding,"[21] concluded Greeley.

So it is with Obama. Because of his even temperament, exercising a calm/cool spirit in the midst of chaos or crisis, Obama has been dubbed by his contemporaries/associates as "No Drama" Obama.[22]

It has been reported that students in Obama's constitutional-law class in 2001 viewed their professor (Obama) as a pragmatist, not an ideologue. One of his students was so impressed by Professor Obama's ability to see both sides of an argument that he turned to Barack Obama, but not for reasons about Obama's politics. Obama wanted his students to consider the impact laws and judicial opinions had on real people. Obama emphasized how people's experiences and backgrounds could influence their perceptions of prejudice and the possible need for government action to curb its effects.

Both men are known for their logic, dispassionately evaluating competing arguments as lawyers and public political actions. Lincoln frequently urged his fellow citizens to be guided by "reason, cold calculating, unimpassioned reason."[23]

Barack Obama's excellent interpersonal skills reflect his basic character in any interactive process and his mindful respect of the human dignity of people. According to Barack Obama, "It's just not my style to go out of my way to offend people or be controversial just for the sake of being controversial. That's offensive and counterproductive. It makes people feel defensive and more resistant to changes."[24]

Comparably, his counterpart Abraham Lincoln embraced interpersonal skills as a source of understanding people and working with them as equals exceeding denouncing others. Lincoln advised his listeners:

> Discourage litigation. Persuade your neighbors to compromise whenever you can. When the conduct of men is designed to be influenced, persuasion, kind, unassuming persuasion, should ever be adopted. . . . Convince him that you are his sincere friend. . . . On the contrary, assume to dictate to his judgement, or to command his action, or to mark him as one to be shunned and despised, and he will retreat within himself, close all the avenues to his head and his heart; and tho' your cause be naked truth itself . . . you shall not more be able to reach him. . . . Such is man and so must he be understood by those who would lead him, even to his own best interest.[25]

Like Lincoln, Obama consumed the great documents of judicial and fundamental civil rights/liberties of humankind by utilizing and studying the Declaration of Independence, the Federalist Papers, and the Constitution as critical American products of governance power. Such documents are resourceful in leading one into understanding Lincoln's presidential views/actions, especially during the Civil War crisis. Both are constitutionalists/lawyers/presidents. According to Obama, his assumption is that "conservative or liberal, we are all constitutionalists."

ALICE RHODES HINSLEY, EdD

Such is the case of Barack Obama's perspective on politics and government as practiced in his servant leadership in parallel to another president: Abraham Lincoln. A study in their relevancy on politics as related to government can define the essence of true servant leadership for this country.

NOTES
Chapter Five
On Politics and Government

1. David W. Blight, "The Theft of Lincoln in Scholarship, Politics, and Public Memory," quoted in Eric Foner, ed., *Our Lincoln: New Perspectives on Lincoln and His World* (2008), 279.
2. David Herbert Donald, *Lincoln* (New York: Simon and Schuster, 1995), 110.
3. "Whig Party," Facts and Summary, www.history.com/topics/whig-party.
4. "Whig Party," history.com.
5. Donald, *Lincoln*, 110.
6. Donald, 187.
7. Donald, 187.
8. Donald, 188.
9. Donald, 189.
10. Donald, 189.
11. Donald, 192.
12. See General References.
13. Larry Bartels, *Unequal Democracy: The Political Economy of the New Gilded Age* (Princeton, NJ: Princeton University Press, 2008).
14. Steve Dougherty, *Hopes and Dreams: The Story of Barack Obama* (New York: Black Dog and Leventhal Publishers, Inc., 2007), 99.
15. Dougherty, 113.
16. David Allen, *Merely the Wisp of a Wish*, 5.
17. Allen, 5.
18. Dougherty, *Hopes and Dreams*, 107.
19. Caren Bohan and Alan E. Isner, ed., www.alertnet.org.
20. Donald J. Phillips, *Lincoln on Leadership: Executive Strategies for Tough Times* (New York: Time Warner Books, 1992), 79.

21. Phillips, 171.
22. Philip Sherwell, "The Secret of Obama's Success," *The Telegraph*, June 7, 2008, www.telegraph.co.uk/news/worldnews/democrats/2091103/US-elections-The-secret-of-Barack-Obamas-success.html.
23. Donald, *Lincoln*, 92.
24. Dougherty, *Hopes and Dreams*, 17.
25. Phillips, *Lincoln on Leadership*, 39–40.

CHAPTER SIX

IN PURSUIT OF THE WHITE HOUSE

My name is new in the field; and I suppose I am not the first choice of a very great many.

—Lincoln

I was never the likeliest candidate for this office.

—Obama

PREFATORY

Rivals, competitors, candidates, contestants, opponents, and politicians alike thrust their livelihoods into the biggest contest of a nation, throw their hats into the reflecting pool, take up arms to fight, get set to run the course of the long racetrack toward the inaugural goal—the finish line—each trying to catch the prize possession being tossed about before the seekers. Expectations, promises, hopes, dreams, ambitions, power, victories, losses, debates, agreements, support, indifference, popularity, patriotism, election, aspiration, inspiration, destiny, appearances, disappearance, challenge, breakthroughs, handshakes, smiles, bidding the media, the people, solitudes, issues, platforms, criticisms, praises—all these are but a few samples in the process of becoming that individual who will be successful or unsuccessful in trying to occupy the executive office of the US, included as one of the three branches of US government. Among the three branches, one is defined as the executive; the other two are judicial and legislative. By general definition, the power of the executive branch is vested in the president of the US, who also acts as head of state and commander in chief of the armed forces. The president is responsible for implementing and enforcing the laws written by Congress, and to that end appoints the heads of the federal agencies, including the cabinet. Under Article II of the Constitution, the president is responsible for the execution and enforcement of the laws created by Congress.

The president also appoints the heads of more than fifty independent federal commissions, such as the Federal Reserve Board or the Securities and Exchange Commission, as well as federal judges, ambassadors, and other federal offices. The president has the power either to sign legislation into law or to veto bills enacted by Congress, although Congress may override a veto with a two-thirds vote of both houses. The executive branch conducts diplomacy with other nations, and the president has the power to negotiate/sign treaties, which must be ratified by two-thirds of the Senate. As a rule, the president can issue executive orders or clarify and further existing laws. The president also has unlimited power to extend pardons/clemencies for federal crimes, except in cases of impeachment.

With the enormity of powers come several responsibilities, among them a constitutional requirement to "from time to time give to the Congress information of the State of the Union, and recommend to their Consideration such measures as he shall judge necessary and expedient."[1]

Regardless of election every four years, the popular vote by the people is not the vote that necessarily or directly elects a president. It is the members of the Electoral College (elected by the people). Apportioned by population to the fifty states—one for each member of their congressional delegate (DC receiving three votes)—these electors then cast the votes for president. There are currently 538 electors.[2]

What a litany of powers, responsibilities, duties, titles, unlimited power, restricted power, vetoes, appointments, etc. that encompass the mounting decision-making and operating efficiency of the president as vested in the executive branch of government. Indeed, the executive branch impacts the other two branches. Likewise, the other two branches (judicial/legislative) impact the executive branch. To ensure that no person or group would amass too much power, the revolutionary founders established a government in which the powers to create, implement, and adjudicate laws were separated. Each branch of government is balanced by powers in the other two coequal branches: the president can veto the laws of the Congress; the Congress confirms or rejects the president's appointments and can remove the president from office in exceptional circumstances, and the justices of the Supreme Court, who can overturn unconstitutional laws, are appointed by the president and confirmed by the Senate.

In creating this balance, the framers of the Constitution hoped to form what they called "a more perfect union"—a government that would not only serve the people but would also be a long-lived exemplar to other nations around the world.[3]

Speaking of government means federal, state, county, district, and local governments that work in the interest of the people of America while the three branches of government collaborate to govern the US.[4]

Becoming president of the United States is an awesome task almost beyond the imagination of the average person—even beyond the fullest concept of those who seek the position until they actually sit in the Oval Office.

Lincoln spoke of the nature of the office of presidency frequently years before he was elected. For example, in his eulogy to the second Whig and twelfth US president, Zachary Taylor (July 25, 1850), while making an informal explanation of the office, Lincoln remarks, "The Presidency, even to the most experienced politicians, is no bed of roses. General Taylor like others, found thorns within it. No human being can fill that station and escape censure."[5]

Shortly after inauguration, a friend asked Lincoln how he liked being president, and he responded in parable form:

> I feel like the man who was tarred/feathered and ridden
> out of town on a rail. To the man who asked how he

liked it he said, 'If it wasn't for the honor of the thing, I'd rather walk.'[6]

On the other hand, what experience or speculations did Obama have about the presidency years before he pursued the White House? Accordingly, Barack reflects:

> The first time I saw the White House was in 1984. I had just graduated from college and was working as a community organizer out of the Harlem campus of the City College of New York. . . . At the end of the day, the students and I took the time to walk down to the National Mall and the Washington Monument, and then spent a few minutes gazing at the White House.[7]

Some years later, Senator Obama describes:

> The inside of the White House doesn't have the luminous quality that you might expect from TV or film. . . . As I stood in the foyer and let my eyes wander down the corridors, it was impossible to forget the history that had been made there—FDR making last-minute changes to a radio address; Lincoln alone, pacing the halls and shouldering the weight of a nation.[8]

On the basis of the impact factor among the three branches, obviously the president has powers but by rule of law cannot rule as a monarchy with imperial style. Instead, each branch monitors and balances the others' actions or powers. The check-and-balance-system intent creates positive and oppositional stands among the three branches, resulting in necessary debates, brokering, rationalizations, deliberations, politics, partisanship hearings, tension, and compromises in the efforts to veto, vote up/down legislation in both houses for or against the president's implementing laws, or envisioning and introducing new paths/changes. Consequently, the president faces huge accountability or responsibility to govern, manage, and establish imprint as the leading nation in the world. Apparently, being presidential is not a position for the timorous, short-sighted, unambitious, passive, uncivil, unpatriotic, or the inability to cope with insurmountable challenges reaching across the depth and breadth of the nation, not to mention global interactions. Above all, maintaining the democracy and Constitution to the best of one's ability is heaped upon the leader of this country, combined with serving as the major leading figure of the free world. Therefore, in the frailty of human hands, the question is inevitable, then, who could possibly want to pursue such a magnanimous feat of decision-making and entrustment combined with accountability.

Through the ages, the White House has been pursued by candidates who wish to become president. In running for the office or seeking the election, the campaign very interestingly begins years before the actual contest. It begins as a preparatory exercise for some through natural pedigree; others approach campaigning through innovative and unsure ways, or whatever. But the element that underscores moving toward the presidency is the campaign, whether subtle or transparent. What is a campaign, one asks? In a limited definitive sense, campaign means a series of operations designed to bring about a particular result. From a conceptual point, a political campaign is an organized effort that seeks to influence the decision-making process within a specific group. In democracies, political campaigns often refer to electoral campaigns, wherein representatives are chosen or referenda are decided. Political campaigns also include organized efforts to alter policy within any institution/organization.

From an historical aspect, political campaigns have a long history within Old World civilization to the Western Hemisphere and the modern world. Primarily, the message of the campaign is what ideas the candidate wants to share with the voters. "I dream my painting and then I paint my dream" (Vincent van Gogh).

To rise from provincial to national recognition indicates aspects of an aspirant's quest in becoming a high-profile front-runner.

Using a variety of techniques to promote themselves, candidates begin even before the formal campaign is evident. Preparing to throw their hats in the running starts early on, so to speak. "*Rising to the loftier race, these things shall be.*"[9] They promote themselves through appearances, legislative accomplishments, media blitz, use of key selling points of the candidate's biography; all "paint their dream" as rising stars.

Deciding to run is the initial stage of campaign, such as talking over prospects of running with family members, getting their approval, gaining endorsements from fellow politicians and influential or celebrated Americans, conferring with friends, elected officials, professional or party associates, community leaders and political leaders; supporters are included in the process. Historically, these are some of the major similarities in the American political process. There are some differences depending upon the times. In modern times within the twentieth and twenty-first centuries, the process of campaigning includes the candidate announcing his/her intention to run publicly, followed by official kickoff events before official campaigning begins. During the eighteenth and nineteenth centuries, it was not a common practice for candidates to openly pursue or chase after political office by announcing their presidential aspirations. However, this is not to say that the candidates simply sat by passively. Quite the opposite, on their own behalf, candidates engaged in appearances, speaking and quietly consulting with influential persons and ordinary citizens.

Perhaps Lincoln and Obama began the process of promoting as they distinguished themselves in legislative accomplishments while serving at state and congressional levels.

While serving at the state level in Springfield, Illinois, Obama's comment was that "the pattern of legislative activity is very similar [as Congress] and the political dynamic was similar because when I first arrived at the state legislature ... no Democrat had much hope of passing any progressive legislation under the iron hand of Pete Phillip [Senate president]."[10] Obama served as an Illinois state senator in Springfield for eight years (1996–2004). Lincoln served his first session in the Illinois House of Representatives from 1834 to 1835 and quickly learned the procedures as well as becoming acquainted with men from different parts of the state.[11] Vandalia was the state capital at the time rather than Springfield.

In contrast to Obama serving as a Democratic state senator, Lincoln identified with the Whigs, but party organization was virtually nonexistent in the legislature when Lincoln took his seat.[12] However, initially Lincoln frequently took the liberty to vote with the majority Democrats on various issues. And Lincoln made a strong impression in his early years as a first-term representative. Accordingly, his young peers and other House members soon noted his knowledge of legal language and his precision in writing. As a result, he was asked to draw up bills and resolutions for them to introduce on the floor, as they enjoyed his humorous stories that he wove so well.[13]

By 1836, Lincoln was reelected to the House of Representatives and chosen (December) as the minority-party (Whig) floor leader at the age of twenty-seven. Additionally, it was during this season that the Sangamon County delegation (largest in General Assembly) secured the removal of the state capital from Vandalia to centrally located Springfield; Lincoln moved to Springfield from New Salem on April 15, 1837. Lincoln, along with Dan Stone, on March 3, 1837, took a moral stand against slavery, stating that: "The institution of slavery is founded on both injustice and bad policy."[14]

That state of Illinois, at the time, was strongly opposed to antislavery agitation, and the legislation was overwhelmingly defeated. Lincoln came to Springfield because he was asked by his legislative mentor and a prominent lawyer, John Todd Stuart, to join him as his law partner in Springfield, about twenty miles from New Salem.[15] Indeed, Lincoln was beginning his rising orbit in politics in the late 1830s of the mid-nineteenth century. Lincoln served successive terms in 1841 in the Illinois House of Representatives General Assembly and did not seek reelection in 1842.

Barack Obama entered into Illinois state politics in 1996 after he successfully challenged the petitions of the other candidates and ran unopposed. His record as an Illinois state senator was as equally impressive as Lincoln's four terms as an Illinois representative. He was in the minority most of the time while serving, but Obama demonstrated outstanding legislative skills. He, too, like Lincoln, was a pragmatic politician, learning how to work among the difficult dilemmas as he stood up for principles while making political progress.

Cosponsoring a bipartisan package on reform legislation in 1998, such as the Gift Ban Act, intensely changed ethics laws by cleaning up enormous and unethical corruption in the state. The young Illinois state senator led the drive in the Senate to increase child-support payments for poor parents, although the Republican governor vetoed it.[16] When the Democrats took control of the State Senate in the 2002 election, Obama was able to introduce and successfully move legislature through with increased success. He was behind legislation creating state-earned tax credit, early childhood education programs expansion, delimit predatory lenders, and require videotaping of police interrogations, along with his ability to gain bipartisan support for progressive and morally clear policies. In reference to race, Obama won widespread approval for his racial-profiling law in 2003. Again, Lincoln and Obama's moral compass on race and/or slavery within the country reflect degrees of similarity.

Accordingly in 2001, Obama approved making gang activity ineligible for the death penalty, arguing that: "There's a strong overlap between gang affiliation and young men of color. . . . I think it's problematic for them to be singled out as more likely to receive the death penalty for carrying out certain acts than are others who do the same thing."[17]

Sundiata Cha-Jua, director of the African American Studies/Research Program at the University of Illinois, observed that in the Illinois Senate, "Obama was clearly one of the best African American politicians in terms of speaking to African American issues."[18]

Additionally, Salim Muwakkil concluded, "His legislative record during his eight years as the State Senator from Illinois, Thirteenth District convinced them that he had the black community's interest at heart, even as he cultivated alliances with other political forces."[19] Summarily, both politicians from Illinois spoke out on the issues of the time even when race or slavery were considered anti-political in the legislative arena. However, speaking of President Lincoln and President Obama in a linear sense is a historical fallacy, simply because the progression of emancipating events and the abolition narrative or civil rights' legislation did not happen in an even course of a chronological (time) line or schedule. It is common knowledge to recognize that the circumstances on basis of slavery to freedom were not correctly pure; there have been "tacks in it and boards torn up"—in the words of Langston Hughes—meaning struggle, setbacks, revisions, reforms, oppositions, and uncertain times for African Americans along the course of history. In short, the road to freedom/equality has not been even or straightforwardly smooth in the course of an African American being elected to the office of president in this great nation. And it is highly unlikely that an African American will immediately follow Obama after he leaves office.

Back in 2005, Senator Barack Obama gave his viewpoint in *Time* magazine on Lincoln, stating, "He never won Illinois' Senate seat. But in many ways, he paved the way for me."[20] He further remarked:

> So when I, a black man with a funny name, born in Hawaii of a father from Kenya and a mother from Kansas, announced my candidacy for the US Senate, it was hard to imagine a less likely scenario than that I would win—except, perhaps, for the one that allows a child born in the backwoods of Kentucky with less than a year of formal education, to end up as Illinois' greatest citizen and our nation's greatest President.[21]

Yes, Lincoln lost his bid for Senate in 1858 to Stephen Douglas.

The Democrats were elated over the defeat of the "Black Republican" contender: Abraham Lincoln. Lincoln's response afterward of his defeat came in a letter he wrote to a friend: "Though I now sink out of view, and shall be forgotten, I believe I have made some marks which will tell for the cause of civil liberty long after I am gone."[22]

The Lincoln-Douglas Debates of 1858 may have ended in temporary defeat for Lincoln, who sought the office of US senator, but he was highly acclaimed as the Republican champion of the Great West resulting from his New York speech in 1860.

A canopy of accomplishments consisting of keynote speaking at the Democratic National Convention in 2004 were enjoyed by Obama. Likewise, the *Chicago Tribune* treated Lincoln favorably after he delivered the 1860 Cooper Union speech. Clearly, the relevance of Lincoln and Obama illuminates from their best-selling autobiographies: Lincoln's 1858 "Debates with Douglas" campaign scrapbook and his 1859 *Autobiographical Sketch*; in addition, Obama's *Dreams from My Father*, 2004 (reprinted), followed by *The Audacity of Hope: Thoughts on Reclaiming the American Dream*.

Their physical appearances are striking; for example, Lincoln's "tall form, striking features, expressive mouth and tawny complexion" reportedly appealed to the people.[23] On the other hand, Obama's youth, athletic good looks, and charisma often received complimentary remarks about this young Illinois senator.

In speech, Lincoln's tone and words were folksy. There is a folksiness with Obama, too, in his syncopated speech "Missed ya." His rhetoric is low and matter of fact, Lincoln's high pitched and analytical, but both laced their talks with occasional quips of humor, and some storytelling came from Lincoln.

A 268-page book entitled *Political Debates between Honorable Abraham Lincoln and Honorable Stephen A. Douglas, in the Celebrated Campaign of 1858, in Illinois* was published in 1860 shortly before the national nominating conventions.

The publicity advanced in the dawn of the official announcements grew tremendously appealing. Coming from political views about them, suggestions of their becoming president by Lincoln and Obama associates, and even how the potential candidates felt about considering the presidency were all inevitable steps in the direction of the head of state, climbing closer in pursuit of the White House. Indeed, people in high places and ordinary places were impressed with Abraham Lincoln and inspired by Barack Obama in those immediate years before either gained the White House.

More specifically, some were intrigued with Barack Obama: "Who is that guy? . . . He's certainly got it," remarked a photographer to a reporter as Senator Obama walked through the crowd of mostly Republican congressional newcomers while attending a reception in the East Room of the White House back in January 2005 after being sworn in to the Senate.[24] Additionally, Senator Dick Durbin, D-IL, a longtime friend and supporter, recalls pulling Obama into a vacant meeting room in Chicago's Union League Club, where both had spoken on a Friday afternoon in November 2006. He felt it was time for his young colleague to decide whether to run for the White House. "There are moments in life when you can pick the time," Durbin said he told Obama. "But when it comes to running for president, the time can pick you. You've been picked. This is your moment."[25]

In 1858, from Washington, Illinoisan Josiah M. Lucas informed Lincoln with prideful overstatement that "many of the leading papers of the country" were proclaiming him "the leading spirit of the Great West."[26]

In Illinois, while Obama was in the State Senate, he sponsored a deluge of bills, wherein 280 were passed out of the 780. Initially he did not fare so well in the State Senate because he was somewhat an unknown; however, his progress soared over a brief period. In 2000, journalist Rick Miller described Obama in these analytical terms: "He likes people to know he went to Harvard." Later, Miller reversed his opinion after Obama's big loss to Bobby Rush, stating, "I just can't emphasize enough how much this guy became respected and how transformative it was. By 2004, he just had this aura about him. . . . The bottom line is pretty much everybody I know had a high opinion of him, Republican or Democrat. In this state, it's hard for anyone to pass a hell of a lot of bills."[27]

Similarly, back in 1834–35, in Illinois, when Lincoln served as a young state representative, he also received special attention. Unlike Obama, he could not boast of credentials from Harvard, and in reality he had just taken up studying and reading borrowed law books so that he could practice law. Therefore, he began law practice in 1836 at twenty-seven years old. Nonetheless, Lincoln, as a first-term representative, made a strong impression on his colleagues in the House. Before the end of the session, Lincoln was asked by his peers to draw up bills and resolutions for them to introduce to the floor. In 1836, he was chosen as the minority-party (Whig) floor leader. "Indeed, he was clearly a rising public man."[28]

"Daddy, are you going to try to be president?" questioned Obama's inquisitive six-year-old daughter, Malia, to her newly installed United States senator father as the family walked the capital grounds to the Library of Congress.[29] Was this the first inkling of Obama's quest for the Oval Office? From the old adage "out of the mouth of babes," the truth shall be heard.

"Vote for Old Abe," urged Lincoln's precocious son, Willie, to neighbors and friends as they passed by his father's house back in Springfield.[30] Like his father before, Willie, no doubt, joined in the political campaign for his father's quest for the Oval Office.

Later, when their fathers would become president, the children of Abraham Lincoln and Barack Obama would become firsts. The three sons of Lincoln became the first children of a president to live in the White House, and the two daughters of President Obama became the first African American children to live in the White House.

There were gestures and suggestions sprouting up frequently surrounding Lincoln's possibilities in pursuit of becoming president.

Historian Donald writes: "The warm reception that Lincoln speeches received in Iowa, Ohio, Indiana, Wisconsin, and Kansas during the last half of 1858 gave plausibility to suggestions that he ought to be nominated for high office."[31]

"The Land o' Lincoln Loves Senator Obama," was also boldly printed on a sign observed at an Illinois AFL-CIO meeting.[32] "For me in my lifetime," a woman told a *Washington Post* reporter, "it is truly possible that an African American man can be the President of the United States."[33]

The first newspaper that seriously proposed Lincoln's name for presidency was the *Illinois Gazette*, followed by more prominent papers who garnered attention to Lincoln. The *Olney* (Illinois) *Times* began running "Abram [sic] Lincoln for President for 1860" below its masthead.[34] The *New York Herald* and the *Reading* (Pennsylvania) *Journal* spoke of possible candidacy favorably as well.[35]

Now, the question of how the wives of Lincoln and Obama viewed the possibilities of their husbands becoming the president of the United States stirs up a bit of curiosity. For Mary Lincoln, the wife of Abraham Lincoln, she happened to be one who intended to become the First Lady of the land ever since she met Mr. Lincoln. Indeed, she enjoyed her role as hostess and impressed most of her visitors with her entertaining, and Mrs. Lincoln was well educated, coming from a prominent pedigreed family in Lexington, Kentucky.

Michelle (Robinson) Obama has been frequently compared to Jacqueline Kennedy—First Lady 1960—where people marveled at Mrs. Kennedy's fashionable wardrobe. On the part of Mrs. Obama, perhaps she kept her husband's (Obama) ego in check. On the other hand, Mr. Lincoln had to keep his wife's (Mary) ego in check.

Michelle Obama informed: "What I am not willing to do is hand my kids over to my mom and say, 'We'll see you in two years.' That's not going to happen."[36]

But Mrs. Lincoln hoped that Mr. Lincoln *would* become president, striding in his own deliberate pace toward reaching the possibility of the White House. Likewise, others in high places believed in the junior senator from Illinois, and former Senate Minority Leader Tom Daschle said that he saw "Obama as a rising star that the Democrats might do well to attach their aspirations to."[37]

Interesting, someday Mrs. Obama was skeptical about Mr. Obama running for office, starting with Senate campaign, by expressing skepticism: "He shouldn't necessarily count on her vote."[38] Yet she found it incredible when he won the US Senate by pleasantly implying to her husband—the new Senator Obama—"I can't believe you pulled it off."[39]

Opposites in some ideology, but alike in their support and love for their husbands, one First Lady stood short/plump framed. The former First Lady stands tall and graceful. Each presidential husband referred to his spouse affectionately as "the love of my life" (Obama), and Lincoln quipped, "that little lady" or "Mother." Indeed, each showed his pride and appeal to these women of strong personality.

As family, associates, media, politicians, and even before prospective candidates fully considered transforming a pipe dream into reality, indeed the groundwork had been laid; cultivating, grooming, and preparing had long commenced. Next came the harvesting of skills, sharpening talents, building character, increasing beliefs, and heeding insights into a magnanimous effort with the thrust of commitment to such an enormous task. Within the ebbing tides and the edgy dreams, the would-be aspirants' rise to higher expectations began. Their associates, politicians, pundits, electorate, and coalitions alike watched them, discussed them, and did everything short of confirming their aspirants' need to run.

For Lincoln, who lost the Senate election in 1858—despite the defeat—his name was heralded among the people of the Great West, especially his exemplary role for the Republicans in the West. Suggestions about his running were surfacing: some suggested that he should run as a candidate for the second place on the Republican ticket with Seward for president and Lincoln for vice president being suggested in the *Hennepin* (Illinois) *Tribune*. The *Chicago Democrat* seemed to be endorsing Lincoln, "The Great Man of Illinois," while urging Republicans to nominate him for either president or vice president, later recommending Lincoln for governor over Norman Judd. "Shouldn't you be vice president first?" asked Malia Obama of her father.[40]

"Run, Barack, run. Barack Obama should run for president. He should run for the good of his party," floated around.[41]

"That would be my favorite guy. . . . I would hope that he would run for president," came the near endorsement by Oprah Winfrey, according to Larry King.[42]

The mania of Obama began to spread. "The man . . . more and more people are saying could be America's first black president" (host who introduced him on *Larry King Live*).[43] Indeed, prophetic sources from media, print, broadcast, their political party associates, and popular culture/public surrounded the future presidents in the approaching years leading up to their eventual inaugurals in their pursuit and now progressing at faster paces; all of this happening in 1858–60 and 2004–2008 consisted of the magical elements chronicling the pre-presidential campaign years.

PRESIDENTIAL CAMPAIGN CHALLENGES

The taste is in my mouth.

—Lincoln

It's only when you hitch yourself up to something bigger than yourself that you realize your potential.

—Obama

What, indeed, were the perspectives of these presidential candidates (Lincoln and Obama) as related to their chances of running for the highest office in the land? After all, did they not have the intellectual capacity to facilitate the skills and abilities needed to preside over this country and process a republic such as America that consists of a vast geographical sketch of land/people from north to south, as well as from east to west? Although both men would inherit the very depths of division in America, the questions loom: How would they think? What actions would they enact? What critical decisions would they make, and just what would they do? Could they effect the best for the country? Resolve problems of cultural/race relations for Obama; preserve the union for Lincoln? End wars, inspire peace, bring the troops home from Iran, win a victory for the Union in a civil war, or emancipate a people from bondage, improve the lot of the current poverty-stricken urban cities, stimulate an economy going bankrupt, restore jobs to the jobless; in short, change, conquer, reunite, reform, and amazingly heal division in the land, by finally reforming the systems of brokenness, messiness, and corruption?

In general, what did Lincoln think about himself in terms of becoming the sixteenth president of the United States of America? In the twenty-first century, what did Obama think about his becoming the forty-fourth president of the United States?

Both had been critical of the previous administrations; for example, Lincoln criticized his predecessor, Democrat James Buchanan, and Obama also heavily criticized his predecessor, Republican George Bush, because President Bush had instigated an unpopular war in the Middle East—the Iraqi War. In the late nineteenth century, President Buchanan had avoided addressing the issues of slavery and secession that led to the Civil War. Essentially, war, disunity, economics, and foreign relations were the critical casualties causing the crisis awaiting whoever the newly elected sixteenth or forty-fourth president should become.

A combination of the man, his agenda, and the times would encompass the presidency on the merits of this particular leader's talent, strategic leadership, relationship with Congress, political judgment, and progressive leadership, just to name a few. Oh, the road to presidency translated into stump speeches, orations, appearances, and shaking hands, as evidence that Lincoln and Obama were possibilities, whether or not either of the men dared to articulate in optic manner about his aspiration.

"America is ready to turn the page. America is ready for a new set of challenges. This is our time. A new generation is ready to lead,"[44] pronounced Senator Barack Obama.

"Let us have faith that right makes might, and in that faith, let us, to the end, dare to do our duty as we understand it,"[45] as orated by Lincoln in his famous Cooper Union speech, February 27, 1859.

Certainly, profound remarks given by Senator B. Obama and Congressman A. Lincoln in the context of their times may easily bear relevancy for all times. Yet their statements were wise words equipped with tones of enlightenment and deep introspection. But most of all, the context of Obama's statement in 2006 as well as Abraham Lincoln's in 1859 indicates the political nature of one who is preparing or thinking about making a move toward a higher aspiration. The question is: Could it be the presidency? Indeed, speculations whirled around and about before either man actually stepped forth to authenticate what the media and others were predicting. Nevertheless, each man moved studiously, cautiously, using a degree of subtlety for certain reasons; perhaps, for personal reasons. Lincoln declared that: "The taste is in my mouth," while remaining unsure because of troubling reasons, such as feeling unqualified, being inexperienced, or lack of status/heritage, perhaps.[46] Although, realistically, Abraham Lincoln believed that he could do as well or better than the fourteenth—President Franklin Pierce—or the incumbent President James Buchanan.

On the other hand, Senator Obama's confidence about climbing higher was heard in his words: "Only when you hitch yourself up to something bigger than yourself . . . that you realize your potential."[47] He, too, must have had similar thoughts as did Lincoln about the incumbent president whose rating was low among the people. George Bush's popularity had slid downward as disenchantment increased in 2007.

But in a matter of two years, Senator Obama would become a potential presidential candidate. While in less years prior to 1860, Lincoln would taste of the candidacy for president as prophetic words turned true.

Senator Obama "should think about the White House" suggested Maureen Dowd, a liberal columnist at the *New York Times*. And in 2006, the senator sort of let the "cat out of the bag," so to speak, by revealing how he felt about the presidency. "My attitude is that you don't want to be just president. You want to change the country. You want to be a great president," according to Obama.[48]

An Obama critic stated, "The essence of Obama's pitch is that it's time to move past the old politics and that he's the embodiment of the new."[49]

Both major parties—Democrat and Republican—were experiencing incredible circumstances of political survival and deflated electability power as related to the 1860 election, as well as in the 2008 election on the basis of the tumultuous times and unrest of economics, war, and disunity crises that shook the land, dividing the country one way or the other. Currently, the Democrats had not been in power since 1999. In 2000 and 2004 Democrats had been unable to gain the force of electability for the Oval Office. In 2000, the Democrat Senator and Vice President Al Gore lost to George Bush (Republican), and again in 2004, the Democrat nominee Senator John Kerry lost to George Bush.

Back in 1860, the record reverses itself wherein two Democrats became the incumbents. In 1853–1857, a Northern Democrat—a Southern sympathizer—Franklin Pierce served as president. Following him, another Northern Democrat and Southern sympathizer, James Buchanan (1857–1861), was elected president when Republican John C. Frémont ran losing to Buchanan in the 1856 election. Indeed, each of those elections during the nineteenth and later in the twenty-first century mirrored the crucial times of the respective eras. Ironically, during the 1860 election and the 2008 election, the possibilities of "firsts" would premier in the presidential outcome. Now, as the election years grew close, aspirants began to gear themselves up for their upcoming candidacy. Many candidates came forth, some angling between maybe or maybe not, between black or white, or the unlikely more than the likely; however, one thing for sure: history will record that the great western state of Illinois has persisted, in spite of obstacles.

At this point, whenever Lincoln was nudged about becoming a candidate for president, he appeared skeptical and ensured that he remained an unannounced presidential hopeful. Back in the 1858 campaign against Stephen Douglas, he humorously confided, "Just think, of such a sucker as me as President."[50] Once writing the admiring editor of the *Rock Island Register*, who wanted to promote Lincoln as a candidate in a Republican paper, Lincoln objected, stating: "I must, in candor, say I do not think myself fit for the Presidency."[51] Indeed, Lincoln was a favorite son of Illinois in the mid-nineteenth century; Obama became a favorite son of Illinois in the early twenty-first century.

Why, then, could not Lincoln and/or Obama rise above the others in this highly competitive contest of strong competitors?

According to historian David Herbert Donald:

> When Lincoln issued such disclaimers about his running for president, he was not being coy, but realistic. To all outward appearances he was less prepared to be President of the United States than any other man who had run for that high office. Without family tradition or wealth, he had only the briefest of formal schooling. Now, fifty years old, he had no administrative experience of any sort, he had never been governor of his state or even mayor of Springfield. A profound student of the Constitution and of the writings of the Founding Fathers, he had limited acquaintance with the government they had established.
>
> He had served only a single, less than successful term in the House of Representatives and for the past ten years had held no public office. Though he was one of the founders of the Republican Party, he had no close friends and only a few acquaintances in the populous Eastern states whose vote would be crucial in the election.[52]

Still, January 6, 1859, in the library of the Illinois State Capitol, some Illinois Republicans noted the acclaim that Lincoln received as a great statesman and popular debater. In late December of 1859, Jesse W. Fell of Bloomington, Illinois, secretary of the State Republican central committee, reported to Lincoln that "everywhere I hear you talked about." These reports encouraged Lincoln's friends to hold a meeting to discuss a proposal "to bring out Abraham Lincoln as a candidate for President." Lincoln was present, but objected adamantly.[53]

In contrast to Lincoln, Senator Obama in 2006 began talking in specific terms about his desire to pursue the White House. Discussions began with his inner circle, according to Mendell. His immediate inner circle consisted of his wife, Michelle Obama, David Axelrod, and Robert Gibbs. Discussions followed with others, such as Rev. Jeremiah Wright and Rev. Jesse Jackson, Newton Minow, and Valerie Jarrett, just to name a few. Minnow urged him, "You ought to go for it now." Later, Robert Gibbs, according to Mendell, made sure to alert reporters that a "Draft Obama for President in 2008" petition was circulating in the crowd on Indianapolis fairgrounds.[54]

Of course, one can readily recognize the apparent stark differences between Obama and Lincoln as potentials in pursuit of the White House and as eventual candidates among strong competitors. In comparison, Obama did not issue similar disclaimers as Lincoln had done, because unlike Lincoln, Obama was a college graduate with stellar formal education, an Ivy Leaguer, and from all outward appearances, he was just as qualified by preparation as anyone else to become president of the United States. He had been a state senator from Illinois who progressed into the United States Senate. He was young—in his forties, like Lincoln—however, he never served as governor nor mayor, but was once a community organizer; later he served as a law professor. On the other hand, like Lincoln, Obama was a lawyer and profound student of the Constitution.

However, one wonders if Barack Obama would have been considered for the presidency in 1860—even with his charm and qualities. Indeed not! But would Lincoln have been considered for the presidency in 2008? Perhaps so! The unequal circumstances of the once-enslaved blacks continued from the final Emancipation Proclamation in 1863 including the Thirteenth, Fourteenth, and Fifteenth

Amendments long after the abolition of slavery—the underlying culprit of racism divides and the struggle of the movement toward equalization/freedom remains with its ups/downs, defeats/triumphs, liberal/conservative, war/peace constructs.

Obama's national emergence toward the highest office in the land personified hope and belief for America to willingly accept major change during this generation. Running for president is possible regardless of race—white, black, Asian American, Hispanic, Northerner, or Southerner—or gender, because all men are created equal—a pillar upon which this nation is founded.

Obama believed that the power of unity prevails among the people of America more than division and that we've got to have faith and believe that change can come.

In the organizational phase of Obama's campaign, David Axelrod engineered a maximum contingency of professionals skilled in the necessity and arts of political science, business management, marketing extremely talented people, advocates, fundraisers, supporters, media, entertainers, strategists, staffers, and a mean use of the internet that effectively reached the PEOPLE! And the campaign began for Barack Obama among strong competitors. His encouraging mantra promised "Yes, we can!" Chicago's West Loop became the initial spot for the idea of his running for the Oval Office, and later, Senator Obama started forming his presidential exploratory committee as Obama's public image grew.

Proudly, he began his candidacy in February 10, 2007, in the shadow of Lincoln in Springfield, Illinois. Barack hit the campaign trail, and the rest is history.

For Lincoln, the presidential campaign phase differed in the mid nineteenth century because in 1859–1860, candidates did not openly campaign for nomination; instead, in those days it was the tradition that the office of president sought after the would-be candidate to run. In other words, because of the huge importance of the office of president, seekers did not run openly; but an internal group of intermediaries worked on behalf of the man considered best to acquire that office. Therefore, Abraham Lincoln did not announce his candidacy, nor did he publicly form an exploratory presidential committee as did Barack Obama in the twenty-first century. Additionally, Lincoln did not have an organized or unified group of campaign workers, advisers, staff, or consultants, such as Obama had.

On the other hand, Lincoln had managers who worked behind the scenes for him, but they were not organized into one operable unit of people because of their lack of trust for each other—they only worked for Lincoln. His lead manager, Judge David Davis, was loyal to Lincoln, for whom Lincoln placed a great amount of confidence in the judge: "I keep no secrets from him," Lincoln invoked.[55] Additionally, Gustave Koerner, a lawyer, served as Lincoln's main connection to the German American constituency, and he relied on Ozias Hatch (Illinois Secretary of State), along with Norman Judd and other key prominent Illinois Republicans, to work quietly for him. In addition, Lincoln confided that he was "not in a position where it would hurt much for me to not be nominated on the national ticket, but it would hurt for me to not get the Illinois delegates" at the Republican Convention.[56] Again, this campaign group for Lincoln was connected only to Lincoln rather than to each other. In fact, they were somewhat cynical toward each other. They did not operate in a close-knit enterprise among themselves because they were suspicious of each other and guarded against undermining motives against them based on their jealousy as well as previous dubious behavior in political deals. For instance, Judge Davis did not trust Norman Judd for his failure once to help Lincoln get elected to the Senate back in 1855.

The competitiveness among Lincoln's group existed, however, in a method that only affected those particular individuals working on his behalf. In spite of the circumstances among them, they devoted their work solely for the interest, good, and protection of Lincoln, and it was their goal to advise, motivate, and promote in order to enhance this possibility or goal. Perhaps they believed in him more than he believed in himself, or so they thought. "He has not known his own power—uneducated in youth, he has always been doubtful whether he was not pushing himself into positions to which he was unequal," came the candid assessment of Lincoln from Nathan M. Knapp, chairman of the Scott County, Illinois, Republican Party.[57]

On the other hand, Obama's assessment came from his leading advisor, David Axelrod, especially to those who doubted Obama's ability and strength to endure the grueling task, measures, and "fish-bowl" conditions that come with the awesomeness of a presidential candidate. When questioned about whether Obama was ready to handle the race, Axelrod replied:

> I don't know, but one thing about running for president is that—and he knows this—it's like putting an x-ray machine on yourself twenty-four hours a day because at the end of the day; the American people know who you are. But with Barack, he's kind of a normal guy in a lot of ways. . . . I think he has an inner toughness, and that is reflected in the road he traveled to get where he is—because you know—he didn't exactly start off in an optimal place. And, I think struggled through a lot of challenges to make himself what he is. I think there's this impression that here's this Harvard-educated, stem-winding intellectual; but he is a guy who was raised by a single mother who wasn't there to help all the time because she couldn't be. And you know, he fought his way through a lot.[58]

The struggle experience encountered during these two future presidents' youths made them alike in many ways wherein their survival was very much balanced on their own young backs far too soon, temporarily experiencing absent parents or indifferent fathers, including causes for periods of loneliness based on certain circumstances, which were strongly endured by each of them. Even so, they handled the situation regardless of whatever.

Now, Lincoln arriving in his fifth decade of life—fifty-something—and Obama, who had come to his fourth decade—forty-something—both at this time in their lives would step forth to seek the presidency of the USA in a presidential campaign among the ablest, strongest, and a contingency of ultraseasoned challengers so etched in the historical periods of America. Some of the strongest ever during their day or time came from elevated backgrounds and different childhoods than either Abraham Lincoln or Barack Obama had ever known. Therefore, it is so unlikely that they should run as candidates, men such as these.

The other candidates were awesomely experienced, to say the least, and were well-known leaders and politicians. Electable—well—it was so apparent that the Democrats needed to win in the 2008 presidential election after eight years of a Republican and the Iraqi War!

As a result, in 2008, the Democratic nominee *must* be an electable candidate like a Joe Biden, Hillary Clinton, Chris Dodd, John Edwards, Dennis Kucinich, Bill Richardson, or did we say a Barack Hussein Obama of Springfield, Illinois? (It's so unexpected, don't you think?)

Indeed, in 2008 Republican presidential candidates were positioning and expecting to maintain their stay in the Oval Office on the basis of a pedestal consisting of electable candidates on the Republican side. Who would be the Republican nominee? Would it be Rudy Giuliani, Mike Huckabee, Duncan Hunter, Ron Paul, Mitt Romney, Tom Tancredo, Fred Thompson, Tommy Thompson, or Senator John McCain?

Among the total pool of candidates came long-term senators, former governors, governors, former war heroes, one former First Lady, former mayors, two 2004 Democrat presidential candidates, former congressmen, US House of Representatives, former US Secretary of Energy, former US Ambassador to United Nations, Chair of Committee on Foreign Policy, Chair of Committee on Rules/Administration, and one who had been a community organizer. In the context of race/ethnicity, the candidates consisted of one African American, and the other seven were white to include one woman Democrat. The common majority of the candidates were lawyers who made up the 2008 Democrat presidential field.

Likewise, the 2008 Republican presidential field consisted of similar political and legal careers as the Democrats.

In the 1860 presidential race, the political perspective was just the opposite, since there was a great need to remove the Democrats from office and replace them with the Republicans in the presidential election after eight years of Democrat control: two Democratic presidential incumbents, Franklin Pierce (1852–1856), followed by James Buchanan (1856–1860), as the nation stood on the edge of divided grounds between North and South threatening the outbreak of a civil war on the conflicting issue of slavery and secession.

In 1860, no Republican had served as president, although General John C. Frémont ran in 1856 and was the new Republican Party's first presidential nominee. Frémont was known as the pathfinder because of his success exploring and surveying transportation routes in the trans-Mississippi west.

In 1860, the four-year newly organized Republican Party consisted of former Whigs, Free Soilers, and anti-slavery Democrats. Their candidates were Senator William H. Seward of New York, as the acknowledged leader; Governor Salmon P. Chase of Ohio; Senator Simon Cameron of Pennsylvania; Associate Justice John McLean of Ohio; and Edward Bates of Missouri. Each of these men had been well-known nationally for years as high-profile politicians and leaders among leaders for many more years than Lincoln, which caused reservations and concerns for Lincoln about his possibility of being accepted as presidential material in comparison to such giants within his own Republican Party. And on the Democrat side, there was the "Little Giant," Senator Stephen A. Douglas, who stood as one of the strongest candidates in northern Illinois and boasted his popular-sovereignty doctrine, including others running on the Democrat ticket: John C. Breckinridge of Kentucky, John Bell of Tennessee, and Edward Everett of Massachusetts.

Regardless of the overwhelming support that Senator Obama garnered or what Lincoln's practical contingency provided in support of him, doubt, suspicion, indifference, and conflicting criticism arose from among many of the prominent Democrats and/or

Republicans about such promising sons of Illinois seeking the presidency within the times. For example, three months before Lincoln's nomination, Illinois Governor William H. Bissell and Orville H. Browning expressed their serious doubt about Lincoln as a candidate for president. Bissell drafted a memo to Salmon P. Chase, stating:

> That our folks have recently taken a notion to talk up Lincoln, [and] he is everything that we can reasonably ask in a man and a politician. Still, I do not suppose that many of our friends *seriously* expect to secure his nomination as candidate for the Presidency. In fact, they would be very well satisfied, probably, if he would secure the second place on the ticket.[59]

Additionally, Orville Browning, an ultraconservative Republican, conferred with Lincoln face to face in Springfield telling him that he preferred Bates of Missouri over Lincoln for the Republican Party's nomination and suggested that Lincoln should support Bates as well.

Ironically, before Obama's candidacy there were some, aside from those who were enthusiastic for him, who doubted the young black senator's bid for presidency. They voiced concerns about him failing in a presidential campaign on the basis of the core requirements needed. One of his key campaign executives, Valerie Jarrett, recalled how "everybody said he'll never be able to get an organization together, no one will come and work for him, and all the other candidates have taken all the good people." In a timely and thoughtful response, Jarrett added, "But you know all our lives people have been telling us you're not good enough, you're not ready so don't even try."[60]

Then, from another interesting perspective, what did the old black vanguard—made up of the former civil rights protest movement luminaries and the esteemed Washington Black Caucus, primarily consisting of black politicians and leaders—think of this obviously ambitious newcomer on the block? Did this special African

American authority consciously display an air of indifference to Senator Obama's pursuit of the White House, which just might resemble a sense of distrust, even rejection, of this new breed of African American polity? Quite honorably, there was a cooperative move coming from the Rev. Jesse Jackson, an African American who ran for president in 1984 and 1988 and one who came from the civil rights movement; he stepped forth and endorsed young Obama in March 2007, a month after this United States senator announced his candidacy in February 2007.

Later, after analyzing the situation of Republican candidates in the 2008 presidential contest, retired US Army General Colin Powell, who served as the first African American secretary of state as appointed by President George W. Bush, crossed party lines (Republican) to endorse a Democrat, Barack Obama, in October 2008. Indeed, the Moses and Joshua generational gap among black Americans became a memorable metaphor symbolizing and comparing previous black activists and politicians of the 1960s to the millennials some forty or more years after Dr. Martin Luther King Jr., leader of the modern Moses era. A transformation moved in wherein the race-specific rhetoric was ceasing to become the fiery rallying cry. And Barack Obama became a skillful interpreter of the new rhetoric, effectively seizing it to herald his widespread message for all to hear at the dawn of the twenty-first century or 2000 decade. He articulated it well. Yet he did not forsake the African American people, but was able to speak for the people of America utilizing less race-specific tones. Instead, his voice emphasized morality and universality for this nation.

Enveloped within the dynamics of the 2008 presidential race, another phenomenal aspect existed: there was a woman running for office—Hillary Clinton. The question is, how did Mrs. Clinton fare in the race as related to blacks, since one of their own stood to be elected: Barack Obama? In fact, both candidates would uniquely become *firsts*, if elected. Quite frankly, loyalty remained among African Americans for Hillary Clinton, as many of them actively placed their support and trust in the former First Lady, wife of

President Bill Clinton (forty-second). It was true that a majority of black voters candidly expressed their desire for Mrs. Clinton to win and become the first woman president of the United States. Of course, she was an outlier among all male contenders since she was the only woman running, while Obama was the only black running among a host of white males and one white female.

But there was another group of relevant elite supporters in existence out there promoting the candidate of their choice. Who was their chosen candidate, then? There were the young, gifted, and famous who set the trend among supporters: Caroline Kennedy, the daughter of President John F. Kennedy (thirty-fifth); Maria Shriver, First Lady of California and another member of the Kennedy dynasty; not to mention the most popular black woman in the media, billionaire Oprah Winfrey, whose praise acknowledged Obama: "His rise is the most moving and exciting political movement that I've seen in my lifetime."[61]

Within this episodic presidential race, many support groups emerged and many variables arose. For example, initially, Congressman (D-GA) John Lewis supported Hillary Clinton, then switched to Senator Barack Obama. Lewis came from the old black vanguard of civil rights leaders and was a superdelegate. Finally, embracing Obama's transformational approach of the new generation versus older generation traditional black interest groups or leaders, Congressman Lewis became compelled to lend his loyal support to this young newcomer, realizing that Barack Obama was a result of the dream of Dr. King and that troop of movers and shakers within the civil rights movement, such as a John Lewis.

The campaign of Barack Obama lasted from 2007 to 2008. Becoming the presumptive and global-wise nominee clearly became a significant domestic issue in 2008, as it did in 1860, although centuries apart. From the nineteenth to the twenty-first centuries in America, success and victories have been won, including the despair of defeats and losses coupled with enduring hopes, and enabling a ride on the shoulders of dreams. As the decades and seasons transition, America remains a global interest and experience, soaring above the principalities of governments in the Western and Eastern Hemispheres, and stands as a nation among all nations. Indeed, America enjoys superior achievement in the New World in comparison to some nations of the Old World. Despite its existence as the leader of the Free World, the posterity of America cannot escape the cross it bore in the enslavement of a people, followed by the inequality and injustices that segregation caused, compounded with a divide between races and a long struggle for civil rights for minorities that yet has not ceased, marring the land. The Declaration of Independence, the Constitution of the United States, including the amendments and the Articles of Confederation—each is definitive of America, or should have been. Unfortunately, they were grossly overlooked as related to the significance of blacks and others of color. They are relevant governmental documents, yet have not always been given the constitutional adherence on behalf of minorities by some who govern in executive office or those who interpret the law. Whenever the question of sacred rights of Negroes, blacks, or African Americans as human beings arises, this republic, a government that consists of no kings, no nobility, just the people (public) as the ultimate source of legitimate power that exercises its powers through elected representatives of a republican government for the colonists,[62] there is a problem. The Constitution of the United States has been the core of the nation's law for over two hundred years. The Bill of Rights is the first group of ten constitutional amendments protecting the fundamental principles of liberty and self-government. Overall, the Constitution responds to new circumstances and conditions wherein political parties are not mentioned in the Constitution, nor is the enslavement of people.

Change is a given. The preamble to the Constitution of the United States remains:

> We the People of the United States, in Order to form a more perfect Union, establish justice, insure domestic tranquility, provide for the common defense, promote the general welfare and secure the blessings of liberty to

ourselves and our posterity, do ordain and establish this Constitution for the United States of America.

According to the Declaration of Independence, the unanimous declaration of the thirteen United States of America reports the Action of Second Continental Congress, July 4, 1776, as given in the text below (R. B. Bernstein, 81). Furthermore:

> We hold these truths to be self-evident, that all men are created equal, that they are endowed by their creator with certain unalienable Rights, that among these are Life, Liberty, and the Pursuit of Happiness—That to secure these Rights, Governments are instituted among men, deriving their just Powers from the Consent of the Governed, that whenever any Form of Government becomes destructive of these Ends, it is the Right of the People to alter or to abolish it and to institute new Government . . . laying its Foundation on such Principles, and organizing its Powers in such Form, as to them shall seem most likely to effect their safety and happiness.[63]

Consequently, the question of blacks belonging to America, the belief of African Americans feeling that America was, indeed, their country, too, has lingered far too long. In protest to the practice of injustice and lack of equality for all, American poet Langston Hughes penned:

> I am the darker brother, they send me to eat in the kitchen when company comes . . . tomorrow, I'll sit at the table when company comes. Nobody'll dare say to me eat in the kitchen then. Besides, they'll see how beautiful I am and be ashamed. I too sing America.[64]

Yes, the possibility and hope of fully belonging economically, politically, culturally, socially, educationally, and being humanly free became the pursuit of a people who sought full participation as citizens in America. Unalienable rights, liberty, and justice were the hope of all the people as they envisioned tomorrow where all could sit at the "table," even the "darker brother."

In 1860, the darker brother was sent to eat in the kitchen, but in 2008, he did not necessarily have to eat in the kitchen. Although, the struggle for freedom was so conspicuous in 1860 when Abraham Lincoln became the presumptive presidential nominee. By 2008 (148 years later), when Barack Obama became the presumptive presidential nominee, the lyrics of Hughes' motif prediction of "better tomorrows" or hoping for a better day when the "darker brother" could join his white brother at the table inspiring the inclusion theory of "I too" almightily symbolizes being free of exclusion. Ringing loudly and clearly confirming America's ideals built on its constitutional truth and power invigorates our collective conscience that we can dare to dream of a better future—all of us.

One hundred forty-eight years later, a more enlightened America stands. It has been a long, long time in the fight of challenges, setbacks, and broken promises, including the remarkable change during the twentieth-century civil rights movement for social justice approximately one hundred years after the nineteenth-century Civil War in 1861 for union and universal freedom. Currently, some forty-three years later, a presidential election loomed forth with one black man among the strong candidates, who could very well become the presumptive nominee. Did the poet muse that "tomorrow" would manifest the "darker brother" actually sitting at the head of the "table" in the position of occupying the desk at the Oval Office? Truly the audacity of hope prevails.

These eventful episodic campaigns of 2008 and 1860 were so awesome, filled with trepidations, resistance, skepticism, criticism, doubt, jealousy, and hostility related to each candidate, especially Abraham Lincoln in 1860 and toward Barack Obama in 2008, even amidst the hope, charisma, dogma, jubilation, intensity, opportunity, emancipation, admiration, and celebration of Obama and Lincoln, who walked as candidates among strong competitors in pursuit of the White House.

Times and complicated timing were indicators of the awesome but complicated 2008 and 1860 elections in America. The core factor is race. Race in the ultimate sense, manifested by the power of the executive office, is expected to represent all of the people in America and to govern with the purpose of unifying America, and shed the dark veil of bondage including exclusion. Traditionally, the primary campaigns begin in the Iowa caucus and New Hampshire primary.

When Lincoln ran in 1860, the fugitive slave Frederick Douglass stood as the most prominent African American leader, as an abolitionist, orator, writer, and intellect who advocated in the interest of the anti-slavery movement. In 1960, one hundred years after slavery, the Baptist minister Dr. Martin Luther King Jr. became the most prominent African American leader, orator, writer, and intellectual advocating in the interest of social justice and change, protesting for civil rights in a movement for equality and end of segregation. From the legal aspect, Thurgood Marshall, serving on the legal defense team of the NAACP during that era, became the leading attorney for civil rights and justice, which enabled the progressive success of the movement.

Some forty-eight years after the 1960 civil rights movement, Barack Obama emerged as the African American presidential candidate who caused a sold-out rally in Portsmouth, New Hampshire, cancelling out the previously scheduled popular Rolling Stones, and in Indianola, Iowa, the Iowa Senator Tom Harkin told a cheering crowd at his Annual Harkin Steak Fry at the Warren County Fairgrounds that "I settled for the second-biggest rock star in America,"[65] meaning Barack Obama. In short, Senator Barack Obama the intellectual became the most celebrated African American among a diversified America.

Why were these two candidates, Obama and Lincoln, so famous or infamous? Who were their opponents? Were they known by mere biographical details? During the 1860 presidential campaign, the Republican candidates who made an indelible mark or impression and considered traditional candidates began with the nearly sixty-year-old William Henry Seward, whose hometown was in Auburn, Upstate New York. Seward believed that his candidacy would be hugely beneficial for America at a time when the issue increased of what to do with the enslavement of black people. Indeed, he had vehemently labeled slavery as an "irrepressible conflict." Personable and an anti-slavery radical, a natural-born politician, as he was so described: "He is beloved by all classes of people, irrespective of partisan predilections," the *New York Herald* wrote.[66] Of course, Seward felt comfortably optimistic about his becoming the inevitable Republican nominee in 1860. Accordingly, the populace sentiment and apparent predictions of print media consistently heaved laurels upon the expected nomination of Senator Seward, which confirmed Seward's faith that he would definitely become Republican nominee because Republican and Democrat papers agreed that:

> The honor in question was [to be] awarded by common expectation to the distinguished Senator from the State of New York, who, more than any other was held to be the representative man of his party, and who, by his commanding talents and eminent public services has so largely contributed to the development of its principles.[67]

Unlike Lincoln, Seward was a college graduate and graduated from Union College in Schenectady, New York, with highest honors and finished his training for the law. He practiced law first, with Judge Elijah Miller. Starting out as a Whig, he was slow to become a Republican. Being a stylishly dressed gentleman added to his flamboyance as a renowned and eloquent oratorical speaker; additionally, the powerful Harlow Weed was Seward's closest friend and ally, and Weed reigned as the dictator of New York state for at least fifty years. Now, Weed continued to manage Seward's consistent successful political campaigns, such as when Seward ran for New York state senator, governor of New York, and eventually a United States senator from New York. Indeed, being more radical on the issue of slavery than Lincoln's moderate position on slavery actually forged some complications for Seward because of his radicalism.

Salmon Chase, governor of Ohio, came forth as another intense runner for the Republican nomination in 1860. Tall in height like Lincoln, Chase was considered a very handsome man. Moreover, Salmon Chase exhibited a dignified impressive mannerism, devoutly religious, well-dressed at all times, and bore the outstanding characteristics of a statesman in every definition of the word or concept. His daughters—nineteen-year-old Kate and eleven-year-old Nettie—were very devoted to their fifty-two-year-old widower father, Salmon Chase. For Kate Chase, his favorite daughter, was consumed with the passion of her beloved father winning the White House, and her father desired to achieve that position of president for his ambitious, political-minded daughter. Salmon Chase, like Seward and Lincoln, found the peculiar institution of slavery problematic, immoral, and unconstitutional. For more than twenty-five years, Chase had steadfastly taken on the cause of the black man and the moral inconsistency that the enslavement of a people created in a country declaring liberty, justice, unalienable rights, and that all men are created equal. Although, on the slavery issue, Chase and Seward were both radical, Chase was more so than even Seward. Furthermore, Chase viewed slavery through the lens of his moral and religious convictions; thus, he was intolerant of its existence in a land that broke from its mother country, England, on the grounds of religion, independence, and the freedom to pursue happiness as a natural law. Salmon Chase was one of the leading authorities on political ideas and demonstrated intellectual brilliance and organizational skills in his leadership of the anti-slavery movement.

Of his pristine virtues, leadership, and intellectualism, Salmon Chase deemed it a natural privilege for his becoming president more than any other candidate because he felt that he had grandly and purposefully contributed so much to his country in his work for such a righteous cause. As stated by Chase in a letter to his abolitionist friend, Gamaliel Bailey:

A very large body of the people—embracing not a few who would hardly vote for any man other than myself as a Republican nominee—seem to desire that I shall be a candidate in 1860.[68]

Also, coming from St. Louis, Missouri, the sixty-six-year-old Judge Edward Bates, a devoted family man who dearly loved his wife and their eight surviving children from among seventeen born to the couple, joined the candidacy.

Judge Bates, actually, withdrew from a political public life because of his great love for domestic family life, and declined requests to run for important offices. After twenty years, he finally considered to run for political office by entering the presidential race of 1860 as a candidate. Bates was quaint in dress because he continued to wear the old Quakers attire. Although he had been a Democrat, coming from his home state of Virginia, he adamantly refused to adhere to the pro-slavery establishment of most Southerners. Bates' acceptance of entering the race resulted from being asked to do so by the prominent Frank Blair family of Silver Springs, Maryland, just a few ways from the bustling District of Columbia. The senior Frank Blair's son, the thirtyish-year-old Frank, recently elected to Congress, specifically nudged Bates for presidency, and the Blair family envisioned Frank Jr. becoming president later on based on his talents, charisma, and a natural politician.

Since Frank Jr. was so young at the time, the influential Republican family decided that the more senior Judge Edward Bates, a well-respected citizen of St. Louis and at one time a shining light at the center of national attention in 1847, would be the ideal person to run as a candidate for the president of the United States. Ironically, Judge Bates was not a member on the Republican ticket of the Republican Party, although he highly endorsed the Republican principle of restricting slavery to the states where it currently existed and that the expansion of slavery must be prevented from spreading into the territories.[69]

The 1860 politics existed without motives and strategies to outwit and outmaneuver each other. Chase and Bates sought to achieve the front-runner positions over Seward. However, only Salmon Chase troubled William Seward in his rigidness.

Just as in the initial stages of the campaign of Barack Obama, and even as it advanced, frequently the youthful junior senator was not a real threat to the other 2008 presidential ambitions. In fact, the assumed front-runner Hillary Clinton's husband, former President Bill Clinton, labeled Obama's campaign as a mere "fairy tale." Nor did Lincoln's opponents, especially Seward, view Lincoln as a formidable threat whatsoever to his presidential ambitions in 1860. The high-mindedness of Judge Bates, Salmon Chase, and Seward ignored the possibility of such an inexperienced candidate as Lincoln becoming the sixteenth president, but entertained in grand confidence about the possibility of one of them becoming the sixteenth president of the United States. Likewise, who would capture the highest office in the land and become the forty-fourth president of the United States of America in 2008: Clinton, Edwards, Biden, Richards? Or Obama! *Well?*

Resistance, indifference, and criticism became a staple among the cynics, both black and white, and other, during the campaign of 2008. Anticipation of change motivated the young, and a sizeable portion of the baby boomers, to accept Barack Obama by placing their confidence on this rising star who represented such hope in fulfilling their dream. What more than this outstanding young man becoming the first African American to clinch the nomination in a majority party at the presidential level. However, somewhere way over in the shadowy crevices of politics lurked unwilling and resisting unenthusiastic blacks, mind you, who did not even partially yield to a Barack Obama in his attempt to carry the torch of leadership as the front-runner—actually becoming the front-runner in the African American race—should he become president of the United States.

Indeed, Obama's presence complicated the high-profile status of certain prominent African American stalwarts who apparently would not move over to let a brother in to take his seat. Although he stood in line after forty-three other presidents, and he had faced unfavorable mounting statistics categorized by traditional racial profiling, when the time came to change, overturn the statistics of being left behind, some in the expected supportive forces closed him out, closed and shut the door in his face when he came knocking, told him it was not his time yet, told him to wait. Maybe by 2016 his time would come, but he needed to go somewhere and sit down now; be more patient or else he was going to act like an "uppity N—," causing him to fail altogether. All of this came from some of his people in high places, I'm just saying.

Just step back, young brother, follow my advice until I allow you to come forth, if ever. Because yesterday I was the HNIC, and right now, I will remain the same to the likes of you. You're just an upstart—a baby compared to me from the 1960s, and so forth.

Now, since there were no candidates of color running in 1860, it did not mean that African Americans were totally unaware of or uninvolved in the white candidates running for president. As stated earlier, Frederick Douglass was the most prominent leading black figure of that time, while his eminence remains as a great American today. Yes, a fugitive slave, transformed abolitionist, Frederick Douglass was widely known in the abolitionist circles as well as outside the circle and abroad.

At the time, free Northern blacks were not too enthusiastic about any of the candidates running, although they were concerned about whom they should support as president on the basis of the freedom cause. As a result, Frederick Douglass' leadership, along with Bishop Daniel Payne and the Reverend Henry McNeal Turner of the African Methodist Episcopal Church, rose as the foremost informed advocates of freedom for their people.

Abraham Lincoln appeared to be their choice because of his consistent, forceful anti-slavery views. However, they did not completely agree with his rather moderate view, such as his acceptance of allowing slavery to remain in Southern states where it existed.

Indeed, that was troublesome for blacks who sought liberation for those enslaved in the Deep South as well. Nonetheless, the most deciding factor of support for Lincoln from free enlightened blacks came as a result of the pro-slavery movement and the Southern

Democrat states who held such vehemence toward Lincoln. The issue of secession from the union if Lincoln were elected convinced blacks that Lincoln was more in their corner, as evidenced by the outcry of haters of Lincoln on the basis of the slavery issue. *If he is so opposed by the Southern Democrats and slaveholders, then we must support him*, came the decision of Frederick Douglass and other prominent blacks of the 1860s election. *In short, Abraham Lincoln is the best choice among them all for us blacks*. Ironically, in the 1850s, enslaved blacks lacked freedom; one hundred years later in the 1950s, Negroes still heavily lacked their full civil rights, which were denied them through the enforced segregation laws since 1857 *Plessy v. Ferguson*. By 1860, Negroes were cautious of the Southern Democrats pushing to maintain slavery by nominating John C. Breckinridge of Kentucky, who vowed to protect slavery in the territories. The Northern Democrats nominated Stephen A. Douglas, and his affirming on a platform that the status of slavery in the territories should be determined by decisions of the Supreme Court did not rest well with Negroes at all.

In 2007, blacks were not prepared among themselves to fully accept the Obama presidential ticket, mainly because they felt it might split the Democrats extensively and result in another Republican win come 2008. Traditionally, loyalty to Bill Clinton by blacks on the basis of the Clintons' very moderate liberalism toward minorities caused many African Americans' reluctance of embracing the young black Senator Obama. Nonetheless, of the black elder statesmen, Rev. Joseph Lowery, former head of the SCLC, and Douglas Wilder, first elected black governor of Virginia, were those blacks who readily endorsed Obama's candidacy.

"I think Obama was right about not waiting for someone to tell him that it was his time."[70] Those were encouraging remarks spoken in terms of Obama's turn being now, thus complimented by one of the respected ministers of the 1960 civil rights movement, Dr. Joe Lowery, confirming that regardless of the progressiveness of blacks since enslavement, unfortunately, many of them still remained reluctant to grasp opportunities in a timely manner:

No matter how much education they have, they never graduated from the slave mentality. The slave mentality compels us to say "We can't win. We can't do." Martin said the people who were saying "later" were really saying "never." But the time to do right is always right now.[71]

Seward, Cameron, Chase, Bates, and Lincoln represented the 1860 presidential field on the Republican ticket while black leaders united in support of the Illinois Republican, Abraham Lincoln. Clinton, Edwards, Dodd, Biden, Richardson, Kucinich, and Obama made up the 2008 Democrat presidential field with more black leaders unified to support the Democrat ticket, moreover, New York Senator Hillary Clinton, as opposed to blacks leaning toward the Republicans, which was the case back in 1860.

In January 2008, with Obama's win of the Iowa caucus, specifically 38 percent of the vote, John Edwards 30 percent, and Hillary Clinton 29 percent, all seemed unbelievable![72] How could this happen "on this January night, at this defining moment in history, you have done what the cynics said we couldn't do,"[73] proclaimed the victorious Barack Obama. Truly, this victory stunned everyone, politicians and nonpoliticians, and upset the Democratic candidates who felt they were much stronger candidates than this most unlikely candidate, Barack Obama! Indeed, in the television debates prior to January 2008, overall, each of the Democratic opponents' common criticism of Barack Obama saw controversy in his candidacy and identified it as being his huge lack of experience in comparison to them. Thus, a shadowy arrogance or silent mocking crept about, indicating that *they* were the only, perhaps, really seriously qualified candidates of the official Democratic Party able to run for president. Questioning his merits to run as an electable Democratic candidate seemed to define him as one among all the candidates that he, Senator Barack Obama, was historically least electable and least politically experienced. The basis of his being unable to exhibit presidential leadership in the event of another tragic terrorist event that happened in 2001 on the United States attempted to deflate his chance even more. No doubt, fellow Americans were doubtful of the junior Illinois senator's ability to handle such a crisis, as opposed to Senator Hillary Clinton (D-NY), who had previously been First Lady of the White House when her husband, Bill Clinton, served as forty-second president of the United States. Then, there was Senator Joe Biden, who was well-experienced in foreign policy, and he verbally criticized the young hopeful by pointing out that Barack Obama was too inexperienced to become a serious presidential candidate for electability on the 2008 Democratic ticket. Indeed, sharp attacks erupted from Senator Joe Biden's remarks about Obama while on the campaign trail during the primaries. The sixty-five-year-old Joe Biden (D-DE) served as chairman of the foreign-relations committee and had served six terms in the Senate to the junior senator's three years. As stated, Obama entered the United States Senate in 2005 as one of its biggest celebrities and one of its politically weakest members.[74]

Earlier on the campaign trail, Biden's sharp remarks about Obama surfaced when the experienced senator described the black senator as "the first mainstream African American who is articulate and bright and clean and a nice-looking guy."[75]

Of course, Biden was forced to quickly withdraw the statement and rendered a profusion of apologies to the senator as well as to other popular African American leaders, namely Rev. Jesse Jackson and Rev. Al Sharpton, because both had been presidential candidates during previous election years: 1984 and 1988 when Jackson ran, and 2004 when Sharpton ran.

Additionally, while campaigning as presidential candidate, Biden frequently denounced the young senator on the issue of Barack Obama's poor foreign-policy judgment and strongly arguing that he voiced the opinions of what Americans realized—that Barack Obama was not ready to be president. Furthermore, Biden emphasized his "I think he can be ready, but, right now, I don't believe he is.... The presidency is not something that lends itself to on-the-job training."[76]

Joseph Biden Jr. was born November 20, 1942, in Scranton,

Pennsylvania, into a working-class, Irish-Catholic family. His education consisted of a bachelor of arts degree in history and political science from the University of Delaware, and a JD (juris doctorate) from Syracuse University College of Law. After receiving his law degree in 1968, Biden worked as a fledgling attorney in Wilmington, Delaware, for four years until his election to the Senate in 1972. Additionally, Senator Biden served as an adjunct professor of constitutional law at Widener University School of Law, beginning in 1991.

Senator Joe Biden had become one of the most respected Senate voices on foreign policy, civil liberties, crime, college-aid loan programs, and an avid supporter of Amtrak. He was chairman of the Senate foreign-relations committee in the 110th Congress (2007–08) and was being considered as a gifted negotiator who helped shape United States security and foreign-relations policies for decades. As a moderate Democrat, Joe Biden often impressively bridged the bipartisan gap. He served as chair of the Senate judiciary committee from 1987 to 1995 and led confirmation fights against Supreme Court nominees such as Robert Bork (not confirmed) and Clarence Thomas (African American who became a justice after the retirement of Justice Thurgood Marshall, first African American justice on the Supreme Court); Thomas was confirmed in 1991.

This United States senator led in the fight against drug use and deterring drugs from entering the country, and crafted many landmark federal crime laws, including the Violent Crime Control and Law Enforcement Act of 1994 and the Violence against Women Act of 2000.

From a personal aspect, his first marriage was to the former Neilia Hunter in 1966. They had three children: Joseph "Beau" Jr., 1969, Robert Hunter, 1970, and Naomi, 1971. Unfortunately, on December 18, 1972, while shopping for a Christmas tree with the children, his wife's car was hit by a truck, killing his wife and baby daughter instantly and injuring the two boys seriously. Remarkably, Biden was persuaded to be sworn into the Senate at the bedside of his two sons. Remaining a widower until 1977, he married Jill Jacobs (a teacher). Senator Biden commuted each day by Amtrak between Delaware and DC for thirty-six continuous years.

Young Joe was a stutterer, becoming terrified to read aloud in class. As a result, he memorized pages of books before class to minimize stuttering in front of his classmates.

Charismatic, gregarious, outspoken, colorful, personable, yet distinguished depicts the personality of Senator Biden. Some of his memorable moments in politics revealing his outspoken nature are given below:

> About six months ago, President Bush said to me, "Well, at least I make strong decisions; I lead." I said, "Mr. President, look behind you. Leaders have followers. No one's following. Nobody."[77]

Senator Biden ran for the presidency in 1988, but aborted his effort when the rival campaign of Dukakis found that Biden had delivered an Iowa speech in which part of it was taken from a British politician. The senator defended the speech, arguing that he had credited the Brit on an earlier occasion. On January 7, 2007, a month before Senator Obama announced his candidacy, Senator Biden declared his candidacy for the 2008 presidential race.

Back in 1972, when Biden was first elected to the US Senate at twenty-nine years old, it made him the youngest US senator in modern history.[78]

Seemingly, Hillary Rodham Clinton stood as the strongest among the Democratic presidential competitors in the presidential campaign. When Hillary Clinton became a United States senator representing New York on November 7, 2000, she received a mirage of media/publicity somewhat equal to Barack Obama, although not quite. Indeed, Mrs. Clinton was popular and had become the candidate most likely to win the nomination over the other Democratic candidates.

Hillary Rodham was born October 26, 1947, eldest child of Dorothy and Hugh Rodham, in Park Ridge, Illinois. She graduated from Wellesley College and entered Yale Law School in 1969. After graduation from law school, she interned with children's advocate Marian Wright Edelman, meeting her future husband, William

"Bill" Clinton of Arkansas. Bill and Hillary married in 1975. Afterward, she joined the faculty of the University of Arkansas School of Law (1975), and later the Rose Law Firm in 1976.

Mrs. Clinton was appointed to the board of the Legal Services Corp by President Carter, and her husband, Bill Clinton, became governor of Arkansas. Their only child, a daughter, Chelsea, was born in 1980. Hillary Clinton was First Lady of Arkansas for twelve years. As the nation's First Lady, Mrs. Clinton continued to balance public service with private life.

In 1993, President Clinton appointed her to chair the Task Force on National Health Care Reform. She is well-known for her 1996 best seller, *It Takes a Village: And Other Lessons Children Teach Us*, and other literary works resulting in her receiving a Grammy Award for her recording of it. Mrs. Clinton became a leading advocate of health-insurance coverage and its expansion, ensuring children are properly immunized, and raising public awareness of health issues.

Hillary Clinton was undeterred by critics, winning many admirers for her staunch support for women around the world and her commitment to children's issues. Hillary Rodham Clinton was a pioneer as the First Lady to be elected to the United States Senate and the first woman elected statewide in New York.

Assuring her maintenance as front-runner for Democratic candidates, Senator Hillary Rodham Clinton demonstrated an indifference toward the young black senator called Barack Obama. With her apparent lead in the competitive pregeneral presidential campaign, Senator Hillary Clinton launched forth, favorably supported by advocates of women's rights; several prominent members of the Black Caucus, especially the late Congresswoman Stephanie Tubbs (D-DC), a close friend of the Clintons; members of the old black vanguard remained loyal to the Clintons; the working middle class of whites in the red states; and loyal patriots to former President Bill Clinton seemed far reaching within the Clinton camp of supporters.

Once more, it was evident that Hillary Clinton and Barack Obama—whomever was nominated by the Democratic Party in

2008—would become "firsts." The tides of time rose and fell upon the sea of the two competitors.

Hillary Clinton purported her untiring commitment to the American people as a servant leader and her unsurpassed patriotism and loyalty to America as a Democratic insurgent who apparently could hold her own with the best of them. Confident, preordained, entitled, and a formidable campaigner, the Clinton machine consisted of her husband—the ever-popular and savvy former President Bill Clinton—tested and proven that they could produce, wielding staggering success in two presidential campaigns, 1992 and 1996, and above all, Hillary's own successful senatorial campaigns.

Obama acknowledged that he was running against the most established brand in the Democratic Party for the last twenty years and that Senator Hillary Clinton was his most tested and proven opponent.

She was, indeed, the front-runner in July 2007, ahead of Obama and the other Democratic candidates. Obama's progress must be fast/hard to catch up with Hillary Clinton and speed by her, if he had any prospect of remaining in the race. Yet the young Illinois senator was consistently gaining popularity and mounting curiosity, which significantly surrounded this race, including his outstanding fundraising, which was so surprisingly successful.

As the campaign progressed, the battle of debates rose to crushing, blasting, and retaliatory opposing tones wrestling against candidates' meritorious service, while voices of hope combined with promises of change and facing challenges persisted.

Senator Clinton's eagerness began in the early 2007 debates during April. Needless to say, the criticisms made by Senator Clinton on Barack Obama increased in attention.

Indeed, when Obama stated that his foreign-policy experience was "probably the strongest experience I have in foreign relations is the fact that I spent four years living overseas when I was a child in Southeast Asia,"[79] according to an *LA Times* report, many found his statement to be naïve and weak in comparison to surrounding candidates whose broader official experience clearly overshadowed Senator Obama's limited foreign-relations record. In response to Obama's claim on foreign policy, there was strong doubt that a four-year stay in Indonesia as a minor child with his mother was experience adequate enough; therefore, in an apparent mock of the naiveté of Obama's claiming foreign policy, Mrs. Clinton quipped back:

> Now, voters will judge whether living in a foreign country at the age of ten prepares one to face the big, complex international challenges the next president will face; I think we need a president with more experience than that. Someone the rest of the world knows, looks up to, and has confidence in. I don't think this is the time for on-the-job training on our economy or on foreign policy.[80]

Later, when Obama began gaining after the Iowa caucus upset of Senator Clinton, she utilized the "red phone" televised ad by overtly emphasizing the former First Lady's experience and covertly emphasizing her femininity by employing the "security mom," focusing on putting the kids to bed and wanting to know that the world is safe while they sleep.[81]

January 3, 2008, the last day before the Iowa caucus crossed Mississippi to Iowa, Obama faced an awesome challenge and task because blacks populate a mere 2.5 percent of the state of Iowa. Was Obama as well-known in Iowa as the other candidates in the race? No, he was not. Catch up to Hillary Clinton, senator from New York, who soared ahead of all the rest, especially the senator from Illinois (Land o' Lincoln): Barack Obama. But like Lincoln back in 1847, who set his energies to rolling way ahead of his opponent, Hardy, Obama's use of technology via the internet energized the task: "A virtually organized Obama machine [was] already up and running."[82]

Because of his fundraising internet operative, he developed a relevant head-start approach by mobilizing support over the internet, which reached far and wide. Obama's ideas on issues and his speeches were delivered on his website—an excellent cyberspace tool operating in the twenty-first century.

Surprisingly, January 8, 2008, brought an astonishing and crushing blow to a supercandidate's stronghold. Indeed, the Iowa caucuses eliminated that blow! Surprisingly and to the amazement of all concerned, Obama won the Iowa caucuses with 38 percent of the vote over John Edwards' 30 percent and Hillary Clinton's 29 percent.[83] "You have done what the cynics said we couldn't do," exclaimed an exuberant Barack Obama after his victory.[84] At this point, Joe Biden and Chris Dodd withdrew from the race after the Iowa caucus in January 2008. Followed by Bill Richardson withdrawing later in January 10, 2008, withdrawals continued rapidly, because on January 30, 2008, John Edwards dropped out of the race after Obama's great victory in the Super Tuesday primary on February 5, 2008.

Afterward, there were two Democratic candidates remaining—Hillary Clinton and Barack Obama—to face the next round of primaries. Clinton and Obama's success became a see-saw experience as they won some and lost some between each other in the New Hampshire, Nevada, and South Carolina primaries.

As Obama trudged forth, becoming perhaps an engaging opponent with whom to be reckoned, after all focusing his mantra and rallying cry "Change" and "Yes We Can" as he convincingly rolled through from one state to the next during the early months of 2008. At each chance possible, Hillary Clinton never failed to attack Obama's claim to *change* and arguably reducing the *ideal*. She enforced: "Making change is not about what you believe; it's not about a speech you make. It's about working hard. I'm not just running on a promise for change. I'm running on [thirty-five] years of change. What we need is somebody who can deliver change. We don't need to be raising false hopes."

Donna Brazile, former Al Gore 2000 campaign manager, warned that Obama's campaign, perhaps, did not realize the Clinton magnitude in their battle for what the Clintons considered as their entitlement; in addition, after a heated debate with her male opponents, Senator Clinton accused the press of showing favoritism toward the other candidates, primarily to Senator Obama.

Essentially, Mrs. Clinton accused the press of giving the other candidates, particularly Obama, "free rein" to go after her.

Indeed, by February 2008, after Super Tuesday, Clinton and Obama were still standing after the other six Democratic candidates had left the race; obviously, Obama's strategies allowed him to persevere. For Barack Obama, did a presidential campaign among strong competitors transform into a presidential campaign between two strong competitors on the Democratic side? The *next* questionable phase is the party nominations.

THE PARTY NOMINATIONS OF 2008 AND 1860

Flashback to 1859. The test of presidential electability was working in Lincoln's favor as 1860 approached. Emerging as the Republican champion of the Great West, Abraham Lincoln became that person. Seward, the front-runner for the party's nomination, appeared vulnerable because of the perception cast because of his radical perspective on the slavery issue, among other things.

At this point in February 2008, the crucial turning point was inevitable: Super Tuesdays, caucuses, pledged delegates, and endorsements all inspired talk of who would be most electable. Electability is defined by voters. Who would get the most votes at this technical juncture? Would it be Obama? Or would it be Clinton?

As 2007 drew to a close, Obama had been campaigning in Iowa and elsewhere for a year. Upon the narrowing down of the Democratic candidacy to just two candidates—the two senators, Barack Obama (D-IL) and Hillary Clinton (D-NY)—the debate scene now featured the two senators. They stood on oppositional stands regarding the driving issues while trying to convince the public who was best to preside over the nation, and who could actually overpower the Republicans after eight years of control. The goal was for the Democrats to regain the Oval Office. But the question was, who or which one—Hillary Clinton or Barack Obama? As a result, the debates between the two initiated a fury of intense maneuvering and opposing stances in efforts to persuade voters that he or she was more electable and the best person to lead the country.

Each represented and stood as firsts. After the first president, George Washington (two centuries ago), such an achievement of electability for Hillary Clinton would mean the *first* woman as president of the United States. On the other hand, the achievement of electability for Barack Obama would mean the *first* African American as president of the United States. Regardless of who won, the presidential race of 2008 would be historic and its significance unprecedented.

The historic intensity of the 1860 presidential election gained its significance on the issue of taking a side on slavery. Running on an anti-slavery platform of the Republican Party of 1860 instigated secession by Southern states because slavery could be consequential should Lincoln be elected. Moreover, if elected, Abraham Lincoln would become the *first* Republican to serve as president of the United States.

The nomination issue soared with insatiable curiosity, mounting enthusiasm, and growing expectations intended for this great country! As a result, strategies, finances, and politics of the times facilitated enormous pressure, correlating with candidates' determination to win. The playing field for the candidates consisted of so many intimidating problems, magical triumphs, and logical decision-making within the turmoil of campaigning as nomination time grew closer; so did the value of the votes that would determine the outcome.

Delegates for Obama consisted of 847 estimated pledged delegates. Delegates for Clinton consisted of 834 pledged delegates by February 2008. Clearly, it appeared that Senator Clinton's lead was slipping away. In addition, Senator Clinton's campaign funds were in trouble at this point and she had to make a $5 million personal loan to her campaign. By contrast, Senator Obama's campaign had plenty of money on the basis of raising an impressive $32 million wherein a vast amount came from the people; donors all over the country contributed via the internet. Indeed, Obama's campaign facilitation and organization surpassed Hillary Clinton's in terms of relevancy and ingenious use of electronic technology reaching the masses.

More states like Maine and Wisconsin waited to be swept up in the competition, and at the arrival of February 9, 2008, Obama won those states over Clinton. Among pledged delegates won after February, Obama had 1,192; Clinton lagged behind him with 1,035, but she led in superdelegates—240 for her and 191 superdelegates for Obama.[85] Here is a compelling case of the role of numbers and how they can affect change—make a difference, of course.

From March through April 2008, the two candidates raced against each other strategizing to gain the votes in efforts to prove his/her electability by the people and for the people. Several other states, Texas, Ohio, Rhode Island, Wyoming, Michigan, Pennsylvania, West Virginia, Indiana, and North Carolina, remained as voting primaries. As a result, in the election/primaries, Clinton won some while Obama won some as he continued to lead in pledged delegates over Clinton.

Come May, the two Democrats became two of the most historical candidates in pursuit of the White House as this 2008 presidential election year paced on. Ironically, the seventy-two-year-old Senator John McCain miraculously won the Republican nomination back in March (4) while the two Democrats furiously slugged along to claim the nomination of their party. The challenge became a battle of who should drop out of the race, now erupting argument that the Democrats were split and the race between the two Democrats seemed to be getting ugly—like damaging and threatening the chances of Democrats ever recapturing the White House in 2008. Is it really Democrat vs. Democrat rather than Democrat vs. Republican? Indeed, Senator John McCain stood alone and free to develop his campaign/platform for the general election without trying to win votes from remaining primaries against other Republican opponents, as did his Democratic rivals as they attacked each other. Issues of race and gender began to creep in, causing unwarranted controversy.

Was the 2008 Democratic Party repeating what happened in 1860 when this same party became vulnerably split among themselves? On June 8, 1860, in Baltimore, Stephen Douglas represented the Northern Democrats, John Breckinridge the Southern Democrats. Unlike Obama and Clinton in 2008, Lincoln and other prominent Republicans did not make campaign speeches whatsoever, nor did Lincoln write public letters seeking supporters for his election.

Others campaigned on behalf of Lincoln as carried on at the state and local level in the North by a vast array of Republican activists. "Lincoln's Young America" was formed, emphasizing old Whig campaign tactics. They built wigwams, raised flagpoles, displayed Lincoln fences and rails, and held torchlight parades in hundreds of villages, towns, and cities. Lincoln's "Rail-Splitter" image, while not decisive in his nomination at Chicago, carried an important symbol of democracy and opportunity for all classes in the West and for farmers and working men in eastern areas like central/western Pennsylvania, which the Republicans needed to win. Lincoln appealed to the people. Obama appealed to the people. Using the simplicity of the key chain in his campaign, one Atlanta businessman sold Obama key chains for three dollars at an Obama rally to lines of people and completely sold out of them, which indicated Obama's popularity, similar to the phenomenal appeal generated by the sixteenth president's "rail splitter" image campaign.

Barack Obama campaigned intensely from the time he announced his candidacy to run for president in February 2007. Similarly, Hillary Clinton ran her campaign with high intensity as the front-runner since she launched her candidacy for president on January 20, 2007. In May 2008, as the campaigning and rallying progressed, the tension mounted between the two Democrats in oppositional and combative competition as each battled for the nomination of the party come August 2008 in Denver, Colorado, at the Democratic National Convention.

Back in 1860 (May) at the Wigwam Convention Hall in Chicago, where the Republican National Convention met, intensity increased as the Republican delegates eagerly turned to the presidential nomination. "Lincoln's managers as cited by Harris, led by David

Davis at Chicago, labored tirelessly to fend off an aggressive Seward effort to win a majority on the first ballot."8

Lincoln's managers insisted that Seward could not win the battleground states of the lower North. Yet the Seward forces believed that the work of their politics the night before the nomination had achieved the desired results: a first-ballot victory. Consequently, the *New York Tribune* editor Horace Greeley, who was against Seward, even conceded that Seward would be nominated over Lincoln even though Greeley preferred the Rail-Splitter. Greeley reported in his newspaper: "From all that I can gather tonight . . . the opposition to Governor Seward cannot concentrate on any candidate, and . . . he will be nominated."87 But Lincoln's managers' confidence in their working to block Seward from receiving the necessary majority on the first ballot was evident when Judge Davis wired Lincoln: "Am very hopeful. Don't [sic] be excited; nearly dead with fatigue."88

In contrast to the 2008 presidential election, the 1860 presidential nomination (Republican) would be won at the Wigwam Convention Hall in Chicago without the candidates being present as of May 1860. Instead, Lincoln, Seward, Bates, and Chase were in their respective states awaiting the outcome or awaiting the announcement of his nomination.

But in the twenty-first century, 2008, the Republican candidate had already received the good graces of the GOP, and John McCain, a war hero (Vietnam POW, 1960s), senior senator from Arizona, beholden of an abundance of wealth, awaited, ironically, who the major competing party would nominate. Would it be New York Senator Hillary Clinton, or the Illinois junior Senator Barack Obama?

Invesco Field in Denver, Colorado, served as the Democratic convention setting in August with only one presumptive nominee awaiting the acceptance by acclamation. Interestingly, customs and circumstances were quite different surrounding the convention aspect of the presidential elections in 1860 and 2008 in America. Nonetheless, April 2008 proved to be an anxious month. On the other hand, in the month of April 1860, Lincoln's support increased greatly, becoming a defining month in 1860. So it would become in

2008 for Democratic and Republican candidates. In 1860, Stephen Douglas (Democrat) stood amidst a dividing party on the basis of sectionalism, such as Northern Democrats, along with a small portion of Southerners supporting Douglas and his popular-sovereignty platform. The Southern Democrats were against Douglas, calling him a traitor to Southern rights. The 1860 Democratic National Convention was held in Baltimore, Maryland. John Breckinridge carried the Southern states, splitting the Democratic vote against Stephen Douglas.

Now, in 2008, Obama and Clinton found themselves in similar circumstance of division like the 1860 Democrats experienced. In April 2008, Hillary Clinton remained in the race when it appeared mathematically clear that she did not have the number of pledged delegate votes needed, as did Obama.

The question was, why didn't she drop out of the campaign? Why didn't Hillary Clinton concede at this point, because obviously she had lost the bid for nomination because she did not have the necessary delegates? Instead, Clinton continued in the race, fighting mightily to convince Michigan and Florida delegates to be seated at the convention. If those two states were seated at the convention, perhaps this action would enable Clinton to barely clinch the nomination over Obama, and she worked hard to defend her electability over Obama.

So the in-fighting became a splitting challenge for the 2008 Democratic National Convention and became extremely problematic for the party's image. However, Clinton took advantage of her constitutional right to hold on to her campaign in expectations of gaining the Democratic nomination rather than Obama, regardless of his gaining the front-runner status by now. The leaders of the DNC feared that the image of division between the two Democratic challengers would prove damaging when whoever became the nominee ran against the established Republican standard-bearer, John McCain, in the fall general election. Such dynamics provided the opportunity for McCain to mold and build his candidacy for the big general election come November. Indeed, such a freewheeling opportunity since March 2004 for John McCain was quite meaningful, because for months, he was unchallenged by a Democratic opponent while Obama and Clinton forcefully challenged each other instead.

So it was in the 1860 presidential contest. The Democrats were split by challenging themselves: Douglas and Breckinridge, with John Bell running on the Constitutional Union Party, while the Republican nominee would stand as one individual after May 16, 1860, when the nomination was made.

Superdelegates were gained by Obama by May 2008, surpassing Clinton in superdelegates.[89] At this point, 217 pledged delegates were left to determine the primary contests. Still in May, Clinton won West Virginia over Obama. Obama, however, had won North Carolina, causing him to lead with 164 pledged delegates when again there were only 217 pledged delegates remaining to be picked up by the candidates. June became the month of the final primaries, which included South Dakota and Montana.

June 7, 2008, the epic struggle between the two Democrats ended with Senator Hillary Clinton conceding to Senator Barack Obama. Barack Obama, the young, forty-seven-year-old senator from Springfield, Illinois, had defeated the established, sixty-one-year-old front-runner senator from New York, Senator Hillary Clinton.[90] Barack Obama had become the presumptive nominee after capturing 2,117 delegate votes required for a majority. With grace and dignity, the former First Lady turned senator, and becoming America's first woman to ever run an authentic and promising campaign for president of the United States, encouraged her supporters to join her in standing behind the first African American to become the presumptive nominee for the president of the United States of America. By June 27, the two came together in their initial post-primary appearance in Unity, New Hampshire. So phenomenal!

In the nineteenth century, a nation hung on breaking up as the shadows of disunion spread over the land in the wake of the first Republican for president in 1860. Could the nominee hold the nation together and remain a United States, or allow the sectional divide to separate North and South over the slavery debate? "The fact that we [Republicans] get no votes in your section is a fact of your making, and not of ours," Lincoln informed Southerners and Southern sympathizers in the North in his Cooper Union speech back in February 1860.[91] Lincoln's constant mindfulness of the South's divisive issues over slavery and secession remained strong and continued his effort to raise the South's conscience to remain as one union. Meanwhile, the Seward candidacy, as front-runner of the Republican Party, was sinking in deep water. During the opening Republican convention on May 16, 1860, a delegate from Pennsylvania wrote a letter for publication in the influential *Chicago Press and Tribune* newspapers warning delegates against the nomination of anyone opposed by the "doubtful states," meaning Pennsylvania, New Jersey, Indiana, and Illinois. The writer was referring to Seward as that "anyone."[92]

Furthermore, the writer asked the delegates a crucial question: "Is the convention going to nominate a candidate without [the] consent of the Republicans of the battleground states?"[93]

According to the managers of Lincoln, Cameron would receive votes from Pennsylvania on the first ballot, but would support Lincoln when the balloting progressed to a choice between Seward and their candidate Lincoln—the Keystone State of Pennsylvania delegates would throw their support to Lincoln.

Additionally, Horace Greeley helped the cause for Lincoln's nomination by pretending he was for Edward Bates when in fact Greeley was for Lincoln, and he used this slick technique revengefully to oppose his old enemies, Seward and Thurlow Weed, Senator Seward's campaign manager. Obviously, Seward's strength as the front-runner would surely decline after the first balloting, and the swing votes from Bates and Chase would go in favor of Lincoln. Seward's chief manager, Thurlow Weed, eventually attempted a deal to nominate Lincoln as vice president on Seward's ticket if Seward was ensured a victory on the first ballot.[94] Of course, Lincoln's managers rejected such an offer immediately because such an action could damage or weaken Lincoln's chances as an authentic presidential candidate. Likewise, in the 2008 campaign, Barack Obama rejected the vice president idea also.

CONVENTION 1860 VS. 2008

Who would clinch the nomination of the Republican Party in 1860? With the party's platform approved, a platform that consisted of seventeen planks, five directly referred to slavery. Others denounced the Democratic Party for forcing the Lecompton Constitution upon Kansas. One of the planks of the platform denied the authority of Congress or the territorial legislature "to give legal existence to slavery" in the territories. It branded "the recent reopening of the African slave trade, under the cover of our national flag, aided by perversions of judicial power, as a crime against humanity and a burning shame to our country and age."[95] Interestingly, the platform did not mention the Fugitive Slave Act, although radicals and abolitionists called for its repeal or revision. But politically, if the Republicans approached this volatile issue in any way, it could cost them key Northern states in this election. Likewise, references to slavery in the District of Columbia were not mentioned either. To insure the German Americans' vote in Illinois and Pennsylvania, the Republicans at Chicago announced their opposition "to any change in our Naturalization Laws or any State Legislation" that would impair the rights of immigrants.[96]

Typically, civil rights, universal freedom, immigration, economy, division, and war filled the character of the country in the nineteenth century without the controversies of abortion and gay marriages surfacing in the twenty-first century. These particular issues were commodities of the state of the country during the 1860 and 2008 elections.

Furthermore, the Republicans carried an economic plank built on the eminence of the days of Henry Clay Whigs, who promoted support for internal improvements for river/harbor and a railroad to the Pacific, free homesteads for bona fide settlers, and an adjustment of "imposts [duties] to encourage the development of the industrial interests of the whole country."[97] Additionally, there was focus on accountability in the federal government and an end to "the systematic plunder of the public treasury by favored partisans of the Buchanan administration."[98]

In 2008, Barack Obama talked about change: "Change that will make a difference in the lives of families—change that will restore balance in our economy and put us on a path to prosperity—it's not just the poll-tested rhetoric of a political campaign—it's the cause of my life."[99]

Building his platform on cutting taxes for 95 percent of Americans, Obama emphasized transforming the economy by making alternative energy a priority, creating new jobs, and freeing the country from the grip of foreign oil and repair alliances abroad.[100] His platform became the opposite of what the Republicans claimed for the American people, and his policies were dissimilar to President Bush's administration.

As the reality of the nomination approached the brink of gaining or losing hope, the historical significance of nomination in an America of the twenty-first century reflected iconic similarities to a nineteenth-century America. Indeed, the roots of the issues wrought upon the nineteenth-century delegation transitioned into the twenty-first-century people. It was a matter of transcending from the Chicago convention site to the convention site in Denver at different times.

The Wigwam Convention Hall in Chicago filled with a robust crowd that was excited, emotional, animated, and anticipating the time for the nominations to be called to herald a new day. The nomination of the *first* or most electable Republican of the 1860 presidential election buzzed in the air amidst huge anticipations and wonder as the delegations crowded the ornate convention center of the day. Space was limited in the Wigwam held in Chicago on May 18, 1860.

Chairman Ashmun gaveled the convention into session. Lincoln supporters packed the Wigwam and "the Rail-Splitters" outside shouted loudly for their hero. Likewise, Seward's supporters were out in force. It is recorded that ten thousand people were in attendance at the convention—an enormous assemblage for that time—indicating intensified impact of this election in 1860 for the Republicans in their precarious political position.

Ashmun called for nominations as the convention progressed. Tension then crept upon the Republican delegates as they anxiously awaited the announcement of nominations. First, William M. Evarts, a New York lawyer, stood to nominate Seward, the New York senator. Next, Norman B. Judd of Illinois nominated Lincoln. Of course, Bates, Chase, and Cameron were nominated, but their nominations did not produce the amount of enthusiasm as did Lincoln and Seward supporters, who roared and yelled in boisterous exuberance garnered with anticipation.

What was different about the 1860 Republican convention from the 2008 Democratic/Republican conventions? The difference: the candidates were not physically present at the Wigwam as would be the case in 2008 wherein the candidates' appearance was the mainstay feature of the national convention at Invesco Field.

Indeed, the tradition changed by the twentieth and twenty-first centuries, when candidates were present at the national conventions of their respective party. In 1860, Seward and Lincoln became the strongest two nominations, causing the crowd of delegates to shout, yell, dance, clap, and become frantically wild after the nominations of Seward and Lincoln, especially Lincoln, at the National Republican Convention.

However, within the din of noise and thunderous roar of the excited delegates, finally a space of calm etched its way in, punctuating the fray of shouts/bellows. At this time, the roll call resumed with New England states on the first votes. But to the dismay of Seward's supporters, those states of Rhode Island, Maine, and Connecticut were not offering their vote to Seward. Instead, Lincoln received the majority of those states' votes and all of Vermont's. Only Massachusetts cast twenty-one of twenty-five votes for Seward; Lincoln received the remaining four.

Seward, of course, received all of his state's votes. New York was the largest, with seventy votes. Kentucky, Virginia, and Indiana gave the majority of their votes to the Rail-Splitter, causing a big downward spiral for Seward. The border states and slave states Delaware and Maryland distributed their votes between Bates and Chase;

Missouri's eighteen votes went to their favorite son, Bates. Texas gave the majority of its six votes to Seward. As a result, Seward did not win on the first ballot. He was defeated. First balloting tally reflected results were Seward, 173; Lincoln, 102; Cameron, 10; Chase, 49; Bates, 48. Seward now needed 233 votes to win. On the second ballot: Lincoln 181 and Seward 184.[101] How close! Lincoln was gaining and gaining very, very closely, perhaps too close for the comfort of Seward's managers, causing them to become extremely anxious.

Would the Seward managers be able to reverse Lincoln's gaining power? Again, the launch of anticipation/wonder remained evident throughout the Wigwam Convention Hall as the third ballot started! At the advent of the third ballot, an epiphany evolved, vanishing oppositions to Lincoln, because New England switched their votes to Lincoln. Chase only received fifteen of his state's votes, Ohio, and twenty-nine of Ohio's votes went to Lincoln—causing Lincoln to need a miraculous two votes to win the great nomination! Momentarily, the voice of David K. Carter of Ohio triumphantly rose and with splendor announced the change of four more Ohio votes for Abraham Lincoln, the man of the west. Afterward, the Wigwam transformed into unprecedented rejoicing and rhythmic clapping, and apparent jubilation swept over the convention hall as the great gathering rose to their feet, inspired and moved by the success of the third-vote balloting in favor of Lincoln—crushing any redeeming hope for the New York senator. Although Seward's managers were stunned at such a transforming and surprising outcome, they composed themselves and displayed the integrity to stand as a unified front in response to their party's deciding vote for Abraham Lincoln, thus calling for all Republicans to rally around Lincoln in the general election.

Ironically, Lincoln was not amidst the rollicking demonstration by the delegates' outburst of approval for the Rail-Splitter's victory, or "Honest Abe's" nomination by the Republican Party. Instead, Lincoln remained at home in Springfield, Illinois, awaiting the results via telegraphic news of his eventual nomination. Rising slowly and calmly from his seat, Lincoln read the message and remarked: "When the second ballot came I knew that this must come."[102]

With a cool and patient countenance, he graciously extended thanks to his friends before striding off toward the house to tell his wife the triumphant news. In Washington, Congress awaited the news and was relieved after hearing that Abraham Lincoln had actually won, because previously an incorrect telegram surfaced stating that the New York Senator Seward had won. But that erroneous report was quickly corrected, stating that Lincoln won unanimously.

The response of the press was rigid and broad. The *Chicago Press and Tribune* newspapers reported: "The entire crowd rose to their feet, applauding rapturously and ladies waving their handkerchiefs, the men waving and throwing up their hats by the thousands, cheering again and again."[103] The *LaPorte* (Indiana) *Herald* hailed Lincoln as a man of the west, born into poverty and obscurity, who "by the most intense labor and application has risen to his high position" and become "a tower of strength" in the region.[104]

The *Davenport* (Iowa) *Gazette* declared that "the people of the West will feel in voting for him as though they were elevating from their own ranks one who thoroughly understands their interests and will faithfully represent them."[105]

From the *New York Times*, Henry J. Raymond wrote: "No one doubts that [Lincoln] has all the intellectual ability, the honesty of purpose, and the fixedness of political principle essential for the presidency. The only apprehension which any of his friends entertain is that he may lack the iron firmness of will and the practical experience of men and factions which the passing crisis will render indispensable in a Republican President."[106]

In the east, the *Concord* (New Hampshire) *Statesman* advised that "the question at Chicago was not who [was] most worthy of our consideration, but what suitable candidate can we present with the strongest probabilities of success."[107]

And the *Boston Courier and Enquirer* offered conciliatory words about Seward's defeat: "The first great representative of Republican principles has been defeated, we have in the nomination of Mr.

Lincoln no expediency candidate, but one who early embraced the Republican cause, has always labored consistently for its successes—has from the beginning stood, and stands now, fair and square on its national and conservative platform."[108]

Additionally, the *Courier and Enquirer* called on all Republicans to rally around Lincoln and go to work to defeat "the sectional and corrupt Democrats."[109]

Seward's foremost political campaign manager's, Thurlow Weed's, *Albany (New York) Evening Journal* encouraged Seward supporters to turn their support to Lincoln, although they had expected Seward to clinch the nomination. Since Lincoln won, the *Albany Evening Journal* promoted Lincoln's selection "as the very next [best] choice of the Republicans of New York."[110]

The media's response echoed the relevance of the Lincoln nomination and interpreted his win as a positive move by the Republicans. Benjamin Harrison, a young Republican candidate for reporter of the state Supreme Court, and who would later become the twenty-third president, described Lincoln's nomination summarily: "Lincoln represented the free labor principle, which is the prominent feature of the Republican creed."[111]

The enormous favorable response and reactions, however, were soon counteracted by unfavorable reactions to the Republicans' nomination of Lincoln. From press to the abolitionists, expressions of adversity over the nomination of Lincoln exploded. The Republican platform was criticized concerning the Dred Scott decision.

The Fugitive Slave Act, and slavery's existence in the District of Columbia, were voiced by William Lloyd Garrison and Wendell Phillips—the leading abolitionists.

The matter of equality of races became a question of the greatest importance for Negro leaders such as Frederick Douglass, H. Ford Douglas, and Rev. Henry McNeal Turner, prompting Frances Ellen Watkins Harper, an abolitionist lecturer and literary person, to write:

> We turn to the free North, but even here oppression tracks us. Indiana shuts her doors to us. Illinois denies

us admission to her prairie homes. Oregon refuses us an abiding-place for the soles of our weary feet.[112]

In retrospect, the Kansas–Nebraska Act (1858) and the *Dred Scott* decision (1851) motivated Lincoln's purpose and return to politics after his long absence and dedicated time spent in his law career. After disagreeing with Stephen Douglas over the Kansas–Nebraska Act, Lincoln reaffirmed his belief that the Declaration of Independence meant that all men were created equal, and that included African American men also: "If the Negro is a man, why then my ancient faith teaches me that all men are created equal and that there can be no moral right in connection with one man's making a slave of another."[113]

Likewise, Frederick Douglass, the leading voice representing Negroes at the time, attacked the same idea of the equality of humans. In 1852, Douglass delivered his oration "The Meaning of July Fourth for the Negro." Earlier, Douglass agreed with William Lloyd Garrison that the Constitution supported slavery. But Douglass eventually broke ties with the Garrisonian abolitionists and became his own interpreter of the Constitution, concluding that it was, indeed, an anti-slavery document rather than a pro-slavery one: "Interpreted as it ought to be interpreted, the Constitution is a Glorious Liberty Document."[114]

Additionally, he viewed the Declaration of Independence as a document that affirmed the rights of humankind—a document purporting humanity.

Indeed, the favorable responses were encouraging to Lincoln and his managers, as well as the majority of the Republican Party. But there were unfavorable commentaries as a backlash to the Republican nomination, in addition to well-known abolitionists like William Lloyd Garrison and Wendell Phillips. And on the Democratic side, the Democratic Party looked upon this Republican nomination with political contempt. As noted in Democrat media such as the *Boston Herald*, a favorable newspaper to Stephen Douglas agreed with some reservations. It voiced, for example, "The

Chicago sectional convention—a thorough geographical body—has crowned its work by nominating a mere local politician questioning whether Abraham Lincoln had shown ability to warrant this distinction over his competitors."[115]

Further raising the issue: "The conduct of the Republican party in this nomination is a remarkable indication of small intellect, growing smaller. They pass over Seward, Chase, and Bates, who are statesmen and able men, and they take up a fourth-rate lecturer, who cannot speak good grammar," came the criticism from the *New York Herald*.[116]

Although Lincoln was a son of Illinois, but not a favorite son among Democratic media in Illinois, such as the *Chicago Times* and Springfield, Illinois, *State Journal-Register*, because both papers voiced Greeley and the Blairs, in addition to other men from Pennsylvania who wanted to prevent the nomination. This transpired in Chicago while adding more unfavorable commentary; the *Chicago Times* loathed this nomination with further grievance:

> The nomination of Lincoln (and we intend to say nothing unkind or disrespectful of him) will be regarded by all who know him, as a degradation of intellectual worth for mere purposes of crafty personal hatred toward others and not because of any fitness on his part for the office.[117]

Of course, its counterpart, the Springfield, Illinois, *State Journal-Register*, acknowledged some appreciation of Lincoln's nomination since he was a leading citizen of Springfield, although otherwise criticized the nominee as an "ultra-radical candidate who subscribed to the sectional 'irrepressible conflict' doctrine." The *State Journal-Register* proclaimed Lincoln the candidate of "Negro equality" and predicted that the Little Giant (Stephen Douglas) in the presidential election would easily repent his 1858 success over the "Black Republican."[118]

On the other hand, other newspapers in the nation, specifically in Louisiana, Virginia, and elsewhere, presented more sobering comments about the nomination of Lincoln by the Republicans: "The Black Republicans have furnished a signal manifestation of their determination to avoid extremes.... We predicted long ago the defeat of Seward in the Chicago Convention.... Republicans believed that Seward could not succeed 'in the doubtful states' without conservative and western support." They concluded by warning Southerners that Lincoln as the Rail-Splitter from Illinois would be a "formidable competitor for the presidency in the election and urged the Democrats in Baltimore to unite behind Douglas."[119]

Cancelling out a prejudice against Lincoln, the Republican Party committee, especially those who had not met him, learned for themselves that Lincoln was an impressive figure and citizen bearing all the qualities of intellect, principle, moral fiber, and a professional lawyer-politician. Hannibal Hamlin of Maine declared the ticket as a Democrat for Lincoln's vice-presidential nominee.

Unfortunately, the Democratic Party was as split as the sectional divide facing the country on the eve of the 1860 presidential election. With three Democratic candidates opposing each other, since the party was unable to repair their differences and unite, the Northern Democrats nominated Stephen Douglas; Southerners nominated John Breckinridge and Bell of Tennessee, with Douglas as the strongest deciding Democrat to compete in general election against Lincoln, Republican nominee. Despite the three Democratic nominees, a powerful possibility and keen predictability existed that Lincoln's nomination would serve the Republicans well in the 1860 election—and America would weather the storm because of the nomination of Abraham Lincoln.

Fast-forward, now, to the Democratic nomination of 2008 approaching its finish line, sprinting toward the final leg of the race that culminates into the long-awaited nomination. Unlike the 1860 nomination, the 2008 candidates were, indeed, visible and not working behind the scenes. Nor did they remain at home, as was the case in 1860. The remaining Democrats' two candidates were Senator Hillary Clinton (D-NY) and Senator Barack Obama (D-IL). That was it! No long list existed anymore. The Republican

Party already had Senator John McCain as the presumptive nominee.

Gracefully, Senator Hillary Clinton gave a final symbolic boost Wednesday, August 2008, at the convention from the floor. The senator from New York moved to suspend the roll call of the states and formalize her former rival's nomination by acclamation.

With this move, the 2008 Democratic National Convention in Denver correlated a global eminence to that of the 1860 Republican National Convention in Chicago on the basis of the exotic nature of its candidates nominated and the mood of the country during such times. As a result of this spectacular nomination of Barack Obama as the Democratic presumptive nominee for president, the young senator became the first African American to lead a major political party into a general election campaign, according to the *Mercury News*.[120]

History repeated and reenacted in 2008—Barack Obama chose his front-runner competitor New York Senator Hillary Clinton as secretary of state. Lincoln chose his front-runner competitor New York Senator William Seward in 1860. Joe Biden was vice president, another strong competitor chosen for the Obama cabinet, similar to Secretary of War Stanton, who once snubbed Lincoln as a lawyer on a patent case in Cincinnati (some years earlier) by expressing his disgust to Lead Counsel Harding of the team: "Where did that long-armed creature come from, and what can he expect to do in this case?"[121] Later he redeemed himself by speaking with approval of Lincoln and admitting that they were in error by underestimating his judicial strength, stating: "Lincoln is capable of more than that . . . no men were ever so deceived as we were in Cincinnati."[122] Joe Biden called Senator Obama inexperienced and made a careless/thoughtless comment about Obama in reference to race, to which Biden had rushed to offer a timely and a sincere apology to his opponent, Barack Obama.

In retrospect, the nomination of the presumptive presidential candidates of both parties and their campaigns that trailed them during the months leading up to the actual election in November 2008 and 2012 for Barack Obama, and the March 2, 1860, and 1864 elections for Abraham Lincoln, are phenomenal events. The phenomenal event of the first African American, Barack Obama, elected as president of the United States means the barrier is broken, if nothing else, and the impossible made possible. Therefore, the spectrum of this election has been etched in the chronicles of time and endless history, never to be erased, removed, scratched out, nor amended, but overwhelmingly stamped forevermore.

When Senator Barack Obama of Illinois officially became the presumptive Democratic Party presidential candidate in 2008, he moved forth to compete with the presumptive Republican Party presidential candidate, senior Senator John McCain of Arizona, who was preceded by Barry Goldwater. Goldwater (1909–1998) was a five-term senator from Arizona and the 1964 Republican Party nominee for president. Although he lost to Democrat incumbent President Lyndon Baines Johnson, still Goldwater is most credited for strongly engaging the renewal of the 1960s political movement of American conservatism, and he was a vocal opponent of the Civil Rights Act of 1964. McCain was a Vietnam prisoner of war, well-known and respected on the political scene in Washington, DC, as compared to Obama, a newcomer. Were the odds stacked against the young, forty-three-year-old presidential candidate in comparison to the seventy-two-year-old presidential candidate with decades of experience beyond Obama's forty-three years? John Sidney McCain III (August 28, 1936–August 25, 2018) had a media reputation as a "maverick" for his willingness, however, to disagree with his party on certain issues; but, he was generally conservative. Yet, Senator McCain demonstrated a bipartisan spirit and patriate representation in his concession speech to President-elect Obama by acknowledging the historic nature of Obama's victory on the basis of what his achievement symbolized for race relations and diversity in America. Indeed, it was a noble and impressive move on the part of Senator McCain as he rose above the limits of partisan practices and stepped forth to congratulate and generously support him as the newly elected leader of the United States. Excerpts follow of Senator John McCain's honorable speech on November 5, 2008.

My friends, we have come to the end of a long journey. The American people have spoken, and they have spoken clearly. A little while ago, I had the honor of calling Sen. Barack Obama—to congratulate him on being elected the next president of the country that we both love. . . .

This is an historic election, and I recognize the special significance it has for African Americans and for the special pride that must be theirs tonight. I've always believed that America offers opportunities to all who have the industry and will to seize it. Sen. Obama believes that, too. But we both recognize that though we have come a long way from the old injustices that once stained our nation's reputation and denied some Americans the full blessings of American citizenship, the memory of them still had the power to wound. A century ago, President Theodore Roosevelt's invitation of Booker T. Washington to visit—to dine at the White House—was taken as an outrage in many quarters. . . . Senator Obama has achieved a great thing for himself and for his country. I applaud him for it. . . .

These are difficult times for our country, and I pledge to him tonight to do all in my power to help him lead us through the many challenges we face.

I urge all Americans who supported me to join me in not just congratulating him, but offering our next president our goodwill and earnest effort to find ways to come together, to find the necessary compromises, to bridge our differences and help restore our prosperity, defend our security in a dangerous world, and leave our children and grandchildren a stronger, better country than we inherited.

Whatever our differences, we are fellow Americans. And please believe me when I say no association has ever meant more to me than that. . . .

> I wish Godspeed to the man who was my former opponent and will be my president....
> Americans never quit. We never surrender. We never hide from history. We make history. Thank you, and God bless you, and God bless America.[123]

Even though McCain had lost to both of the former presidents during the 2004 and 2008 presidential campaigns, later, at the funeral of the late senator on September 1, 2018, at the National Cathedral, the forty-third and the forty-fourth presidents (Bush and Obama) eulogized Senator John McCain upon his request given to each of them during the senator's closing days of his bout with brain cancer.

Likewise, the forty-second president, President Bill Clinton, was present and paid final respect and honor to the fallen senator. The forty-fifth president was not present.

Back in 1861, March 4, during President Lincoln's inauguration, when the president-elect and President Buchanan entered the capitol from the north through the passageway to attend the swearing-in ceremony of Vice President Hannibal Hamlin, upon Lincoln's appearance on the platform, the audience burst forth in loud applause. Then, after being introduced by Edward Baker, Lincoln rose to speak; however, he hesitated momentarily because he did not know where to rest his tall stovepipe hat. Observantly, his once-Democratic opponent Senator Stephen A. Douglas detected Lincoln's hesitation and promptly rushed to assist him by gaining permission from the president to take his hat, and the senator continued to hold it during the ceremony while Lincoln spoke. Later, during the Fort Sumter surrender, Lincoln consulted with Senator Douglas and showed him the war proclamation that Lincoln expected to issue on April 15, 1861, which indicates that Senator Stephen Douglas, too, seemed to forget their past differences, such as the 1858 Lincoln-Douglas Debates, among other political rivalry that once separated them. Thereafter, in his immediate press release, Senator Douglas summarily announced that he was in agreement with President Lincoln and supported/sustained the president in the constitutional functions that meant preserving the Union, maintaining the government, and defending the federal capitol. Therefore, Senator Douglas returned to Illinois and heroically and emphatically persuaded Democrats to support the newly elected Republican president in his preparation for war and proclamation calling for seventy-five thousand volunteer troops to rise up against the take-over of Fort Sumter in South Carolina by the secessionists. Indeed, Stephen Douglas demonstrated his bipartisan engagement as he reached across party lines to support his former opponent's goal to preserve the Union, which was similar to Senator John McCain's bipartisan maneuvers. Incidentally, Senator Douglas, the 1860 Democrat nominee, lost his bid for president to the Republican nominee, Abraham Lincoln.

Stephen Douglas died unexpectedly on June 3, 1862, two days before Lincoln's message (July 5) was read to Congress in response to the attack on Fort Sumter.

In moving forward, while on the campaign trail, John McCain chose Sarah Palin as his vice-presidential candidate, who served as the first woman governor of Alaska (2006–2009), and she was only in her thirties. Earlier, in 1982, Palin enrolled in the University of Hawaii. Perhaps McCain was making some kind of statement aimed at his opponent, Obama, implying that McCain was more progressive minded by choosing a woman as his running mate as opposed to Obama, who had just recently defeated the Democratic front-runner who happened to be a woman as well, Hillary Clinton; instead, Joe Biden was chosen by Obama as his vice president. So initially, it appeared that John McCain's selection worked favorably for his campaign, because suddenly, all eyes were upon this attractive and former beauty queen who spoke loudly and clearly against Barack Obama as she struck out at him while promoting her conservative views and frequently referring to Obama as a socialist on the basis of his moderate liberal platform on universal healthcare, especially other issues in interest of the people. However, Sarah Palin became somewhat of a liability to the McCain campaign because she did not appear informed enough, causing her to make several serious public misrepresentations in interviews and such, including behind-the-scene missteps within McCain's entourage of advisors. In fact, one of the most influential leaders in the Republican Party, former Vice President Dick Cheney, stated publicly in a television interview about McCain's selecting Sarah Palin as his running mate:

> Picking Sarah Palin as a running mate was a mistake. . . . Is the person capable of being the president of the United States? . . . I like Governor Palin. I've met her. I know her. She was an attractive candidate. . . . But based on her background—she had only been governor for two years. I don't think she passed the test . . . of being ready to take over. And, I think that was a . . . a mistake.[124]

Indeed, the campaigns were rough and tough between the two candidates, who aggressively promoted their platforms, designing their programs and visualizing their ideas to the voters in hopes of persuading America to ensure that one of them claimed a victory in 2008. This goal streamed continuously on the radar screen via media for both candidates, and their debates reflected their competitive contexts in the waning months on the campaign trail.

The debates drew large crowds of enthusiastic and anxious viewers who were primarily voters to whom the candidates must appeal and sell his stock of ideas, hoping that the American voter would invest and bond with them. Yes, the charisma of the debates carried interesting and questionable interactions on the debate stage during the three debates that transpired between Senators Barack Obama and John McCain. Three debates were scheduled to take place within the two campaigns of 2008 and 2012. Indeed, the campaigns were intense and oppositional. Interestingly, while on the campaign trail in Minnesota, Senator McCain encountered an astonishing ordeal when one of his supporters informed him that she did not trust Obama because she believed that he was an Arab. The senator responded without hesitation as he quickly removed the microphone from her and defended his opponent. "No, ma'am, he's a decent family man, citizen, that I just happen to have disagreement with on fundamental issues." Of course, McCain's response was considered one of the finer moments of the campaign and still viewed several years later as a marker for civility in American politics.[125]

In 2012, Willard Mitt Romney, born in Detroit, Michigan, and former governor of Massachusetts (2003–2007), at the age of sixty-five, became the first Mormon to become a presidential nominee of a major party: the Republican Party. His estimated worth is over $250 million.[126]

Evidently, Obama knew how to challenge the barriers and divides encountered on the campaign trail against his Republican opponents, first with John McCain. Meanwhile, Obama's popularity and competence rose with a stable lead among a strong, multiracial coalition that he so expertly built. As a result, the Democrat was elected as the forty-fourth president of the United States, an unprecedented achievement and performance combined with a global victory that nations of the world accepted and emphatically embraced as a keystone of diversity shaped in democracy.

Hopeful supporters, as the second term came around, that the incumbent President Obama would consider running again did become a reality. So in 2012, Obama and Biden ran against Mitt Romney and Paul Ryan, GOP candidates. And in 1864, incumbent Republican President Lincoln and Andrew Johnson were on the ticket; however, clouds of doubt hung over his reelection—even the president himself contemplated that he might be defeated badly over Democratic nominee General George McClellan, who was once Lincoln's general back in 1862. Regardless, Lincoln weathered the storm, and in December 1864, Major General William Tecumseh Sherman's "March to the Sea," a victorious military campaign over the Confederate army (Savannah), aided in saving the Union at a critical time. In the postelection of 2008, Obama met with some trepidation when a select group of leading Republican Congress people conspired to limit his presidency to only one term and strategize that Obama would not be elected for a second term come 2012. During the forty-fourth's presidency, it is common knowledge that a majority of GOP lawmakers failed in bipartisanship or to join Obama in achieving his goals or reforms that he wanted passed and legislated against or overthrew his proposals, including healthcare reform. According to Ed Rendell, Senate Minority Leader Mitch McConnell remarked: "Our No. 1 priority is to make this president a one-term president."[127]

Indeed, other partisan issues and major controversies arose, specifically in 2016 at the height of the presidential election year, marking Obama's last year as president. The president nominated Judge Merrick Garland of Maryland following the February 2016 death of Associate Justice of the Supreme Court Antonin Scalia. However, Republican Senate leaders refused to hold any votes on a potential nomination during President Obama's last year in office, even though Democrats argued that there was adequate time before election to vote on President Obama's nominee, which eventually resulted in Judge Garland's nomination expiring on January 3, 2017, therefore clearly paving the way for the forty-fifth president—a Republican—to fill the judicial vacancy. Just as Obama faced this controversial judicial appointment, so did President Lincoln in 1864 during election year when Chief Justice Roger B. Taney died (October 12, 1864), who was known for his conservative pro-slavery rule on the Dred Scott decision. Lincoln nominated Salmon P. Chase on December 15, 1864, and he was confirmed and installed on February 1, 1865. Meanwhile, Chief Justice Chase favorably received the first African American, John S. Rock's, opportunity to practice before the Supreme Court.

***

In reflecting on Obama's successful campaigns of 2008 and 2012, it is obvious that he gained more electoral votes than either of his opponents: McCain or Romney. His popularity soared highest when he ran in 2008, but his populist position took a slight dip in his second bid for presidency. Yet he beat his opponents (McCain and Romney) one state after another while vigorously giving attention to the coalition that he had built.

When Obama debated Senator John McCain or Governor Mitt Romney, he displayed skill and wit that brought national attention to his lead and that he was equal to either regardless of their years of experience in comparison to him. Barack Obama stood his ground with confidence, aggressiveness, and knowledge on any of the issues debated: foreign policy, Wall Street, corporations, the economy, jobs, Joe the Plumber/issues of tax policies, universal healthcare, war, Iraq, and the question of role of government—big or small, etc. He understood how to limit his opponent's platform and strength as being the best candidate by establishing considerable doubt about McCain as well as Romney as president.

His brilliance, compelling biography, inspirational oratory, authenticity, charm, humility, and care made him phenomenally effective. Is that why Barack Obama arrived at forty-fourth president of the US? Again, did those above expressed qualities lead him to his victory as the president-elect of the United States in 2008?

We can ponder over those questions, yet the mystique lies in the weight of an answer, if there really is one appropriate enough. Nonetheless, the factual reality is that for eight years (2008 until 2016), America made an incredible statement to the world when the forty-fourth fulfilled his pursuit of the White House.

Lest we forget:

The sixteenth president, Abraham Lincoln, was reelected in 1864; in 1860, he became the first (original) Republican elected president of the United States.

The forty-fourth president, Barack Obama, was reelected in 2012; in 2008, he became the first African American elected president of the United States.

NOTES

Chapter Six
In Pursuit of the White House

1. See General References, *Britannica Encyclopedia* (2009).
2. *Britannica Encyclopedia* (2009).
3. See www.whitehouse.gov/executive branch/, retrieved April 29, 2009.
4. Our Government, accessed April 29, 2009.
5. Carol Kelly-Gangi, ed., *Abraham Lincoln: His Essential Wisdom* (n.p.: Fall River, 2007), 38.
6. Kelly-Gangi, 43.
7. Barack Obama, *The Audacity of Hope: Thoughts on Reclaiming the American Dream* (New York: Crown Publishers, 2006), 41.
8. Obama, 44.
9. See hymn "Rising to the Loftier Place."
10. John K. Wilson, *Barack Obama: This Improbable Quest* (Boulder, CO: Paradigm Publishers, 2008), 144.
11. William C. Harris, *Lincoln's Rise to the Presidency* (Lawrence, KS: University of Kansas Press, 2007), 16–17.
12. Harris, 17.
13. Harris, 17.
14. Harris, 18.
15. Harris, 18.
16. Wilson, *Barack Obama*, 145.
17. Wilson, 146–47.
18. In Wilson, *Barack Obama: This Improbable Quest*, "Media Matters," May 20, 2007.
19. In Wilson, "Barack Obama Made a Smashing National Debut," 147.
20. *Time* magazine, July 4, 2005, 74.

21. *Time*, 74.
22. In Harris, *Lincoln's Rise to the Presidency* (AL to Anson G. Henry, November 19, 1858), CW (Collected Works) 3:339, 149.
23. Harris, 168.
24. Steve Dougherty, *Hopes and Dreams: The Story of Barack Obama* (New York: Black Dog and Leventhal Publishers, Inc., 2007), 100.
25. See "Obama Rises from Political Obscurity," Politics News, May 5, 2008, www.comcast.net.articles/newspolitics/5October200 80510/Obama.Odyssey.
26. Harris, *Lincoln's Rise to the Presidency*, 151.
27. Wilson, *Barack Obama*, 150.
28. William Miller, *Lincoln's Virtues: An Ethical Biography* (New York: Vintage Books, 2008), 116.
29. David Mendell, *Obama: From Promise to Power* (New York: Amistad Publishing, 2007), 303.
30. John Sellers, ed., *The Diary of Horatio Nelson Taft 1861–1865* (February 20, 1862), vol. 1, January 1–April 11, 1862.
31. David Herbert Donald, *Lincoln* (New York: Simon and Schuster, 1995), 235.
32. Dougherty, *Hopes and Dreams*, 122.
33. Dougherty, 122.
34. Donald, *Lincoln*, 235.
35. Donald, 235.
36. Mendell, *Obama*, 381.
37. Dougherty, *Hopes and Dreams*, 107.
38. Mendell, *Obama*, 302.
39. Mendell, 303.
40. Dougherty, *Hopes and Dreams*, 114.
41. David Brooks, *New York Times*, in Dougherty, 20.
42. Dougherty, 26.
43. Dougherty, 27.

44. Dougherty, 100.
45. Donald, *Lincoln*, 239.
46. Donald, 241.
47. Dougherty, *Hopes and Dreams*, 70.
48. Mendell, *Obama*, 376.
49. Dougherty, *Hopes and Dreams*, 109.
50. Donald, *Lincoln*, 235.
51. Donald, 235.
52. Donald, 236.
53. Donald, 242.
54. Mendell, *Obama*, 377.
55. Donald, *Lincoln*, 242.
56. Donald, 242.
57. Donald, 242.
58. Mendell, *Obama*, 385–86.
59. Harris, *Lincoln's Rise to the Presidency*, 159.
60. Jabari Asim, *What Obama Means: For Our Culture, Our Politics, Our Future* (New York: William Morrow, 2009), 194.
61. Oprah Winfrey.
62. R. B. Bernstein, Introduction. The Constitution of the United States with the Declaration of Independence and the Articles of Confederation, 9.
63. Action of Second Continental Congress, July 4, 1776, 81.
64. See Langston Hughes, "I, Too, Sing America."
65. Dougherty, *Hopes and Dreams*, 9–10.
66. "New York Herald," in Doris Kearns Goodwin, *Team of Rivals: The Political Genius of Abraham Lincoln* (New York: Simon and Schuster, 2005), 12.
67. Goodwin, 13.
68. Goodwin, 20.
69. Goodwin, 25.
70. Asim, *What Obama Means*, 191.
71. Asim, 191–92.

72. "2008 Presidential Campaign," *The Dream Fulfilled: Barack Obama: A Historical Retrospective* (New Jersey, 2009), multimedia, 82.
73. *The Dream Fulfilled*, 82.
74. Wilson, *Barack Obama*, 151.
75. Gil Kaufmann and Sabrina Rojas Weiss, "Joseph Biden Chosen as Barack Obama's Running Mate," *Think MTV*, August 23, 2008, http://mtv.com/news/articles.
76. *Rolling Stone* magazine (2004).
77. Deborah White, "Profile of Vice President Joe Biden," US Liberal Politics Newspaper, July 29, 2009.
78. See *LA Times*, November 20, 2007, retrieved August 14, 2009, abcnews.com/politicalradar/2007/11/clinton_mockso.html.
79. *LA Times*.
80. Tedra Osell, "Hillary Clinton Should Run on Her Own Merits," *Jewcy*, March 20, 2008, retrieved August 14, 2009, www.jewcy.com/post/hillary_clinton_should_run_her_own_merits.
81. "Clinton's 'Red Phone' Ad," *New York Times*, March 1, 2008.
82. *The Dream Fulfilled*, 85.
83. *The Dream Fulfilled*, 82.
84. *The Dream Fulfilled*, 83.
85. *The Dream Fulfilled*, 85.
86. Harris, *Lincoln's Rise to the Presidency*, 225.
87. Harris, 206.
88. Harris, 206.
89. *The Dream Fulfilled*, 90.
90. *The Dream Fulfilled*, 90.
91. Harris, *Lincoln's Rise to the Presidency*, 201.
92. Harris, 201.

93. Harris, 206.
94. Harris, 202.
95. Harris, 205.
96. Harris, 206.
97. Harris, 206.
98. Harris, 206.
99. Dougherty, *Hopes and Dreams*, 139.
100. *Jet* magazine (September 2008), 10.
101. Harris, *Lincoln's Rise to the Presidency*, 214.
102. Harris, 211.
103. Harris, 210.
104. Harris, 213.
105. Harris, 213.
106. Harris, 214.
107. Harris, 214.
108. Harris, 214.
109. Harris, 214.
110. Harris, 215.
111. Harris, 214.
112. Benjamin Quarles, *Lincoln and the Negro* (New York: Da Capo Press, 1962); Frances Ellen Watkins Harper, "An Appeal to Christians throughout the World," 55.
113. Orville Vernon Burton, *The Age of Lincoln: A History* (Boston: Hill and Wang, 2007), 113.
114. Frederick Douglass, "What to the Slave Is the Fourth of July?" at Corinthian Hall, Rochester, New York, July 5, 1852.
115. Harris, *Lincoln's Rise to the Presidency*, 215.
116. Harris, 215.
117. Harris, 216.
118. Harris, 216.
119. Harris, 216–17.
120. See Dan Balz and Anne E. Kornblut, *Washington Post*, August 2008.

121. Miller, *Lincoln's Virtues*, 417.
122. Miller, 427.
123. National Public Radio Politics Newsletter, November 5, 2008, 2:12 a.m. ET.
124. *The Telegraph*, "About Dick Cheney on Sarah Palin."
125. National Public Radio Politics Newsletter.
126. See *General References/Britannica Encyclopedia*, s.v. "Mitt Romney."
127. See Ed Rendell about Senator Minority Leader Mitch McConnell.

CONCLUSION

A CONCLUSION AND A TRANSITION

Just as the dawn lifts up to greet a new day, greatness races by in seconds—minutes—until it reaches its closing spectrum and prepares to bow out, bid farewell, while contemplating, perhaps, another horizon rising somewhere over in the distant yonder. Heretofore, the odyssey permits the soul/self to wander—meander through fields and hills of dreams/failures in search of a purpose-driven venture to parts unknown and known until arriving at a startling conclusion for better or worse. So, for the forty-fourth president and the sixteenth president, the conclusion is confirmed . . .

Both presidents—Barack Obama and Abraham Lincoln—made indelible marks upon the sands of time, and without a doubt, their names are etched in history as second to none. The legacy continues—Obama 2016, Lincoln 1865—each entangled in the ending of the most exotic odyssey from obscurity to historic notability, whose closing grandeur invokes a solemn uncertainty, a feeling of tension surrounded by skepticism while silently signaling, "It's not my turn anymore . . . and whose turn is it now?"

2016. 1865. No doubt those years reverberate like a majestic anthem praising the efforts and effects of the forty-fourth and sixteenth.

Will the anthem's praise ring in lasting brilliance loud and clear?

Or will it reverse to a woeful dirge, wailing lamentations, drowning in the weeping willows' tears of sorrow?

O, Lord, did the sheltering canopy just collapse and fall—suffocating the breath of freedom and silencing the longing sighs of hope, equality, dignity?

In 2016, can the path be retraced? Back to the 1865–66 trailblazing hallmarks of the Thirteenth, Fourteenth, and Fifteenth Amendments of the Constitution; tread the long road of one hundred years to 1964–65 with the justice of the Voting Rights Act and passage of the Civil Rights Act; wind back to 1954 landmarking *Brown v. Board of Education* in its overturn of 1896 *Plessy v. Ferguson*; retain liberation for women of 1920 suffrage and 1973 *Roe v. Wade* ... add Ledbetter!

2008. Flashback: The ebbing tides ride in and Barack Obama takes his turn, strides into the Oval Office as the forty-fourth president of the United States—an African American—fulfilling term number one, 2008–2012, then second term, 2012–2016, like his sixteenth predecessor. Remarkable. Awesome.

2017–2018 ... Are we now stumbling through incredulous swampland filled with mulchy, miry, and muddy threats of disruption/corruption, separation vs. collaboration, division vs. unity, anger vs. charity, fear and suspicions, propaganda of supremacy?

Lest we forget the revolution of coming together and lifting up diversity for stabilization rather than becoming victimized and politicized, or we sink deeper into the wretched depths of the unheard. Those transforming social changes of justice cannot be erased or replaced with separatism and division by heaping too much power upon those already empowered in the coffers of money, secured status, preferential gender, dominant majority, and privileged accessibility/o pportunity. If so, the nation fails in social change/transformation and trust.

It may be imperative that we cling to a Barack Obama and the likes of him—the forty-fourth—not just as a memory or illusion, but to complement such significance with a retrospective guiding lens to recent past decades of a Franklin Delano Roosevelt, thirty-second; Harry Truman, thirty-third; Dwight Eisenhower, thirty-fourth; John F. Kennedy, thirty-fifth; Lyndon Baines Johnson, thirty-sixth; Jimmy Carter, thirty-ninth; Ronald Reagan, fortieth; George H. W. Bush, forty-first; Bill Clinton, forty-second; and George W. Bush, forty-third, as modern presidential leadership who executed some reasonable objective decisions for positive progress when they took their turn in the Oval Office. In reflection, Abraham Lincoln—sixteenth—remains the contemporary president regardless of his serving in the nineteenth century; still, his relevance for all ages is opportune enough for his successors to eagerly embrace and attempt to emulate, in many instances, this unpretentious Illinois son of meek and humble beginnings for his sagacious wisdom, calm temperament, and effective, deliberative decision-making, including his impressive capacity for moral and political growth and understanding. As pointed out by Horace Greeley, "There was probably no year of his life when he was not a wiser, cooler, and better man he had been the year before."[1] Although, among the many successors, none have so profoundly captured an emulous passion for Lincoln as the forty-fourth has done.

Small wonder, then, that attention has been given to the forty-fourth president according to the astonishing and striking parallels that exist between the two: sixteenth and forty-fourth. Indeed, those parallels are not casual coincidences, but actual facts—no alternative facts—which make authentic statements about both of them and their place in history. Of course, anytime one is compared to a great historical/popular figure such as a Dr. King, Thurgood Marshall, St. Paul, Moses, Mother Teresa, Eleanor Roosevelt, Mary McLeod Bethune, Muhammed Ali, Prince, Beethoven, Shakespeare, or a Lincoln, such a compliment can be one of the most coveted distinctions one can merit.

Although, frequently the many skeptics and naysayers raise the question, what has Obama done for us as president? Or, has he really looked out for us black folk, poor folks, and so on and so and so? Of course, each president is examined and assessed by the people, which means questioning the effectiveness of the person who sits in the Oval Office. During the term of a president, the people want to know or see/feel results that are beneficial to them as common folk or the ordinary inclusion of middle class and poor people alike. The

---

[1] Donald T. Phillips, *Lincoln on Leadership: Executive Strategies for Tough Times* (New York: Warner Business Books, 1992).

American people, indeed, are the voters and stakeholders in the United States of America—whatever their occupation, career, or post may happen to be—including children, the masses of poverty-stricken, minorities, the immigrants, all genders, the veterans of foreign wars, active-duty service personnel, those suffering with disease, mental/physical challenges, the homeless, and even the more fortunate and rich. After all, the United States consists of a diverse group of people who are Americans and should be considered as such. America is the people whom the elected president represents and should work or govern in the best interest of the nation and its people. Lincoln believed this and Obama believes this.

Consequently, the answers to the question about what Obama has done for the people or how he looked out for them lies in what the forty-fourth president accomplished while serving in office. There are domestic issues and global challenges that the president must face and attempt to resolve—especially as the assumed leader of the Free World—through commanding strategies, negotiable compromising, and deliberative decision-making, while avoiding rash, naked, power-driven decisions resulting in authoritative dictatorship. To accomplish the ultimate goal is the driving force toward a reliable and realistic outcome in government. In essence, what are the most outstanding accomplishments of this president—one Barack Obama—that have earned him the status of a consequential president, a transformer, or so forth? I conclude that the list is extensive and impressive on the basis of complications that arose as he labored to successfully accomplish what he did. Nor were his accomplishments gained for selfish purposes, but his was a labor of love for the American people. To his amazement, perhaps, when he first entered the Oval Office, he won the Nobel Peace Prize in 2009 on the basis of his unusual diplomatic tactics and collaboration among nations of people. Additionally, upon arriving in office as president, he faced the 2008 financial crisis that he promptly and vigorously approached, and in 2009, Congress approved his $787 billion economic stimulus package, resulting in economic growth and employment rights:

- Included tax cuts
- Extended unemployment benefits
- Funded public-works projects, thus ending the 2008 recession as the measurable outcome
- Signed Credit Card Accountability, Responsibility, and Disclosure Act

In addition to his approach and accomplishments in the area of economics/employment, President Obama:

- Bailed out the United States auto industry, March 30, 2009, which saved three million jobs for workers
- Cut the unemployment rate from 10 percent to 4.7 percent over six years[2]

President Obama influenced peace, security, and safety measures for America, as well as globally, in his agenda of accomplishments, such as:

- Ended war in Iraq
- Drew down of troops in Afghanistan
- Captured and slew Osama bin Laden
- Reversed Bush era of torture policies
- Began normalizing relations with Cuba
- Signed the Hate Crimes Prevention Act
- Helped negotiate landmark Iran nuclear deal

Furthermore, Barack Obama supported and led in humanitarian, justice, equality, and education policies and actions in the following outcomes:

- Appointed the first Hispanic ever to serve as a

---

[2] Todd Perry, "28 of Barack Obama's Greatest Achievements as President of the United States," Good, July 23, 2017, www.good.is/articles/obamas-achievements-in-office.

justice by nominating Sonia Sotomayor to US Supreme Court
- Supported the LGBT community's advocacy for marriage equality
- Signed the Deferred Action for Childhood Arrivals (DACA), allowing as many as five million people living in the United States illegally to avoid deportation and receive work permits
- Dropped the veteran homeless rate by 50 percent
- Increased Department of Veteran Affairs funding
- Repealed the military's "Don't Ask, Don't Tell" policy
- Signed the Lilly Ledbetter Fair Pay Act to combat pay discrimination against women
- Supported veterans through a $78 billion tuition-assistance GI bill
- Launched My Brother's Keeper, a White House initiative designed to help young minorities achieve their full potential
- Commuted the sentences of approximately 1,200 drug offenders to reverse "unjust and outdated prison sentences"[3]

Indeed, the list of accomplishments by the forty-fourth president remarkably distinguishes his ability and persuasive leadership to fulfill a superlative record of quest and victory resulting in great accomplishments for the American people. That was his promise, and he aimed to bring it into fruition. He believed in the cause to elevate his fellow citizens, the downtrodden and the ordinary, and make a difference. His courage and fortitude were like unto the sixteenth, President Lincoln, who achieved accomplishments that actually helped to change the nation and move it toward a strong foundation in the preservation of citizen rights and American values. Small wonder that the forty-fourth took on similar missions to care for the people in ways

---

[3] Todd Perry, "28 of Barack Obama's Greatest Achievements."

that were sustainable, universal ventures—goals that were results oriented, such as clean energy and good health as activated:

- Expanded embryonic stem-cell research
- Improved school nutrition within the Healthy, Hunger-Free Kids Act
- Helped put the US on track for energy independence by 2020
- Signed the Affordable Care Act (critics of the health insurance often referred to as Obamacare), which provided health insurance to over twenty million uninsured Americans, even though his recent predecessors were unsuccessful in accomplishing affordable universal healthcare

Unfortunately, because some of his accomplishments were humanitarian in nature, his critics and opponents label him as a socialist in an attempt to discredit and dismantle the Affordable Care Act.

One hundred fifty-one years ago, this country came out of a civil war between the North and South over the enslavement of a people, followed by a rebirth of freedom, along with liberation from oppression. A Union formed after a secession that threatened a United States of America—instead of a Confederate States (South) or Federal States of America (North)—as well as delivered the amendment of number thirteen, sealing "Forever free" for an emancipated people, accompanied by Reconstruction to rebuild the war-torn damages, to reconstruct the ugly, scarred face of oppression, and to restore the beauty of liberty for all as recorded in the Declaration of Independence.

And then came number seventeen, Andrew Johnson (1865)—seventeenth president—who was no match for Lincoln, number sixteen. Johnson, a white supremacist, blatantly refused to take that special turn to step up to maintain the finer policies and labors of the sixteenth president. Contrarily, his bigoted ignorance hindered equal growth and civil rights progress. Consequently, rebellion rose again—the plantation revisited as a way of life, immediate terrorism by the Ku Klux Klan emerged as unspoken law and order against the newly freed black citizens, shameless white supremacy returned to power, and destruction of reconstruction overtook the land.

"With malice toward none." The attitude of inferiority about others while many promoted superiority of themselves for obvious reasons of race mirrors the 1870s. At the foot of the Lincoln Memorial in 1963, Dr. King envisioned a time when we would "not be judged by the color of our skin, but by the content of character," resounding as an affirmation of the instructive words echoed by Lincoln: "With malice toward none."

Yes, all the way from 2008 to 2016, President Barack Obama went forth—took his turn—as the forty-fourth, lest we forget. The question is, where do we go from here? Whose turn is it now—after the forty-fourth?

Is there now a mystical parallel, or just an unequivocal contrast amidst the transition, 2017 to 2018 (forty-four to forty-five)?

Does the reality show or cast feature disturbing/questionable players where controversy overwhelms the hemisphere? Conflict of interest prances around. Irrationality erases rationality. Scandal overtakes the dignity of respect, indifference/detachment replaces interest/attachment; authority overstated, arrogance over humility—alas, the joyful tweet of the morning songbird is muted—translated into the mournful darkness and nocturnal twitter, even threatening the cry of the nightingale. All this means is the sum total of constant wild gestures centered around narcissism and pretentious greatness obviously prevailing.

After the forty-fourth, the cavalcade of white power—zillionaires—trumps and grins across the towering gilded stage in numbers justifying and conserving the rich, powerful, and famous cabined together.

Tomorrow, and tomorrow, and tomorrow creeps in this petty

pace from day to day to the last syllable of recorded time, and all our yesterdays have lighted fools the way to dusty death. Out, out brief candle! Life's but a walking shadow, a poor player that struts and frets his hour upon the stage. . . . It is a tale told by an idiot, full of sound and fury, signifying nothing.
—Macbeth's soliloquy, Shakespeare

Fellow citizens, we cannot escape history. We of this Congress and this administration, will be remembered in spite of ourselves. No personal significance, or insignificance, can spare one or another of us. The fiery trial through which we pass, will light us down, in honor or dishonor, to the latest generation.
—Abraham Lincoln, December 1, 1862

My fellow citizens: I stand here today humbled by the task before us, grateful for the trust you have bestowed, mindful of the sacrifices borne by our ancestors. . . . Forty-four Americans have now taken the presidential oath. The words have been spoken during rising tides of prosperity and the still waters of peace. Yet, every so often the oath is taken amidst gathering clouds and raging storms. . . . America has carried on not simply because of the skill or vision of those in high office, but because we the people have remained faithful to the ideals of our forbearers, and true to our founding documents. So it has been. So it must be with this generation.
—Barack Obama, January 20, 2009

Number forty-four documents his odyssey to the Oval Office, and in his exodus, the universal wisdom of the ancient books reminds us of the future as echoed:

> From the Old Testament in the Book of Numbers, Israel's journey is documented through the wilderness . . . the

critics say that Numbers would be a bleak account of the Israelites... if it were not outweighed by faith and Divine protection.

Meaning there is *Good News*: "And the government will be on His shoulders. And He will be called Wonderful Counselor, Mighty God, Everlasting Father, Prince of Peace" (Isaiah 9:6, NIV).

BIBLIOGRAPHY

Asim, Jabari. *What Obama Means: For Our Culture, Our Politics, Our Future*. New York: William Morrow, 2009.

Bartels, Larry M. *Unequal Democracy: The Political Economy of the New Gilded Age*, 2nd ed. Princeton, NJ: Princeton University of Press, 2008.

Burton, Vernon O. *The Age of Lincoln*. Boston: n.p., 2007.

Business Insider. President Obama, DNC Keynote Speech (2000).

Donald, David Herbert. *Lincoln*. New York: Simon and Schuster, 1995.

Dougherty, Steve. *Hopes and Dreams: The Story of Barack Obama*. New York: Black Dog and Levanthal Publishers, 2007.

Fisher, Robert, and Peter Romanofsky. "Community Organizing for Urban Social Change: A Historical Perspective." Greenwood Press, 1981.

Foner, Eric, ed. *Our Lincoln: New Perspectives on Lincoln and His World*. New York: W. W. Norton and Co., 2008.

Foner, Eric. *The Fiery Trial: Abraham Lincoln and American Slavery*. New York: W. W. Norton and Co., 2010.

Garfinkle, Norton, and Harold Holzer. *A Just and Generous Nation: Abraham Lincoln and the Fight for American Opportunity*. New York: Basic Books, 2015.

Goodwin, Doris Kearns. *Team of Rivals: The Political Genius of Abraham Lincoln*. New York: Simon and Schuster, 2005.

Harris, William C. *Lincoln's Rise to the Presidency*. Lawrence, KS: University of Kansas Press, 2007.

Holzer, Harold, and Sara Vaughn Gabbard, eds. *Lincoln and Freedom: Slavery, Emancipation, and the Thirteenth Amendment*. Carbondale, IL: Southern Illinois University, 2007.

Kelly, Carol-Gangi, ed. *Abraham Lincoln: His Essential Wisdom*. New York: Barnes and Noble, 2007.

Kline, Ted. "Is Bobby Rush in Trouble?" *Chicago Reader*. March 17, 2000.

Mann, Susan, and Yu-Yin Cheng, eds. *Under Confucian Eyes: Writings on Gender in Chinese History*. Berkeley, CA: University of California Press, 2001.

McNamara, Carter, ed. [Not Necessarily Systematic] Training and Development Processes. Authenticity Consulting, LLC (1997–2008).

McPherson, James M., ed. *To the Best of My Ability*, Updated Edition. New York: Dorling Kindersley Publishing, Inc., 2001.

Miller, William Lee. *Lincoln's Virtues: An Ethical Biography*. New York: First Vintage Books, 2002.

NaGourney, Adam. "Barack Obama." *New York Times*. November 4, 2008.

Obama, Barack. *Dreams from My Father: A Story of Race and Inheritance*. New York: Crown Publishers, 2004.

Obama, Barack. *The Audacity of Hope: Thoughts on Reclaiming the American Dream*. Portland, OR: Broadway Books, 2007.

"Obama Rises from Political Obscurity to Verge of History." Politics News. See www.comcast.net.articles/newspolitics/5October20080510/Obama.Odyssey.

Perry, Todd. "28 of Barack Obama's Greatest Achievements as President of the United States." Good. July 23, 2017. www.good.is/articles/obamas-achievements-in-office.

Quarles, Benjamin. *Lincoln and the Negro*. New York: Da Capo Press, 1990.

Ryan, Lizza. "The Agitator." *The New Republic*. March 19, 2007.

Sellers, John, ed. *The Diary of Horatio Nelson Taft, 1861–1865* (February 20, 1862), vol. 1 (January 1–April 11, 1862).

Sherwell, Phillip. "The Secret of Obama's Success." *Telegraph*. June 7, 2008. www.telegraph.co.uk.

Smith, Daniel. "Female Householding in Late Eighteenth-Century America and the Problem of Poverty." *Journal of Social History* (Fall 1994) 1.

The Dream Fulfilled: A Historical Retrospective. New Jersey: The Multimedia Publishers, 2009.

Time magazine. *President Obama: The Path to the Whitehouse*. Des Moines, IA: Time Books, 2008.

Washington Post. "Robert F. Kennedy." See www.snopes.com/politics/obama/kennedy.asp.25Jan2016

Wills, Garry. *Lincoln at Gettysburg: The Words That Remade America*. New York: Simon and Schuster, 1992.

Wilson, David McKay. "When Worlds Collide." Harvard Education Letter. Nov/Dec. 2008.

Wilson, John K. *Barack Obama: This Improbable Quest*. Boulder, CO: Paradigm Publishers, 2008.

Youngman, Sam, and Aaron Blake. "Obama's Crime Votes are Fodder for Rivals." *The Hill*. March 14, 2007.

ABOUT THE AUTHOR

As an African American woman, Alice Rhodes Hinsley, EdD, who is unique in the field of presidential narratives, purposefully writes about Abraham Lincoln with admiration and understanding of Lincoln's significant contribution to America. She states that the sixteenth president began the long, historic, and winding pathway that led to the fulfilling election event of the forty-fourth president: Barack Obama.

With Hinsley's avid interest in presidential narrative, she engages in critical research/study in this subject area and is a member of the Lincoln Forum, Gettysburg, Pennsylvania.

She is an educator with decades of meritorious pedagogical skills in classroom experience at the secondary level, including leadership positions in teaching and learning areas of public school education. Additionally, she serves in higher education as an adjunct professor in general education and communication at Morris Brown College.

Dr. Hinsley lives in Atlanta, Georgia. She is the proud mother of one son, who is a member of the clergy and a military veteran.